HAMMOND

The Comparative
WORLD ATLAS

Mapmakers for the 21st Century

INTERPRETING MAPS

Designed to enhance your knowledge and enjoyment of maps, these pages explain map scales and projections, describe how to locate information quickly and show you how to weave together the sections of this atlas to gain a more dynamic world view.

GLOBAL RELATIONSHIPS

Beginning with general world physical and political maps, subsequent chapters highlight a variety of the earth's natural features, dealing first with its structure and then with its air, water and land components. Next, maps, charts and graphs unveil the complex relationships between people and their environments. Coverage includes: demographic trends, population distribution and growth, and global energy production; the consequences of pollution: acid rain, deforestation, ozone depletion and global warming; comparisons of GNP per capita and literacy and life expectancy around the globe.

MAPS OF THE WORLD

This new collection of regional maps artfully balances political and physical detail, while proprietary map projections present the most distortion-free views of the continents yet seen. Special thematic maps are included in each continental section. Numbers following each entry indicate map scale (M = million).

Europe ar
Northern A

Asia

North Ame

Africa,
Polar Reg

South Ame

Australia a
Pacific

INDEX

A Master Index lists places and features appearing in this atlas, complete with page numbers, population of places, and latitude and longitude.

Contents

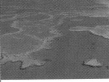

THE COMPARATIVE WORLD ATLAS

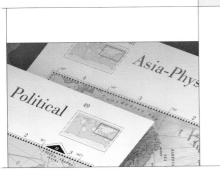

QUICK REFERENCE GUIDE

The world at your fingertips: a concise, current, alphabetical listing of the world's continents and countries; U.S. and Canadian states, provinces and territories; and the size, population and capital of each. Page numbers and reference keys for each entry are visible at a glance.

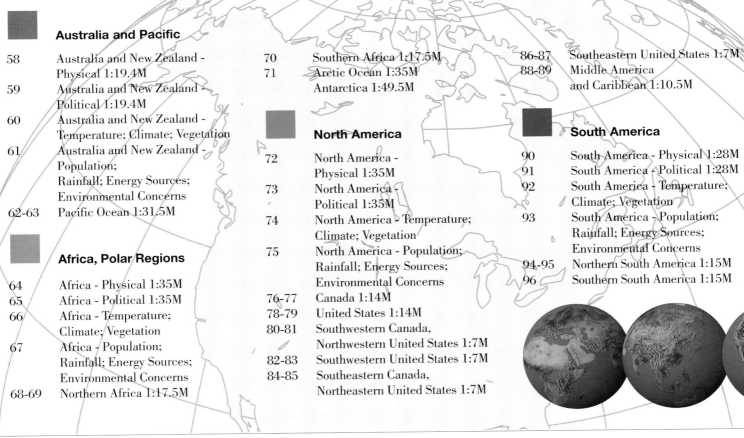

LIBRARY OF CONGRESS
CATALOGING-IN-PUBLICATION DATA

Hammond World Atlas Corporation.
Hammond comparative world atlas.
p. cm.
Revision of 2002 ed.
Includes index.

ISBN 0-8437-0853-0 (hc)
ISBN 0-8437-0852-2 (sc)
1. Atlases.
I. Title. Hammond comparative world atlas
II. Title.
G1021. H2738   2004
912--DC22
             2004052374
             CIP
             MAPS

Using This Atlas

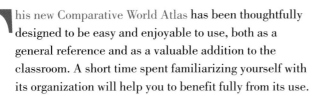

This new Comparative World Atlas has been thoughtfully designed to be easy and enjoyable to use, both as a general reference and as a valuable addition to the classroom. A short time spent familiarizing yourself with its organization will help you to benefit fully from its use.

Quick Reference Guide (p.8)
This concise guide lists continents, countries, states, provinces and territories in alphabetical order, complete with the size, population and capital of each. Page numbers and alpha-numeric reference keys are visible at a glance.

Master Index (p.97)
When you're looking for a specific place or physical feature, your quickest route is the Master Index. This 2,600-entry alphabetical index lists both the page number and latitude-longitude coordinates for major places and features found on the Regional Maps.

Structure of the Earth

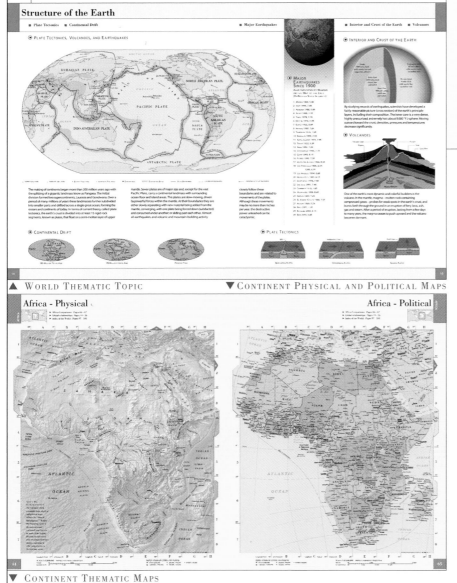

▲ WORLD THEMATIC TOPIC   ▼ CONTINENT PHYSICAL AND POLITICAL MAPS

▼ CONTINENT THEMATIC MAPS

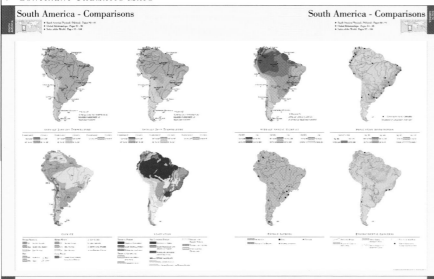

MAP PROJECTIONS
This chapter explores some of the most widely used examples of how mapmakers project the earth's curved surface onto a flat plane. Included is Hammond's new Optimal Conformal Projection which keeps scale distortion over selected areas to the minimum degree possible.

GLOBAL RELATIONSHIPS
Double spread World Physical and World Political maps are accompanied by Land Elevation/Ocean Depth Profiles and Comparative Land Areas and Population graphics. World thematic maps, charts and diagrams highlight important social, cultural, economic and geographic factors affecting today's world. Here, readers can explore complex relationships among such topics as population growth, environmental problems, climate and agriculture or compare worldwide standards of living, resources and manufacturing.

CONTINENT COMPARISONS
Eight thematic maps are shown for each continent (except Antarctica) enabling the map reader to visualize a variety of topics for the same region or to compare similar topics for different regions.

MAP SCALES
A map's scale is the relationship of any length on that map to an identical length on the earth's surface. A scale of 1:7,000,000 means that one inch on the map represents 7,000,000 inches (110 miles, 178 kilometers) on the earth's surface. Thus, a 1:7,000,000 scale is larger than a 1:14,000,000 scale just as 1/7 is larger than 1/14.

Along with these proportional scales, each map is accompanied by a linear (bar) scale, useful in making accurate measurements between places on the maps.

In this atlas, the most densely populated regions are shown at a scale of 1:10,500,000. Other major regions are presented at 1:14,000,000 and smaller scales, allowing you to accurately compare areas and distances of similar regions.

REGIONAL MAPS

This atlas section is grouped by continent starting with facing-page physical and political maps. Following two pages of thematic topics, in-depth regional maps offer abundant detail including boundaries, cities, transportation networks, rivers and major mountain peaks. Map backgrounds are shown in a pleasing combination of elevation coloration and relief shading, with boundary bands defining the extent of each nation's internal and external limits.

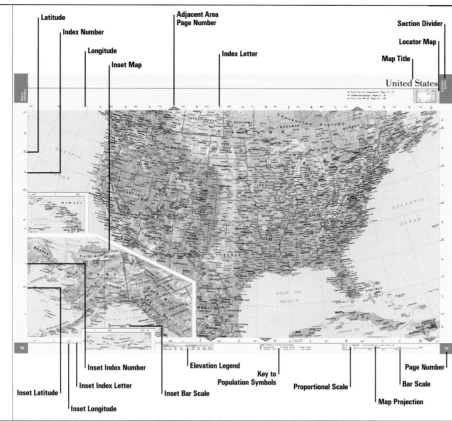

Latitude
Index Number
Longitude
Inset Map
Adjacent Area Page Number
Index Letter
Section Divider
Locator Map
Map Title
United States

Inset Index Number
Inset Index Letter
Inset Latitude
Inset Longitude
Inset Bar Scale
Elevation Legend
Key to Population Symbols
Proportional Scale
Page Number
Bar Scale
Map Projection

PRINCIPAL MAP ABBREVIATIONS

ARCH.	ARCHIPELAGO	FT.	FORT	NAT'L	NATIONAL	PT.	POINT
AUT.	AUTONOMOUS	G.	GULF	NO.	NORTHERN	R.	RIVER
B.	BAY	GD.	GRAND	NP	NATIONAL PARK	RA.	RANGE
C.	CAPE	GT.	GREAT	OBL.	OBLAST	REP.	REPUBLIC
CAN.	CANAL	HAR.	HARBOR	OCC.	OCCUPIED	RES.	RESERVOIR,
CAP.	CAPITAL	I., IS.	ISLAND(S)	OKR.	OKRUG		RESERVATION
CHAN.	CHANNEL	INT'L	INTERNATIONAL	PASSG.	PASSAGE	SA.	SIERRA
CR.	CREEK	L.	LAKE	PEN.	PENINSULA	SD.	SOUND
DES.	DESERT	LAG.	LAGOON	PK.	PEAK	SO.	SOUTHERN
FD.	FIORD, FJORD	MT.	MOUNT	PLAT.	PLATEAU	STR.	STRAIT
FED.	FEDERAL	MTN.	MOUNTAIN	PN	PARK NATIONAL	TERR.	TERRITORY
FK.	FORK	MTS.	MOUNTAINS	PRSV.	PRESERVE	VOL.	VOLCANO

CITY POPULATIONS

In addition to population symbols locating cities and towns on the regional maps, the Master Index provides at a glance the population of all major cities as well as the country's capital.

WORLD STATISTICS

These statistical tables list the dimensions of the earth's principal mountains, islands, rivers and lakes, along with other useful geographic information.

MASTER INDEX

This provides an A to Z listing of names found on the world, continent and regional maps. Each entry is accompanied by a page location and population of places, as well as latitude and longitude coordinates.

Boundary Policies

This atlas observes the boundary policies of the U.S. Department of State. Boundary disputes are customarily handled with a special symbol treatment, but de facto boundaries are favored if they seem to have any degree of permanence, in the belief that boundaries should reflect current geographic and political realities. The portrayal of independent nations in the atlas follows their recognition by the United Nations and/or the United States government.

A Word About Names

Our source for all foreign names and physical names in the United States is the decision lists of the U.S. Board of Geographic Names, which contain hundreds of thousands of place names. If a place is not listed, the Atlas follows the name form appearing on official foreign maps or in official gazetteers of the country concerned. For rendering domestic city, town and village names, this atlas follows the forms and spelling of the U.S. Postal Service.

Hammond Also Uses

accepted conventional names for certain major foreign places. Usually, space permits the inclusion of the local form in parentheses. To make the maps more readily understandable to English-speaking readers, many foreign physical features are translated into more recognizable English forms.

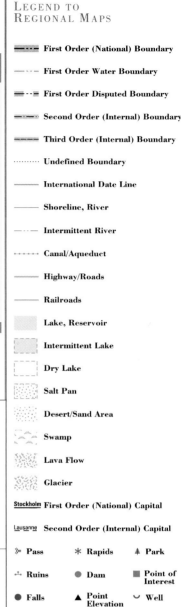

LEGEND TO REGIONAL MAPS

First Order (National) Boundary
First Order Water Boundary
First Order Disputed Boundary
Second Order (Internal) Boundary
Third Order (Internal) Boundary
Undefined Boundary
International Date Line
Shoreline, River
Intermittent River
Canal/Aqueduct
Highway/Roads
Railroads
Lake, Reservoir
Intermittent Lake
Dry Lake
Salt Pan
Desert/Sand Area
Swamp
Lava Flow
Glacier
Stockholm First Order (National) Capital
Lausanne Second Order (Internal) Capital

≻ Pass   ✳ Rapids   ♣ Park
⚲ Ruins   ● Dam   ■ Point of Interest
● Falls   ▲ Point Elevation   ‿ Well

6,000 m. / 19,700 ft.	
4,000 / 13,000	
2,000 / 6,500	
1,500 / 5,000	
1,000 / 3,300	
500 / 1,600	
200 / 700	
Sea Level	
Below Sea Lev.	

The colors in this bar represent elevation ranges of land areas above or below sea level. Boundaries between colors are laveled both in feet and meters. Selective shading highlights those regions with significant relief variations.

Map Projections

■ **Basic Principles and Terms**   ■ **Examples of Popular Map Projections**

There is only one way to represent a sphere with absolute precision: on a globe. All attempts to project our planet's surface onto a plane unevenly "stretch or tear" the sphere as it is flattened, inevitably distorting shapes, areas, distances and/or directions.

To make a flat map cartographers place an imaginary grid pattern on the globe. Points and lines on this pattern are then transferred, or "projected," to a corresponding flat surface pattern, which has been previously constructed, from one of a wide variety of mathematical formulas devised for this purpose. To understand some of the most widely used map projections, it is necessary to briefly describe this imaginary grid pattern that has been imposed on the Earth to locate features, and places and to measure their special relationship to each other.

The Earth rotates around its axis once a day. Its end points are the North and South poles; the line circling the Earth midway between the poles is the Equator. The arc from the Equator to each pole is divided into 90 degrees of latitude. The Equator itself represents 0° latitude and is divided into 360 degrees of longitude. Lines circling the globe from pole to pole, which intersect with the Equator at 90-degree angles, are called meridians, or great circles. The meridian passing through the Greenwich Observatory near London was chosen by international agreement as the prime meridian, or 0° longitude, in 1884. Meridians and lines of latitude (parallels) form the global coordinate grid, or graticule. The distance from the prime meridian to a given point to the west or east, expressed in degrees is its geographic longitude. Similarly, distances north or south of the Equator represent geographic latitude. Although all meridians are equal in length, parallels become shorter as they approach the poles. Thus, while the distance between two parallels (one degree of latitude) is approximately 112 km everywhere on Earth, the distance between two meridians (one degree of longitude) varies between 112 km at the Equator and zero at the poles where the meridians converge. Each degree of longitude and latitude is divided into 60 minutes. One minute of latitude equals one nautical mile (1.85 km).

On a flat surface, any regular set of parallels and meridians upon which a map can be drawn makes a map projection. However, since representing a sphere on a flat plane always creates distortion, only the parallels or the meridians or some other set of lines can be true (i.e. the same length as on a globe at corresponding scale).

The larger the area covered by the map the larger the amount of distortion; thus, distortion is greatest on world maps. Many maps seek to preserve either true area relationships (equal-area projections) or true angles and shapes (conformal projections). Other maps are more concerned with achieving true distance and directional accuracy. Instead of trying to preserve any single true relationship, some maps achieve an overall balance by compromise.

WORLD MAP PROJECTIONS

A globe's surface can be transformed to fit within any outline on a flat surface. In fact, such shapes as diamonds, hearts, stars and even stylistic butterflies have enclosed a map of the earth. However, three traditional shapes - rectangles, circles and ovals - are used to portray most maps of the world.

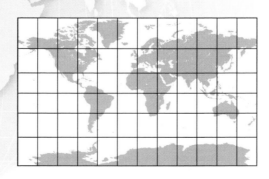

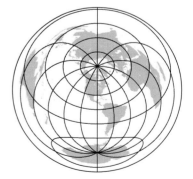

Mercator Projection
A rectangular- shaped map with vertical meridians and horizontal parallels, it is the only map on which a straight line, drawn anywhere on the map, indicates true direction along its entire length. The map has reasonably true shapes and distances within 15 degrees of the equator, but distortion increases dramatically into the higher latitudes.

Miller Cylindrical Projection
Similar in appearance to the Mercator Projection, the Miller Cylindrical lessens distortions in the higher latitudes by closing up the spacing between parallels. Although this destroys the unique navigational property of the Mercator, it does present a more realistic view of land areas in the northern parts of Europe, Asia and North America.

Azimuthal Equidistant Projection
A circular-shaped projection whose oblique view is the only projection in which directions and distances are depicted accurately from the projection's center point to any other place on the globe. Any straight line passing through the center is a great circle route. Distortion of areas and shapes increases away from the center.

⊙ OTHER MAP PROJECTIONS

Since continents and smaller regions occupy only a part of the entire earth's surface, other projections can be employed to minimize distortion and, where possible, preserve true shapes, areas, distances or directions. But, although smaller in size, the areas being mapped are still parts of a sphere and the flattening process will still result in distortions in the maps.

Albers Equal-Area
Projection

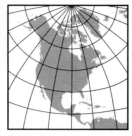

Lambert Conformal Conic
Projection

Optimal Conformal
Projection

Gnomonic Projection

Viewing the surface of the globe from its center point creates this projection with very bad distortions away from the map's center. However, this projection has a unique quality - all great circles (shortest lines between points on a sphere) are shown as straight lines. Therefore, the path of the shortest distance between any two points on the map is a straight line.

Conic Projections

These maps are created by mathematically projecting points and lines from a globe onto a cone which caps the globe. The cone can be placed either tangent to the globe at a preselected parallel or it can intersect the globe at two preselected parallels. The use of two standard parallels, one near the top of the map, the other near the bottom of the map, reduces the scale error. In one type of conic projection, Albers, the parallels are spaced evenly to make the projection equal-area. In the Lambert Conformal Conic Projection the parallels are spaced so that any small quadrangle of the grid will have the same shape as on the globe.

Lambert Azimuthal Equal-Area Projection

Mathematically projected on a plane surface tangent to any point on a globe, this is the most common projection (also known as Zenithal Equal-Area) used for maps of the Eastern and Western hemispheres. It is also a good projection for continents, as it shows correct areas with little distortion of shape.

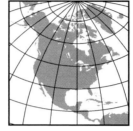

Lambert Azimuthal
Equal-Area Projection

Polyconic Projection

Best suited for maps with a long north-south orientation, this projection is mathematically based upon an infinite number of cones tangent to an infinite number of points (parallels) on the globe. All meridians are curved lines except for the central meridian, which shows true distance and direction.

Polyconic Projection

Hammond's Optimal Conformal Projection

As its name implies, this new conformal projection presents the optimal view of an area by reducing shifts in scale over an entire region to the minimum degree possible. While conformal maps generally preserve all small shapes, large shapes can become very distorted because of varying scales, causing considerable inaccuracy in distance measurements. Consequently, unlike other projections, the Optimal Comformal does not use one standard formula to construct a map. Each map is a unique projection - the optimal projection for that particular area. The result is the most distortion-free conformal map possible.

Gnomonic Projection

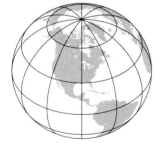

Orthographic Projection

This projection looks like a picture of a globe. It is neither conformal nor equal-area. Although the distortion on the peripheries is extreme, we see it correctly, because the eye perceives it not as a map but as a picture of a three-dimensional globe. Obviously, only a hemisphere (half globe) can be shown.

Mollweide Projection

An early example of an oval-shaped (also called pseudocylindrical) projection is this equal-area map of the earth within an ellipse. Shapes are elongated in the lower latitudes. Since its presentation in 1805 it has been an inspiration for similar oval-shaped maps and has even been "interrupted" to minimize distortion of continental or ocean areas.

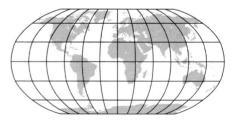

Robinson Projection

This modern, oval-shaped projection uses tabular coordinates rather than mathematical formulas to make the world "look right." Although not true with respect to shapes, sizes, distances or directions, its compromising features show a better balance of size and shape in high latitude lands and very low distortion near the equator.

Quick Reference Guide

■ Countries and Other Areas   ■ Statistics

T his concise alphabetical reference lists continents, countries, states, territories, possessions and other major geographical areas, complete with the size, population and capital or chief town of each. Page numbers and alpha-numeric reference keys (which refer to the grid squares of latitude and longitude on each map) are visible at a glance. The population figures are the latest and most reliable figures obtainable.

Place	Square Miles	Square Kilometers	Population	Capital or Chief Town	Page/Index Ref.
A Afghanistan*	250,000	647,500	29,547,078	Kabul	49/F 6
Africa	11,701,147	30,306,000	875,027,307	....	65
Alabama, U.S.	52,237	135,293	4,447,100	Montgomery	87/G 3
Alaska, U.S.	615,230	1,593,444	626,932	Juneau	78/W12
Albania*	11,100	28,749	3,544,808	Tiranë	44/C 3
Alberta, Canada	255,285	661,185	2,974,807	Edmonton	76/E 3
Algeria*	919,591	2,381,740	33,357,089	Algiers	68/F 2
Andorra*	174	450	69,865	Andorra la Vella	42/E 5
Angola*	481,351	1,246,700	10,978,552	Luanda	70/C 3
Antarctica	5,500,000	14,245,000	....		71
Antigua and Barbuda*	170	440	68,320	St. John's	89/J 4
Argentina*	1,068,296	2,766,890	39,144,753	Buenos Aires	96/C 4
Arizona, U.S.	114,006	295,276	5,130,632	Phoenix	82/D 4
Arkansas, U.S.	53,182	137,742	2,673,400	Little Rock	83/J 4
Armenia*	11,506	29,800	3,325,307	Yerevan	45/C 4
Asia	17,159,867	44,444,100	3,861,712,437	....	49
Australia*	2,967,893	7,686,850	19,913,144	Canberra	59
Austria*	32,375	83,851	8,174,762	Vienna	42/G 4
Azerbaijan*	33,436	86,600	7,868,385	Baku	45/D 4
B Bahamas, The*	5,382	13,939	299,697	Nassau	89/F 2
Bahrain*	240	622	677,886	Manama	52/F 3
Bangladesh*	55,598	144,000	141,340,476	Dhaka	53/E 4
Barbados*	166	430	278,289	Bridgetown	89/J 5
Belarus*	80,154	207,600	10,310,520	Minsk	43/G 5
Belgium*	11,780	30,513	10,348,276	Brussels	42/E 3
Belize*	8,865	22,960	272,945	Belmopan	88/D 4
Benin*	43,483	112,620	7,250,033	Porto-Novo	68/F 5
Bhutan*	18,147	47,000	2,185,569	Thimphu	53/E 3
Bolivia*	424,163	1,098,582	8,724,156	La Paz; Sucre	94/F 7
Bosnia & Herzegovina*	19,781	51,233	4,007,608	Sarajevo	44/C 3
Botswana*	231,803	600,370	1,561,973	Gaborone	70/D 5
Brazil*	3,286,470	8,511,965	184,101,109	Brasília	91/D 3
British Columbia, Canada	365,946	947,800	3,907,735	Victoria	76/D 3
Brunei*	2,228	5,770	365,251	Bandar Seri Begawan	56/E 4
Bulgaria*	42,823	110,912	7,517,973	Sofia	44/D 3
Burkina Faso*	105,869	274,200	13,574,820	Ouagadougou	68/E 5
Burundi*	10,745	27,830	6,231,221	Bujumbura	70/E 1
C California, U.S.	158,869	411,470	33,871,648	Sacramento	82/B 3
Cambodia*	69,900	181,040	13,363,421	Phnom Penh	56/C 3
Cameroon*	183,568	475,441	16,063,678	Yaoundé	68/H 7
Canada*	3,851,787	9,976,139	32,507,874	Ottawa	76
Cape Verde*	1,556	4,030	415,294	Praia	12/H 5
Central African Republic*	240,533	622,980	3,742,482	Bangui	69/J 6
Chad*	495,752	1,283,998	9,538,544	N'Djamena	69/J 4
Chile*	292,258	756,950	15,827,180	Santiago	91/B 6
China, People's Rep. of*	3,705,386	9,596,960	1,294,629,555	Beijing	54/G 4
China, Republic of (Taiwan)	13,892	35,980	22,749,838	Taipei	55/M 7
Colombia*	439,733	1,138,910	42,310,775	Bogotá	94/D 3
Colorado, U.S.	104,100	269,618	4,301,261	Denver	82/F 3
Comoros*	838	2,170	651,901	Moroni	65/G 6
Congo, Democratic Republic of the	905,563	2,345,410	58,317,930	Kinshasa	65/E 5
Congo, Republic of the*	132,046	342,000	2,998,040	Brazzaville	65/D 4
Connecticut, U.S.	5,544	14,358	3,405,565	Hartford	85/F 3
Costa Rica*	19,730	51,100	3,956,507	San José	88/E 5
Côte d'Ivoire*	124,502	322,460	17,327,724	Yamoussoukro	68/D 5
Croatia*	22,050	56,538	4,435,960	Zagreb	44/C 2
Cuba*	42,803	110,860	11,308,764	Havana	89/F 3
Cyprus*	3,571	9,250	775,927	Nicosia	52/B 1
Czech Republic*	30,387	78,703	10,246,178	Prague	44/B 2
D Delaware, U.S.	2,396	6,206	783,600	Dover	84/F 4
Denmark*	16,629	43,069	5,413,392	Copenhagen	43/C 4
District of Columbia, U.S.	68	177	572,059	Washington	84/E 4
Djibouti*	8,494	22,000	466,900	Djibouti	69/P 5
Dominica*	290	751	69,278	Roseau	89/J 4
Dominican Republic*	18,815	48,730	8,833,634	Santo Domingo	89/H 4
E East Timor	5,743	14,874	1,019,252	Dili	57/H 7
Ecuador*	109,483	283,561	13,971,798	Quito	94/C 4
Egypt*	386,659	1,001,447	76,117,421	Cairo	69/L 2
El Salvador*	8,124	21,040	6,587,541	San Salvador	88/C 5
England, U.K.	50,356	130,423	49,138,831	London	42/D 3
Equatorial Guinea*	10,831	28,052	523,051	Malabo	68/G 7
Eritrea*	46,842	121,320	4,447,307	Asmara	69/N 5
Estonia*	17,413	45,100	1,401,945	Tallinn	43/G 4
Ethiopia*	435,184	1,127,127	67,851,281	Addis Ababa	69/N 5
Europe	4,066,019	10,531,000	729,075,181	....	39
F Fiji*	7,055	18,272	880,874	Suva	62/G 6
Finland*	130,128	337,032	5,214,512	Helsinki	43/G 3
Florida, U.S.	59,928	155,214	15,982,378	Tallahassee	87/H 4
France*	211,208	547,030	60,424,213	Paris	42/E 4
French Guiana	35,135	91,000	191,309	Cayenne	95/H 3
French Polynesia	1,522	3,941	266,339	Papeete	63/L 6
G Gabon*	103,347	267,670	1,355,246	Libreville	68/H 7
Gambia, The*	4,363	11,300	1,546,848	Banjul	68/B 5
Gaza Strip	139	360	1,324,991	Gaza	52/B 2
Georgia*	26,911	69,700	4,909,633	T'bilisi	45/C 4
Georgia, U.S.	58,977	152,750	8,186,453	Atlanta	87/G 3
Germany*	137,803	356,910	82,424,609	Berlin	42/F 3
Ghana*	92,100	238,540	20,757,032	Accra	68/E 6
Greece*	50,942	131,940	10,647,529	Athens	44/D 4
Greenland, Denmark	840,000	2,175,600	56,384	Nuuk (Godthåb)	73/N 2
Grenada*	131	340	89,357	St. George's	89/J 5
Guadeloupe	687	1,779	444,515	Basse-Terre	89/J 4
Guam	209	541	160,796	Hagåtña	62/D 3
Guatemala*	42,042	108,889	14,280,596	Guatemala	88/C 4
Guinea*	94,927	245,860	9,246,462	Conakry	68/C 5
Guinea-Bissau	13,946	36,120	1,388,363	Bissau	68/B 5
Guyana*	83,000	214,970	705,803	Georgetown	94/G 3
H Haiti*	10,714	27,750	7,656,166	Port-au-Prince	89/G 4
Hawaii, U.S.	6,459	16,729	1,211,537	Honolulu	78/S 9
Honduras*	43,277	112,087	6,823,568	Tegucigalpa	88/D 4
Hong Kong, China	402	1,040	7,483,009	Victoria	55/K 7
Hungary*	35,919	93,030	10,032,375	Budapest	44/C 2
I Iceland*	39,768	103,000	282,151	Reykjavík	39/B 2
Idaho, U.S.	83,574	216,456	1,293,953	Boise	80/E 5
Illinois, U.S.	57,918	150,007	12,419,293	Springfield	84/B 4
India*	1,269,339	3,287,588	1,065,070,607	New Delhi	53/C 4
Indiana, U.S.	36,420	94,328	6,080,485	Indianapolis	84/C 3
Indonesia*	741,096	1,919,440	238,452,952	Jakarta	56/E 6
Iowa, U.S.	56,275	145,752	2,926,324	Des Moines	81/K 5
Iran*	636,293	1,648,000	69,018,924	Tehran	52/F 2
Iraq*	168,753	437,072	25,374,691	Baghdad	52/D 2
Ireland*	27,136	70,282	3,969,558	Dublin	42/C 3
Ireland, Northern, U.K.	5,459	14,138	1,685,267	Belfast	42/C 3
Israel*	8,019	20,770	6,199,008	Jerusalem	52/B 2
Italy*	116,305	301,230	58,057,477	Rome	39/F 4
J Jamaica*	4,243	10,990	2,713,130	Kingston	89/F 4
Japan*	145,882	377,835	127,333,002	Tokyo	55/Q 4
Jordan*	34,445	89,213	5,611,202	Amman	52/C 2
K Kansas, U.S.	82,282	213,110	2,688,418	Topeka	83/H 3
Kazakhstan*	1,049,150	2,717,300	16,798,552	Astana	46/G 5
Kentucky, U.S.	40,411	104,665	4,041,769	Frankfort	87/G 2
Kenya*	224,960	582,646	32,021,856	Nairobi	69/N 7
Kiribati*	277	717	100,798	Tarawa	62/H 5
Korea, North*	46,540	120,539	22,697,553	P'yŏngyang	55/N 3
Korea, South*	38,023	98,480	48,598,175	Seoul	55/N 4
Kuwait*	6,880	17,820	2,257,549	Kuwait	52/E 3
Kyrgyzstan*	76,641	198,500	4,965,081	Bishkek	46/H 5
L Laos*	91,428	236,800	6,068,117	Vientiane	49/K 8
Latvia*	24,749	64,100	2,332,078	Riga	43/G 4
Lebanon*	4,015	10,399	3,777,218	Beirut	52/B 2
Lesotho*	11,718	30,350	1,865,040	Maseru	70/E 6
Liberia*	43,000	111,370	3,390,635	Monrovia	68/D 6
Libya*	679,358	1,759,537	5,631,585	Tripoli	69/J 2
Liechtenstein*	62	160	33,436	Vaduz	42/F 4
Lithuania*	25,174	65,200	3,584,836	Vilnius	43/F 4
Louisiana, U.S.	49,651	128,595	4,468,976	Baton Rouge	86/E 4
Luxembourg*	999	2,587	462,690	Luxembourg	42/F 4

Place	Square Miles	Square Kilometers	Population	Capital or Chief Town	Page/Index Ref.
M					
Macedonia, Former Yugoslav Republic of *	9,781	25,333	2,071,210	Skopje	44/D 3
Madagascar*	226,657	587,041	17,501,871	Antananarivo	70/K10
Maine, U.S.	33,741	87,388	1,274,923	Augusta	85/G 2
Malawi*	45,745	118,480	11,906,855	Lilongwe	70/F 3
Malaysia*	127,316	329,750	23,522,482	Kuala Lumpur	56/D 4
Maldives*	116	300	339,330	Male	49/G 9
Mali*	478,764	1,240,000	11,956,788	Bamako	68/E 4
Malta*	124	320	403,342	Valletta	44/B 4
Manitoba, Canada	250,946	649,951	1,119,583	Winnipeg	76/G 3
Marshall Islands*	70	181	57,738	Majuro	62/G 3
Maryland, U.S.	12,297	31,849	5,296,486	Annapolis	84/E 4
Massachusetts, U.S.	9,241	23,934	6,349,097	Boston	85/F 3
Mauritania*	397,953	1,030,700	2,998,563	Nouakchott	68/C 4
Mauritius *	718	1,860	1,220,481	Port Louis	13/M 7
Mexico *	761,601	1,972,546	104,959,594	Mexico	88/A 3
Michigan, U.S.	96,705	250,465	9,938,444	Lansing	84/C 2
Micronesia, Federated States of*	271	702	108,155	Palikir	62/D 4
Minnesota, U.S.	86,943	225,182	4,919,479	St. Paul	81/K 4
Mississippi, U.S.	48,286	125,060	2,844,658	Jackson	87/F 3
Missouri, U.S.	69,709	180,546	5,595,211	Jefferson City	83/J 3
Moldova*	13,012	33,700	4,446,455	Chişinău	44/E 2
Monaco*	0.7	1.9	32,270	....	42/F 5
Mongolia*	606,163	1,569,962	2,751,314	Ulaanbaatar	54/G 2
Montana, U.S.	147,046	380,849	902,195	Helena	80/F 4
Morocco*	172,414	446,550	32,209,101	Rabat	68/C 1
Mozambique*	309,494	801,590	18,811,731	Maputo	70/G 4
Myanmar (Burma)*	261,969	678,500	42,720,196	Yangon	49/J 7
N					
Namibia*	318,694	825,418	1,954,033	Windhoek	70/C 5
Nauru	8	21	12,809	Yaren (district)	62/F 5
Nebraska, U.S.	77,358	200,358	1,711,263	Lincoln	83/G 2
Nepal*	54,363	140,800	27,070,666	Kathmandu	53/D 3
Netherlands*	14,413	37,330	16,318,199	The Hague; Amsterdam	42/F 3
Nevada, U.S.	110,567	286,367	1,998,257	Carson City	82/C 3
New Brunswick, Canada	28,355	73,440	729,448	Fredericton	85/H 2
Newfoundland and Labrador, Canada	156,649	405,721	512,930	St. John's	77/K 3
New Hampshire, U.S.	9,283	24,044	1,235,786	Concord	85/G 3
New Jersey, U.S.	8,215	21,277	8,414,350	Trenton	84/F 3
New Mexico, U.S.	121,598	314,939	1,819,046	Santa Fe	82/F 4
New York, U.S.	53,989	139,833	18,976,457	Albany	84/F 3
New Zealand*	103,736	268,676	3,993,817	Wellington	59/H 6
Nicaragua*	49,998	129,494	5,232,216	Managua	88/D 5
Niger*	489,189	1,267,000	11,360,538	Niamey	68/G 4
Nigeria*	356,668	923,770	137,253,133	Abuja	68/G 6
North America	9,355,975	24,232,000	508,788,254	....	73
North Carolina, U.S.	52,672	136,421	8,049,313	Raleigh	87/H 3
North Dakota, U.S.	70,704	183,123	642,200	Bismarck	81/H 4
Northern Ireland, U.K.	5,459	14,138	1,685,267	Belfast	42/C 3
Northwest Terrs., Canada	1,322,905	3,426,328	37,360	Yellowknife	76/D 2
Norway*	125,181	324,220	4,574,560	Oslo	43/C 3
Nova Scotia, Canada	21,425	55,491	908,007	Halifax	85/H 2
Nunavut, Canada	733,590	1,900,000	26,795	Iqaluit	76/G 2
O					
Ohio, U.S.	44,828	116,103	11,353,140	Columbus	84/D 3
Oklahoma, U.S.	69,903	181,048	3,450,654	Oklahoma City	86/D 3
Oman*	82,031	212,460	2,903,165	Muscat	52/G 4
Ontario, Canada	412,580	1,068,582	11,410,046	Toronto	76/H 3
Oregon, U.S.	97,132	251,571	3,421,399	Salem	80/C 4
P					
Pakistan*	310,403	803,944	153,705,278	Islamabad	49/F 7
Palau*	177	458	20,016	Koror	62/C 4
Panama*	30,193	78,200	3,000,463	Panamá	88/E 6
Papua New Guinea*	178,259	461,690	5,420,280	Port Moresby	62/D 5
Paraguay*	157,047	406,752	6,191,368	Asunción	91/C 5
Pennsylvania, U.S.	46,058	119,291	12,281,054	Harrisburg	84/E 3
Peru*	496,223	1,285,220	28,863,494	Lima	94/C 5
Philippines*	115,830	300,000	86,241,697	Manila	57/H 3
Poland*	120,725	312,678	38,626,349	Warsaw	39/F 3
Portugal*	35,552	92,080	10,119,250	Lisbon	42/C 6
Prince Edward Island, Canada	2,184	5,657	135,294	Charlottetown	85/J 2
Puerto Rico, U.S.	3,508	9,085	3,957,988	San Juan	89/H 4
Q					
Qatar*	4,247	11,000	840,290	Doha	52/F 3
Québec, Canada	594,857	1,540,680	7,237,479	Québec	77/J 3
R					
Réunion, France	969	2,510	766,153	St-Denis	13/M 7
Rhode Island, U.S.	1,231	3,189	1,048,319	Providence	85/G 3
Romania*	91,699	237,500	22,355,551	Bucharest	44/D 2

Place	Square Miles	Square Kilometers	Population	Capital or Chief Town	Page/Index Ref.
Russia*	6,592,735	17,075,200	144,112,353	Moscow	46/H 3
Rwanda*	10,169	26,337	7,954,013	Kigali	70/E 1
S					
Saint Kitts and Nevis*	104	269	38,836	Basseterre	89/J 4
Saint Lucia*	239	620	164,213	Castries	89/J 5
Saint Vincent & the Grenadines*	131	340	117,193	Kingstown	89/J 5
Samoa*	1,104	2,860	177,714	Apia	63/H 6
San Marino*	23.4	60.6	28,503	San Marino	42/G 5
São Tomé and Príncipe*	371	960	181,565	São Tomé	68/F 7
Saskatchewan, Canada	251,865	652,330	978,933	Regina	76/F 3
Saudi Arabia*	756,981	1,960,582	25,100,425	Riyadh	52/D 4
Scotland, U.K.	30,414	78,772	5,062,011	Edinburgh	42/C 2
Senegal*	75,749	196,190	10,852,147	Dakar	68/B 5
Serbia and Montenegro*	39,517	102,350	10,663,022	Belgrade	44/D 3
Seychelles*	176	455	80,832	Victoria	13/M 6
Sierra Leone*	27,699	71,740	5,883,889	Freetown	68/C 6
Singapore*	244	632.6	4,767,974	Singapore	56/C 5
Slovakia*	18,859	48,845	5,423,567	Bratislava	44/C 2
Slovenia*	7,836	20,296	1,938,282	Ljubljana	44/B 2
Solomon Islands*	10,985	28,450	523,617	Honiara	62/E 6
Somalia*	246,200	637,658	8,304,601	Mogadishu	69/Q 6
South Africa*	471,008	1,219,912	42,718,530	Cape Town; Pretoria	70/D 6
South America	6,879,916	17,819,000	368,926,272	....	91
South Carolina, U.S.	31,189	80,779	4,012,012	Columbia	87/H 3
South Dakota, U.S.	77,121	199,744	754,844	Pierre	81/H 4
Spain*	194,884	504,750	40,280,780	Madrid	42/D 5
Sri Lanka*	25,332	65,610	19,905,165	Colombo; Sri Jayeward-enepura Kotte	53/D 7
Sudan*	967,494	2,505,809	39,148,162	Khartoum	69/L 5
Suriname*	63,039	163,270	436,935	Paramaribo	95/G 3
Swaziland*	6,703	17,360	1,169,241	Mbabane	70/F 6
Sweden*	173,731	449,964	8,986,400	Stockholm	43/D 3
Switzerland	15,943	41,292	7,450,867	Bern	42/F 4
Syria*	71,498	185,180	18,016,874	Damascus	52/C 1
T					
Taiwan	13,892	35,980	22,749,838	T'aipei	55/M 7
Tajikistan*	55,251	143,100	7,011,556	Dushanbe	46/H 6
Tanzania*	364,699	945,090	36,588,225	Dar es Salaam	70/F 2
Tennessee, U.S.	42,146	109,158	5,689,283	Nashville	87/G 3
Texas, U.S.	267,277	692,248	20,851,820	Austin	86/C 4
Thailand*	198,455	513,998	64,865,523	Bangkok	56/C 2
Togo*	21,927	56,790	5,556,812	Lomé	68/F 6
Tonga	289	748	110,237	Nuku'alofa	63/H 7
Trinidad and Tobago*	1,980	5,128	1,096,585	Port-of-Spain	89/J 5
Tunisia*	63,170	163,610	10,032,050	Tunis	68/G 1
Turkey*	301,382	780,580	68,893,918	Ankara	44/F 4
Turkmenistan*	188,455	488,100	4,863,169	Ashkhabad	46/F 6
Tuvalu	10	26	11,468	Funafuti	62/G 5
U					
Uganda*	91,135	236,040	26,404,543	Kampala	69/M 7
Ukraine*	233,089	603,700	47,732,079	Kiev	44/E 2
United Arab Emirates*	29,182	75,581	2,523,915	Abu Dhabi	52/F 4
United Kingdom*	94,525	244,820	60,270,708	London	42/D 2
United States*	3,618,765	9,372,610	293,027,571	Washington, D.C.	78
Uruguay*	68,039	176,220	3,440,205	Montevideo	96/E 3
Utah, U.S.	84,904	219,902	2,233,169	Salt Lake City	82/E 3
Uzbekistan*	172,741	447,400	26,410,416	Tashkent	46/G 5
V					
Vanuatu*	5,699	14,760	202,609	Port-Vila	62/F 6
Vatican City	0.17	0.44	911	....	42/G 5
Venezuela*	352,143	912,050	25,017,387	Caracas	94/E 2
Vermont, U.S.	9,614	24,900	608,827	Montpelier	85/F 2
Vietnam*	127,243	329,560	82,689,518	Hanoi	49/K 8
Virginia, U.S.	42,326	109,625	7,078,515	Richmond	87/J 2
Virgin Islands, British	59	153	22,187	Road Town	89/J 4
Virgin Islands, U.S.	136	352	108,775	Charlotte Amalie	89/H 4
W					
Wales, U.K.	8,017	20,764	2,903,085	Cardiff	42/D 3
Washington, U.S.	70,637	182,949	5,894,121	Olympia	80/C 4
West Bank	2,263	5,860	2,311,204	....	52/C 2
Western Sahara	102,703	266,000	267,405	....	68/B 3
West Virginia, U.S.	24,231	62,758	1,808,344	Charleston	84/D 4
Wisconsin, U.S.	65,499	169,643	5,363,675	Madison	84/B 2
World	(land) 57,505,734	148,940,000	6,375,882,069	....	12
Wyoming, U.S.	97,818	253,349	493,782	Cheyenne	80/F 5
Y					
Yemen*	203,849	527,970	20,024,867	Sanaa	52/E 6
Yukon Territory, Canada	186,660	483,450	28,674	Whitehorse	76/D 2
Z					
Zambia*	290,583	752,610	10,462,436	Lusaka	70/E 3
Zimbabwe*	150,803	390,580	12,671,860	Harare	70/E 4

World – Physical

■ World Physical Map   ■ Land Elevation and Ocean Depth Profiles

LAND ELEVATION AND OCEAN DEPTH PROFILES

1

2

3

4

5

6

7

8

9

10

ARCTIC OCEAN

Svalbard Franz Josef Land Severnaya Zemlya 80°
Nordkapp Novaya Kara Sea New Siberian Is.
BARENTS Zemlya Yamal
SEA Pen. Arctic Circle 60°
Kola Pen. Yenisey Tower Tunguska Lena Kolyma Ra.
White Sea Oh West Central Aldan BERING SEA
Stockholm Siberian Siberian Anadyr Kamchatka Pen.
L. Ladoga Plain Plateau L. Baykal SEA OF OKHOTSK 3
Moscow Irtysh Amur Sakhalin
EUROPE Kirgiz Steppe A S I A Kuril Is.
Carpathians Dnipro Altai Mts. NORTHWEST
Volga Aral Balkhash Gobi Hokkaido PACIFIC 40°
Black Sea Sea Tian Shan Honshu BASIN
Rome Caucasus Caspian Sea of NORTH
Istanbul El'brus Amu Darya Takla Japan JAPAN
Taurus Mts. 5,642 m Makan Beijing Tokyo TRENCH PACIFIC
Zagros Mts. Hindu Kush Kunlun Shan Yellow East
Tehran Himalaya Huang Sea China 4
Cairo Tigris India Satluen Sea Ryukyu Is.
Euphrates Mt. Everest Ganges RYUKYU TRENCH -7,507 m Tropic of Cancer
Persian Gulf 8,848 m Taiwan PHILIPPINE OCEAN 20°
Red Sea Hills Karachi Narmada Red PHILIPPINE MARIANA
Arabian Hainan Luzon SEA Mariana Is. TRENCH CENTRAL
RICA Arabian Pen. ARABIAN Mumbai BAY SOUTH Manila BASIN Challenger Deep Marshall PACIFIC 5
L. Chad Rub' al Khali SEA (Bombay) OF CHINA Palawan -11,033 m Is. BASIN
Gulf of Aden BENGAL Andaman SEA Sulu Caroline Is. MELANESIAN
Ethiopian Socotra CARLSBERG Is. Mekong Sea Mindanao
Plateau C. Comorin Malay Celebes BASIN 0°
SOMALI RIDGE Sri Lanka Pen. Sea Halmahera
Congo BASIN Maldive Equator Borneo Celebes Bismarck Arch.
Basin Kilimanjaro Is. Sumatra SEA New New
Kinshasa 5,895 m INDIAN Chagos Java Sea Guinea Britain Solomon Is.
Victoria Seychelles Arch. Jakarta Java Banda Sea 6
L. Tanganyika OCEAN Cocos Is. JAVA TRENCH -7,450 m Arafura Torres Str.
Comoros Sea Cape CORAL New
Lusaka Zambezi Is. Timor Gulf York SEA Hebrides
Madagascar Sea of Pen. Great Barrier Reef Fiji Is.
Réunion Carpentaria New
Mauritius BROKEN AUSTRALIA Caledonia 20°
Johannesburg PLATEAU Great Victoria Great North C. 7
Kalahari Desert Dividing Sydney North
Orange C. Leeuwin Great Murray Mt. Kosciusko TASMAN
Good Hope Australian Darling 2,228 m SEA North 40°
SOUTHWEST INDIAN RIDGE Bight Melbourne South
SOUTHEAST Tasmania
Kerguélen INDIAN 8
McDonald Is. RIDGE
KERGUELEN AUSTRALIAN-ANTARCTIC BASIN 60°
PLATEAU
ENDERBY ABYSSAL PLAIN C. Adare
C. Batterbee 9
ROSS SEA
ANTARCTICA 80°
10

© HAMMOND WORLD ATLAS CORPORATION

POPULATION OF CITIES AND TOWNS
◉ OVER 5,000,000   ⊙ 500,000 - 1,999,999
◉ 2,000,000 - 4,999,999   ○ UNDER 500,000

SCALE 1:81,700,000   ROBINSON PROJECTION STANDARD PARALLELS 38°N AND 38°S
MILES   0   1000   2000   3000
KILOMETERS 0   1000   2000   3000

Glockner 12,457 K2 28,250 Dhaulagiri Everest 29,028 FEET 30,000
Etna Margherita 16,795 Kilimanjaro Elbrus Tirich Mir 25,230 26,810 Kanchenjunga Namcha Barwa Gongga 24,790 25,000
11,053 19,340 Dashan 18,510 Ararat Damavand 28,208 25,445 20,000
Gerlachovka 15,157 16,946 18,605 Kinabalu Jaya 16,503 Klyuchevskaya Cook 12,349 15,000
8,707 East African Caucasus Elburz Semeru 13,455 Yu 13,113 Fuji 12,389 15,584 10,000
Carpathian Mts. Highlands Mts. Luser 11,371 Kerinci 12,467 12,060 Kosciusko Southern Alps 5,000
Qattara Depression Dead Sea Lake Assal -512 Caspian Sea 7,310 Aleutian Ra. SEA LEVEL
-436 Lake Eyre -39 5,000
Agulhas Basin Mozambique Enderby Abyssal Southwest Indian Ridge Mid-Indian Ninetyeast South
Basin Ocean Basin Ridge Australian Basin 10,000
-18,040 -19,680 -16,400 Chagos -18,040 -18,040 Weber 15,000
Trench New Basin Kuril- 20,000
Java -17,220 Sunda -27,960 Yap Mariana Kamchatka Hebrides Aleutian 24,600
Trench Trench -3,120 Philippine -27,912 Trench Trench Trench Trench 25,000
Planet Deep -18,010 Trench Gap -32,088 26,240 Tonga 30,000
-25,344 Challenger Deep -36,810 Horizon Deep 35,424 Trench 35,000

World – Political

■ World Political Map ■ Comparative Populations ■ Comparative Land Areas

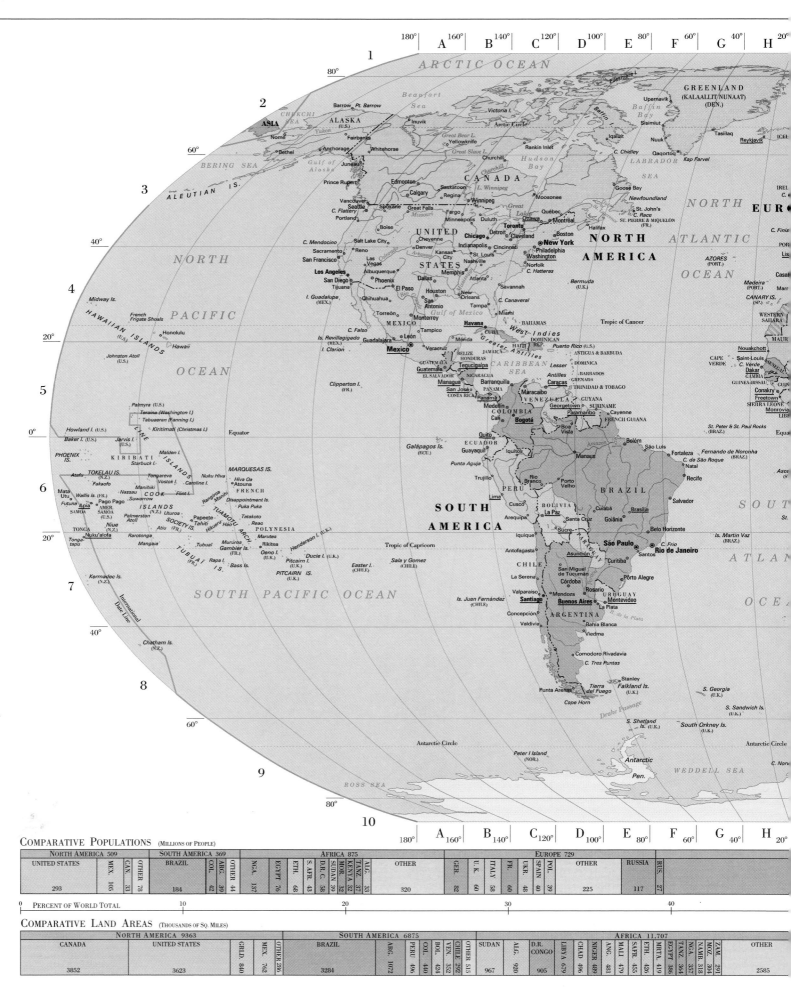

COMPARATIVE POPULATIONS (MILLIONS OF PEOPLE)

NORTH AMERICA 509				SOUTH AMERICA 369				AFRICA 875												EUROPE 729										
UNITED STATES	MEX.	CAN.	OTHER	BRAZIL	COL.	ARG.	OTHER	NGA.	EGYPT	ETH.	S. AFR.	D.R.C.	SUDAN	MOR.	KENYA	TANZ.	ALG.	OTHER		GER.	U.K.	ITALY	FR.	UKR.	SPAIN	POL.	OTHER	RUSSIA	RUS.
293	105	33	78	184	42	39	44	137	76	68	43	58	39	32	32	37	33	320		82	60	58	60	48	40	39	225	117	27

0 — PERCENT OF WORLD TOTAL — 10 — 20 — 30 — 40

COMPARATIVE LAND AREAS (THOUSANDS OF SQ. MILES)

NORTH AMERICA 9363					SOUTH AMERICA 6875							AFRICA 11,707																
CANADA	UNITED STATES	GR.LD.	MEX.	OTHER	BRAZIL	ARG.	PERU	BOL.	VEN.	CHILE	OTHER	SUDAN	ALG.	D.R. CONGO	LIBYA	CHAD	NIGER	ANG.	MALI	S.AFR.	ETH.	MRTA.	EGYPT	TANZ.	NGA.	MOZ.	NAMB.	ZAM.	OTHER
3852	3623	840	762	286	3284	1072	496	424	352	292	515	967	920	905	679	496	489	481	479	455	426	419	386	364	357	304	318	291	2585

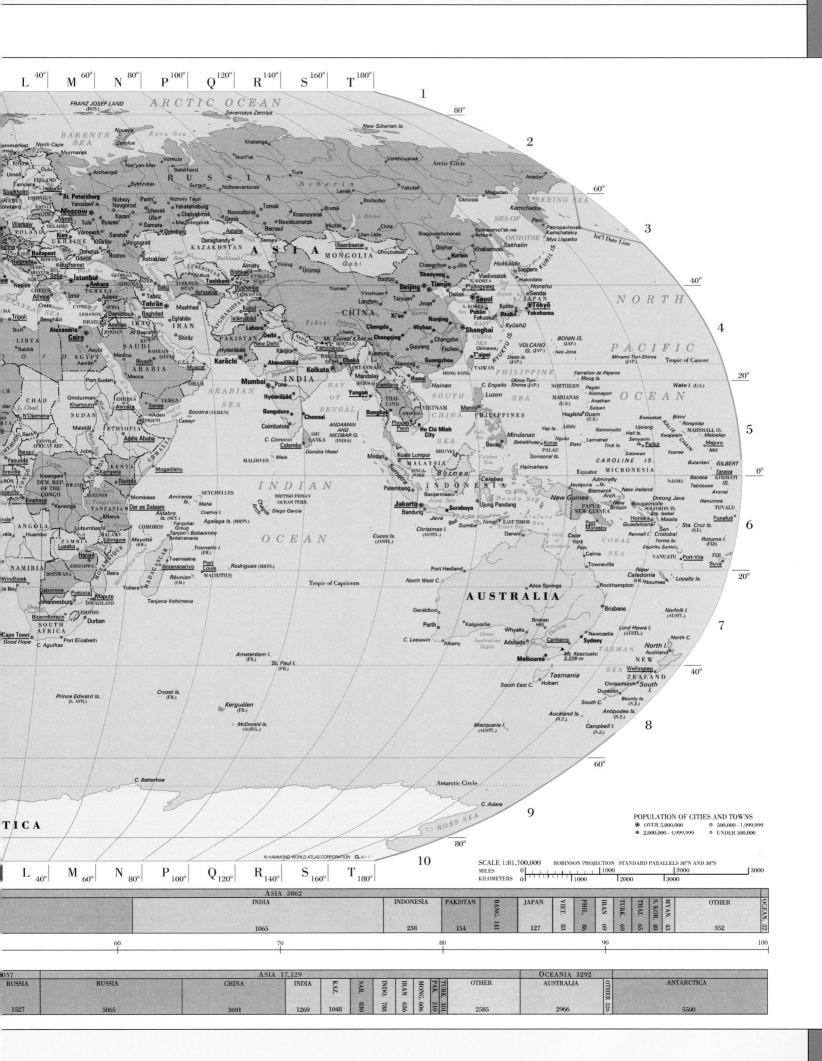

Structure of the Earth

■ **Plate Tectonics** ■ **Continental Drift**

⊙ Plate Tectonics, Volcanoes, and Earthquakes

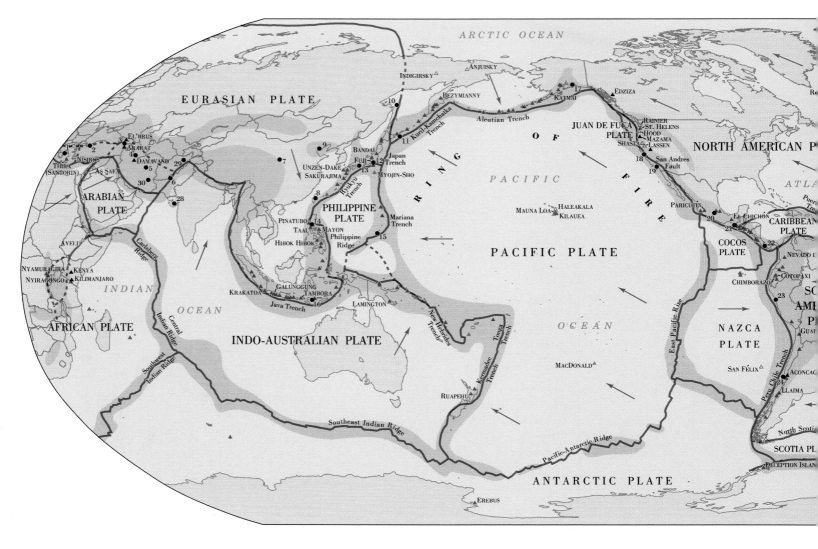

| ▲ Active Volcanoes | △ Dormant Volcanoes | ▲ Extinct Volcanoes | ▴ Submarine Volcanoes | ● Earthquakes | ▨ Earthquake Zones | — Plate Boundaries | - - - Uncertain Bou |

The making of continents began more than 200 million years ago with the splitting of a gigantic landmass know as Pangaea. The initial division formed two supercontinents, Laurasia and Gondwana. Over a period of many millions of years these landmasses further subdivided into smaller parts and drifted across a single great ocean, forming the oceans and continents of today. In terms of current theory, called plate tectonics, the earth's crust is divided into at least 15 rigid rock segments, known as plates, that float on a semi-molten layer of upper mantle. Seven plates are of major size and, except for the vast Pacific Plate, carry a continental landmass with surrounding ocean floor and island areas. The plates are slow-moving, driven by powerful forces within the mantle. At their boundaries they are either slowly separating with new material being added from the mantle, converging, with one plate being forced down (subducted) and consumed under another; or sliding past each other. Almost all earthquakes, and volcanic and mountain-building activity

⊙ Continental Drift

180 Million Years Ago   70 Million Years Ago   Present Time

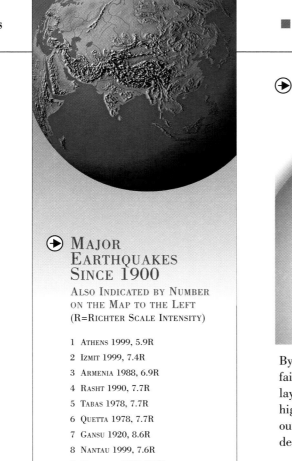

⊕ INTERIOR AND CRUST OF THE EARTH

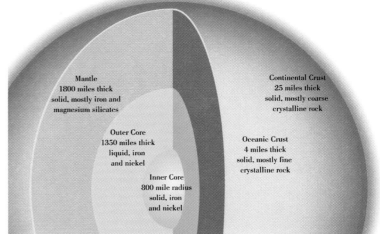

By studying records of earthquakes, scientists have developed a fairly reasonable picture (cross section) of the earth's principle layers, including their composition. The inner core is a very dense, highly pressurized, extremely hot (about 9,000 °F.) sphere. Moving outward toward the crust, densities, pressures and temperatures decrease significantly.

⊕ VOLCANOES

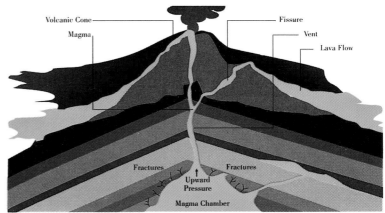

One of the earth's most dynamic and colorful builders is the volcano. In the mantle, magma – molten rock containing compressed gases – probes for weak spots in the earth's crust, and bursts forth through the ground in an eruption of fiery lava, ash, gas and steam. After a period of eruption, lasting from a few days to many years, the magma ceases to push upward and the volcano becomes dormant.

⊕ MAJOR EARTHQUAKES SINCE 1900

ALSO INDICATED BY NUMBER ON THE MAP TO THE LEFT (R=RICHTER SCALE INTENSITY)

1 ATHENS 1999, 5.9R
2 IZMIT 1999, 7.4R
3 ARMENIA 1988, 6.9R
4 RASHT 1990, 7.7R
5 TABAS 1978, 7.7R
6 QUETTA 1978, 7.7R
7 GANSU 1920, 8.6R
8 NANTAU 1999, 7.6R
9 TANGSHAN 1976, 7.8R
10 SAKHALIN 1995, 7.5R
11 KURIL ISLANDS 1994, 7.9R
12 TOKYO 1923, 8.3R
13 KOBE 1995, 7.2R
14 CABANATUAN 1990, 7.7R
15 GUAM 1993, 8.1R
16 FLORES 1992, 7.5R
17 SOUTHERN ALASKA 1964, 8.4R
18 SAN FRANCISCO 1906, 8.3R; 1989, 6.9R
19 LOS ANGELES 1994, 6.6R
20 MEXICO CITY 1985, 8.1R
21 GUATEMALA 1976, 7.5R
22 SAN JOSÉ 1991, 7.4R
23 CHIMBOTE 1970, 7.8R
24 VALPARAÍSO 1906, 8.6R
25 NAPLES 1980, 7.2R
26 EL ASNAM (CHLEF) 1980, 7.5R
27 AGADIR 1960, 5.7R
28 BHUJ 2001, 7.9R
29 BAGHLĀN 2002, 6.1R
30 BAM 2003, 6.6R

← DIRECTION OF PLATE MOVEMENT

closely follow these boundaries and are related to movements of the plates. Although these movements may be no more than inches per year, the destructive power unleashed can be cataclysmic.

⊕ PLATE TECTONICS

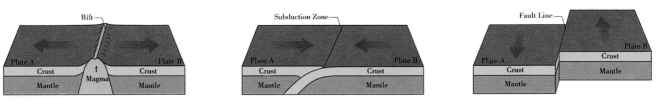

SEPARATING PLATES   CONVERGING PLATES   SLIDING PLATES

Atmosphere and Oceans

■ Ocean Currents   ■ Hurricanes

➤ OCEAN CURRENTS

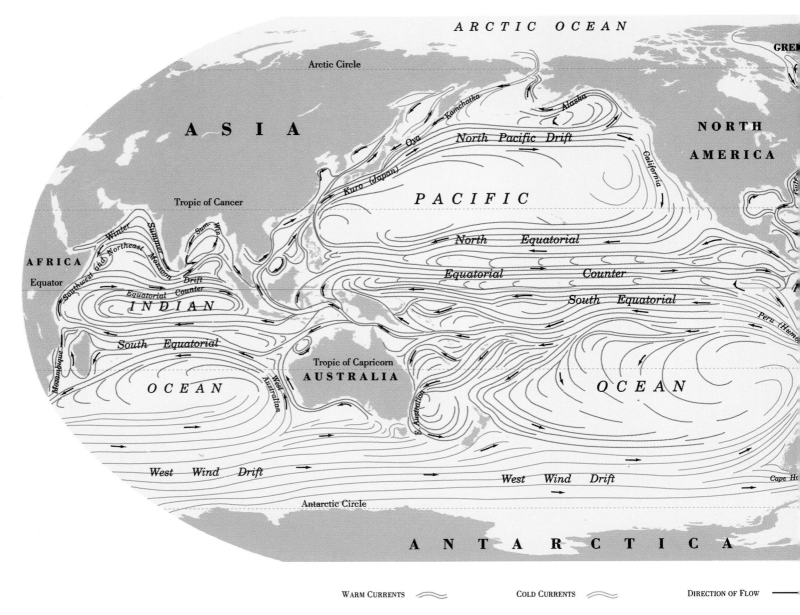

WARM CURRENTS ≋   COLD CURRENTS ≋   DIRECTION OF FLOW

➤ HURRICANES

Hurricane or Typhoon

Hurricanes are great whirling storms accompanied by violent destructive winds, torrential rains and high waves and tides. They originate over the oceans, and usually move from lower to higher latitudes with increasing speed, size and intensity. Movement over land quickly reduces their force. Hurricane winds cause severe property damage, but drowning is the greatest cause of hurricane deaths. Floods can be the hurricane's most serious threat.

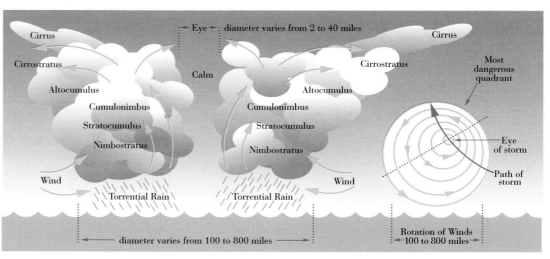

Illustrations not to scale

⊙ AIR PRESSURE AND WINDS

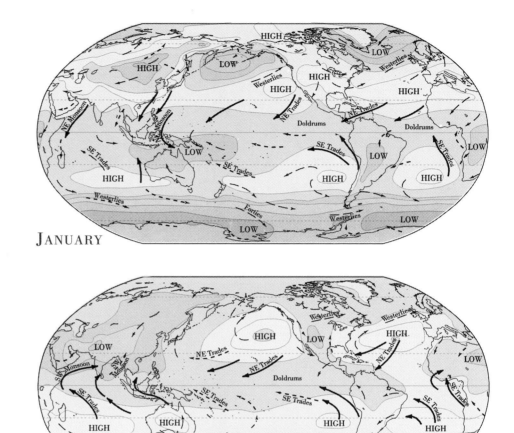

JANUARY

JULY

PRESSURE IN MILLIBARS					WINDS	
OVER 1038	1020 TO 1026	1002 TO 1008	984 TO 990		LESS OFTEN	— →
1032 TO 1038	1014 TO 1020	996 TO 1002	UNDER 984		MORE OFTEN	- - - ▸
1026 TO 1032	1008 TO 1014	990 TO 996			CONSTANT	⟶

⊙ WARM AND COLD FRONTS

A front is the boundary surface between two air masses which have different characteristics, primarily different temperatures. Depending upon the amount of moisture in the warm air, warm fronts usually produce steady, moderate precipitation over a broad area ahead of the front on the ground. Cold fronts tend to move faster than warm fronts. They are generally confined to a narrower frontal zone but may contain dense thunderheads and severe storms.

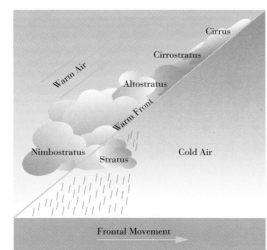

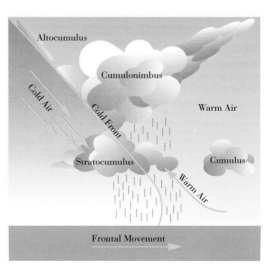

Left: Warm Front. Right: Cold Front.

Climate

■ **Climate Regions**　　■ **Average Temperatures**

⊙ CLIMATE REGIONS

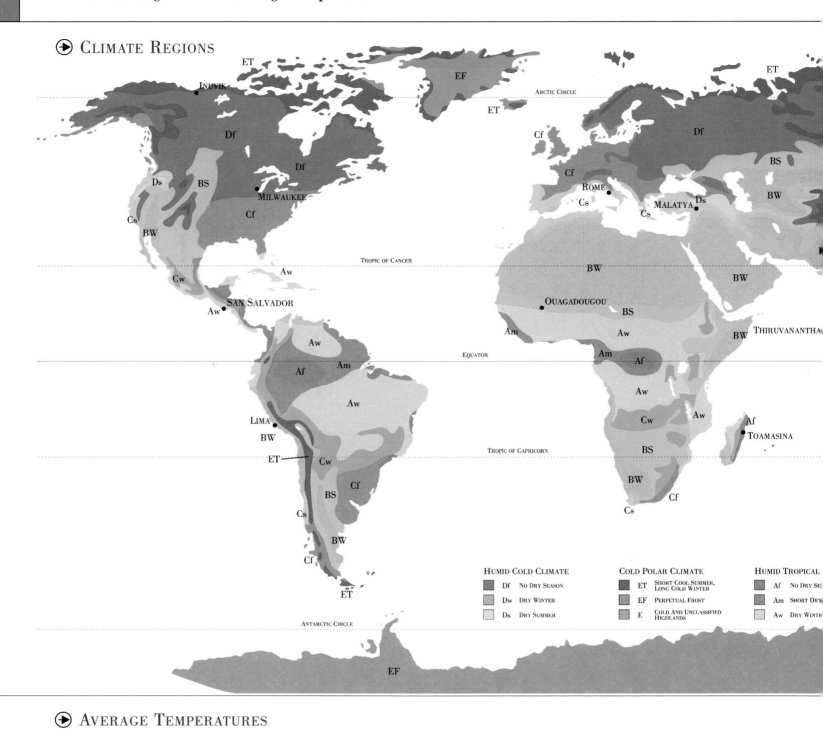

ET

EF

ET

INUVIK

Df

Cf

Cf

Df

BS

Df

ROME

BW

Cs

MALATYA

Ds

Df

MILWAUKEE

Ds

Cs

Cf

BS

Cs

BW

ARCTIC CIRCLE

TROPIC OF CANCER

BW

BW

Cw

Aw

Aw

SAN SALVADOR

OUAGADOUGOU

BS

Am

Aw

BW

THIRUVANANTHA

Aw

Aw

Am

Af

EQUATOR

Aw

Af

Am

Af

Cw

Aw

Af

LIMA

TOAMASINA

BW

TROPIC OF CAPRICORN

BS

ET

Cw

BW

BS

Cf

Cf

Cs

Cs

BW

Cf

ET

ANTARCTIC CIRCLE

EF

HUMID COLD CLIMATE

	Df	NO DRY SEASON
	Dw	DRY WINTER
	Ds	DRY SUMMER

COLD POLAR CLIMATE

	ET	SHORT COOL SUMMER, LONG COLD WINTER
	EF	PERPETUAL FROST
	E	COLD AND UNCLASSIFIED HIGHLANDS

HUMID TROPICAL

	Af	NO DRY SE
	Am	SHORT DRY
	Aw	DRY WINTE

⊙ AVERAGE TEMPERATURES

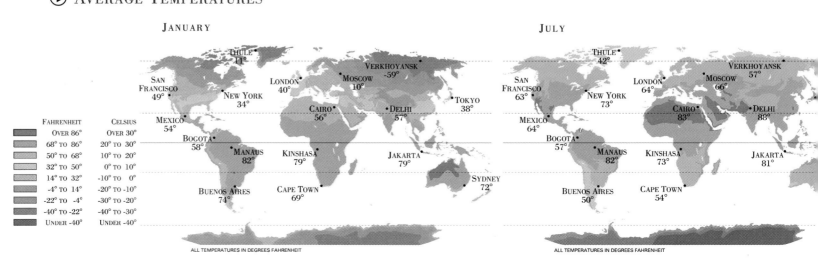

JANUARY

THULE 11°

VERKHOYANSK -59°

SAN FRANCISCO 49°

LONDON 40°

MOSCOW 10°

NEW YORK 34°

TOKYO 38°

MEXICO 54°

CAIRO 56°

DELHI 57°

BOGOTA 58°

MANAUS 82°

KINSHASA 79°

JAKARTA 79°

BUENOS AIRES 74°

CAPE TOWN 69°

SYDNEY 72°

JULY

THULE 42°

VERKHOYANSK 57°

SAN FRANCISCO 63°

LONDON 64°

MOSCOW 66°

NEW YORK 73°

DELHI 88°

MEXICO 64°

CAIRO 83°

BOGOTA 57°

MANAUS 82°

KINSHASA 73°

JAKARTA 81°

BUENOS AIRES 50°

CAPE TOWN 54°

FAHRENHEIT	CELSIUS
OVER 86°	OVER 30°
68° TO 86°	20° TO 30°
50° TO 68°	10° TO 20°
32° TO 50°	0° TO 10°
14° TO 32°	-10° TO 0°
-4° TO 14°	-20° TO -10°
-22° TO -4°	-30° TO -20°
-40° TO -22°	-40° TO -30°
UNDER -40°	UNDER -40°

ALL TEMPERATURES IN DEGREES FAHRENHEIT

ALL TEMPERATURES IN DEGREES FAHRENHEIT

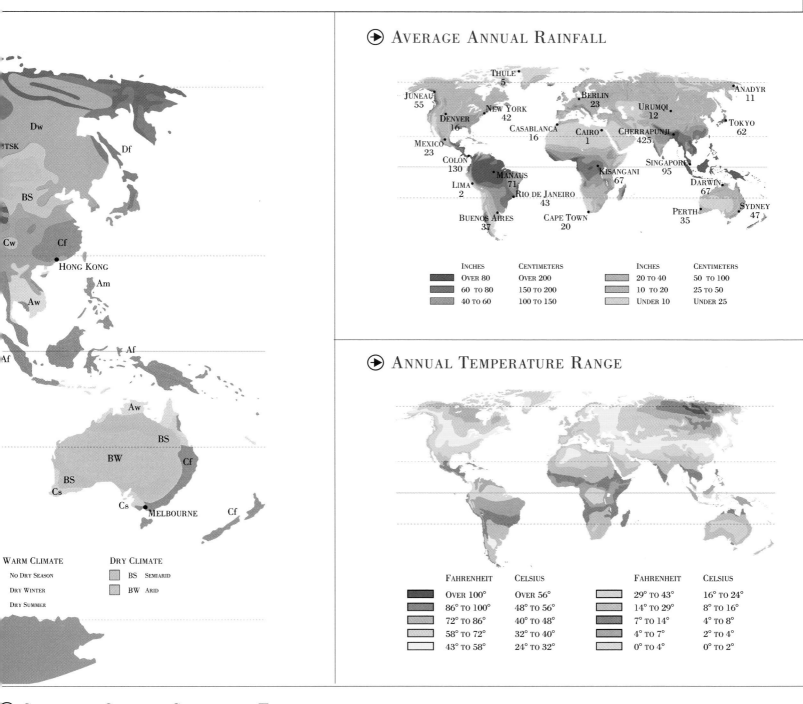

AVERAGE ANNUAL RAINFALL

THULE 5
JUNEAU 55
BERLIN 23
ANADYR 11
URUMQI 12
NEW YORK 42
DENVER 16
TOKYO 62
CASABLANCA 16
CAIRO 1
CHERRAPUNJI 425
MEXICO 23
COLON 130
SINGAPORE 95
KISANGANI 67
MANAUS 71
LIMA 2
RIO DE JANEIRO 43
DARWIN 67
PERTH 35
SYDNEY 47
BUENOS AIRES 37
CAPE TOWN 20

INCHES	CENTIMETERS	INCHES	CENTIMETERS
OVER 80	OVER 200	20 TO 40	50 TO 100
60 TO 80	150 TO 200	10 TO 20	25 TO 50
40 TO 60	100 TO 150	UNDER 10	UNDER 25

ANNUAL TEMPERATURE RANGE

FAHRENHEIT	CELSIUS	FAHRENHEIT	CELSIUS
OVER 100°	OVER 56°	29° TO 43°	16° TO 24°
86° TO 100°	48° TO 56°	14° TO 29°	8° TO 16°
72° TO 86°	40° TO 48°	7° TO 14°	4° TO 8°
58° TO 72°	32° TO 40°	4° TO 7°	2° TO 4°
43° TO 58°	24° TO 32°	0° TO 4°	0° TO 2°

Dw
Df
TSK
BS
Cw
Cf
HONG KONG
Am
Aw
Af
Af
Aw
BS
BW
Cf
BS
Cs
Cs
MELBOURNE
Cf

WARM CLIMATE
NO DRY SEASON
DRY WINTER
DRY SUMMER

DRY CLIMATE
BS SEMIARID
BW ARID

SELECTED CLIMATE STATIONS - TEMPERATURES AND RAINFALL

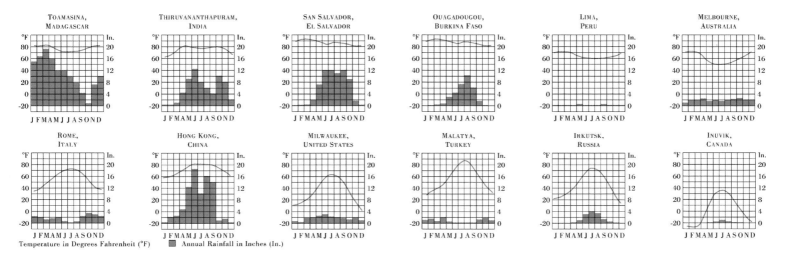

TOAMASINA, MADAGASCAR
THIRUVANANTHAPURAM, INDIA
SAN SALVADOR, EL SALVADOR
OUAGADOUGOU, BURKINA FASO
LIMA, PERU
MELBOURNE, AUSTRALIA

ROME, ITALY
HONG KONG, CHINA
MILWAUKEE, UNITED STATES
MALATYA, TURKEY
IRKUTSK, RUSSIA
INUVIK, CANADA

Temperature in Degrees Fahrenheit (°F)   ■ Annual Rainfall in Inches (In.)

Vegetation and Soils

⊕ NATURAL VEGETATION

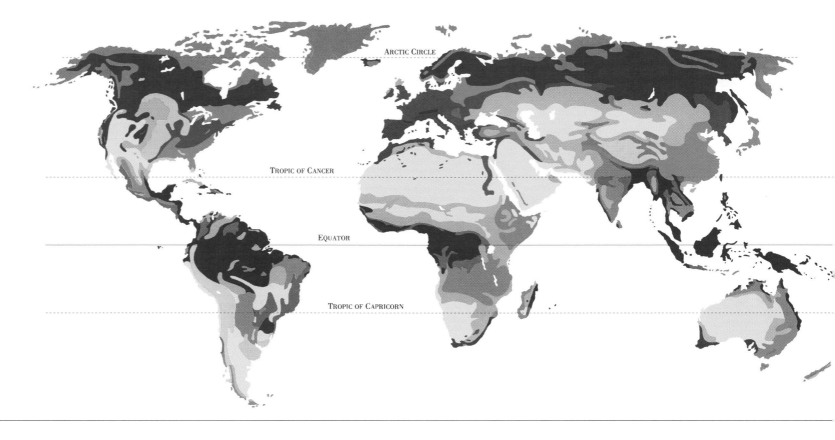

NEEDLELEAF FOREST
Found in higher latitudes with shorter growing seasons, and dominated by pure stands of softwood, evergreen conifers (cone-bearing trees) such as pine, fir and spruce. The light undergrowth consists of small shrubs, mosses, lichens and pine needles.

BROADLEAF FOREST
Found in the middle latitudes, this forest of deciduous (seasonal leaf-shedding) trees includes the hardwoods maple, hickory and oak. The forest floor is relatively barren, except for thick leaf cover during colder months.

MIXED NEEDLELEAF AND BROADLEAF FOREST
A transitional zone between northern softwoods and temperate hardwoods.

WOODLAND AND SHRUB (MEDITERRANEAN)
A mid-latitude area of broadleaf evergreens, dense growths of woody shrubs and open grassy woodland, characterized by pronounced dry summers and wet winters.

SHORT GRASS (STEPPE)
A mid-latitude, semi-arid area usually found on the fringe of desert regions, with continuous short-grass cover up to 8" (20 cm.) tall, used chiefly to graze livestock.

TALL GRASS (PRAIRIE)
Mid-latitude, semi-moist areas with continuous tall-grass cover up to 24" (61 cm.) in height, used for agricultural purposes. Rainfall is insufficient to support larger plants.

TROPICAL RAIN FOREST (SELVA)
A dense, evergreen forest of tall, varied hardwood trees with a thick broadleaf canopy and a dark, moist interior with minimal undergrowth.

LIGHT TROPICAL FOREST (TROPICAL SEMIDECIDUOUS OR MONSOON FOREST)
As above, with more widely spaced trees, heavier undergrowth, larger concentrations of single species. Dry season prevents most trees from remaining evergreen. Found in monsoon areas.

TROPICAL WOODLAND AND SHRUB (THORN FOREST)
Longer dry season results in low trees with thick bark and smaller leaves. Dense undergrowth of thorny plants, brambles and grasses. Transition belt between denser forests and grasslands.

TROPICAL GRASSLAND AND SHRUB (SAVANNA)
Stiff, sharp-edged grasses, from 2' to 12' (0.6 m. to 3.7 m.) high, with large areas of bare ground. Scattered shrubs and low trees in some areas.

WOODED SAVANNA
A transitional area where savanna joins a tropical or shrub forest, with low trees and shrubs dotting the grasslands.

DESERT AND DESERT SHRUB
Barren stretches of soft brown, yellow or red sand and rock wastes with isolated patches of short grass and stunted bushes, turning bright green when fed by infrequent precipitation.

RIVER VALLEY AND OASIS
River valleys are lush, fertile lands, with varied vegetation. An oasis is a fertile or verdant spot found in a desert near a natural spring or pool.

HEATH AND MOOR
A heath is open, uncultivated land covered with low, flowering evergreen shrubs such as heather. Moors are often high and poorly drained lands, with patches of heath and peat bogs.

TUNDRA AND ALPINE
An area of scarce moisture and short, cool summers where trees cannot survive. A permanently frozen subsoil supports low-growing lichens, mosses and stunted shrubs.

UNCLASSIFIED HIGHLANDS
Sequential bands or vertical zones of all vegetation types, which generally follow the warm-to-cold upward patterns found in corresponding areas of vegetation. (Map scale does not permit delineation of these areas.)

PERMANENT ICE COVER
Permanently ice and snow-covered terrain found in polar regions and atop high mountains.

⊕ TYPES OF SOILS

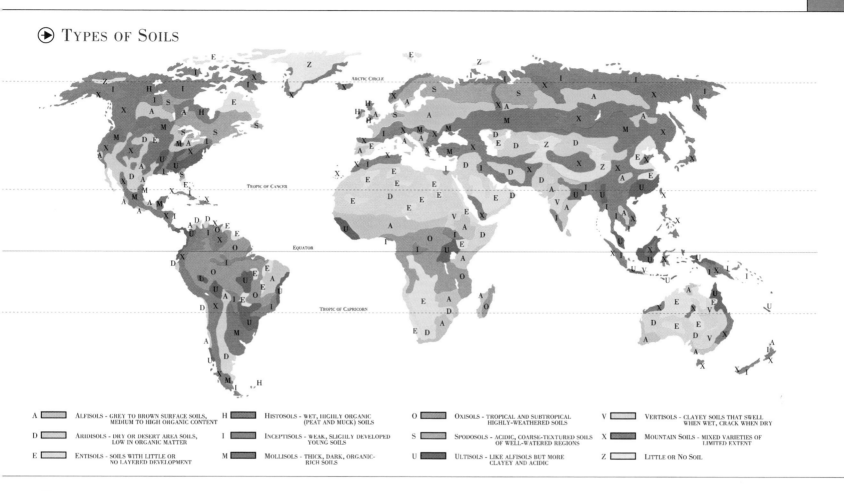

A ▭	ALFISOLS - GREY TO BROWN SURFACE SOILS, MEDIUM TO HIGH ORGANIC CONTENT	
D ▭	ARIDISOLS - DRY OR DESERT AREA SOILS, LOW IN ORGANIC MATTER	
E ▭	ENTISOLS - SOILS WITH LITTLE OR NO LAYERED DEVELOPMENT	
H ▭	HISTOSOLS - WET, HIGHLY ORGANIC (PEAT AND MUCK) SOILS	
I ▭	INCEPTISOLS - WEAK, SLIGHLY DEVELOPED YOUNG SOILS	
M ▭	MOLLISOLS - THICK, DARK, ORGANIC-RICH SOILS	
O ▭	OXISOLS - TROPICAL AND SUBTROPICAL HIGHLY-WEATHERED SOILS	
S ▭	SPODOSOLS - ACIDIC, COARSE-TEXTURED SOILS OF WELL-WATERED REGIONS	
U ▭	ULTISOLS - LIKE ALFISOLS BUT MORE CLAYEY AND ACIDIC	
V ▭	VERTISOLS - CLAYEY SOILS THAT SWELL WHEN WET, CRACK WHEN DRY	
X ▭	MOUNTAIN SOILS - MIXED VARIETIES OF LIMITED EXTENT	
Z ▭	LITTLE OR NO SOIL	

⊕ TYPES OF VEGETATION

Needleleaf Forest

These typically coniferous soft-wood forests of Europe, Asia and North America cover about 9 percent of the earth's land.

Broadleaf Forest

Located in the most pleasant habitable climatic regions, temperate broadleaf forests have suffered the greatest destruction by people.

Mixed Forest

These hardwood and softwood forests, when added to the broadleaf forest area, are home to over half the world's population.

Prairie

Unique to the Americas, tall grass prairie lands have been success-fully cultivated to become great grain fields of the world

Steppe

Slightly more moist than desert, steppe areas are sometimes cultivated but more often used for livestock ranching and herding.

Tropical Rain Forest

Teak, mahogany, balsawood, quinine, cocoa and rubber are some of the major products found in the world's tropical rain forest regions.

Savanna

A place of winter droughts and summer rainfall, these tropical grass and shrub areas are home to a wide variety of big-game animals.

Mediterranean

In addition to southern Europe and northern Africa, this vegetation also can be found in California, Chile, South Africa and Western Australia.

Desert Shrub

One-fifth of the world's land is desert and desert shrub, too dry for farming and ranching, and populated largely by nomads and oases-dwellers.

Tundra

Found along the Arctic fringe of North America and Eurasia, tundra is of little economic significance except for mineral exploitation.

Environmental Concerns

⊕ DESERTIFICATION AND ACID RAIN DAMAGE

EUROPE

NORTH AMERICA

ASIA

AFRICA

SOUTH AMERICA

AUSTRALIA

▬ AREAS OF PRODUCTIVE DRYLANDS DESERTIFIED BY EARLY 1980'S

● AREAS OF DAMAGE FROM ACID RAIN AND OTHER AIRBORNE POLLUTANTS

⊕ GREENHOUSE EFFECT

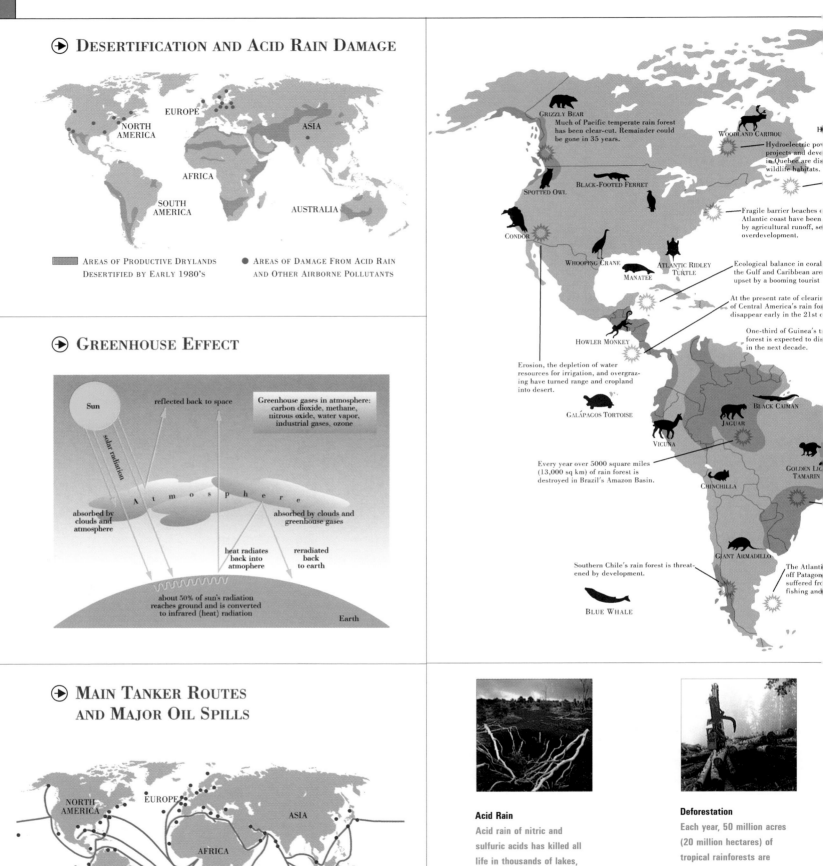

Sun

reflected back to space

Greenhouse gases in atmosphere: carbon dioxide, methane, nitrous oxide, water vapor, industrial gases, ozone

solar radiation

A t m o s p h e r e

absorbed by clouds and atmosphere

absorbed by clouds and greenhouse gases

heat radiates back into atmophere

reradiated back to earth

about 50% of sun's radiation reaches ground and is converted to infrared (heat) radiation

Earth

GRIZZLY BEAR
Much of Pacific temperate rain forest has been clear-cut. Remainder could be gone in 35 years.

WOODLAND CARIBOU

Hydroelectric po projects and deve in Quebec are dis wildlife habitats.

SPOTTED OWL

BLACK-FOOTED FERRET

Fragile barrier beaches Atlantic coast have been by agricultural runoff, se overdevelopment.

CONDOR

WHOOPING CRANE

MANATEE

ATLANTIC RIDLEY TURTLE

Ecological balance in cora the Gulf and Caribbean are upset by a booming tourist

At the present rate of clearin of Central America's rain for disappear early in the 21st c

One-third of Guinea's t forest is expected to di in the next decade.

HOWLER MONKEY

Erosion, the depletion of water resources for irrigation, and overgraz- ing have turned range and cropland into desert.

GALÁPAGOS TORTOISE

BLACK CAIMAN

JAGUAR

VICUNA

GOLDEN LI TAMARIN

CHINCHILLA

Every year over 5000 square miles (13,000 sq km) of rain forest is destroyed in Brazil's Amazon Basin.

GIANT ARMADILLO

Southern Chile's rain forest is threat- ened by development.

The Atlanti off Patagon suffered fr fishing and

BLUE WHALE

⊕ MAIN TANKER ROUTES AND MAJOR OIL SPILLS

NORTH AMERICA

EUROPE

ASIA

AFRICA

SOUTH AMERICA

AUSTRALIA

—— ROUTES OF VERY LARGE CRUDE OIL CARRIERS   ● MAJOR OIL SPILLS

Acid Rain

Acid rain of nitric and sulfuric acids has killed all life in thousands of lakes, and over 15 million acres (6 million hectares) of virgin forest in Europe and North America are dead or dying.

Deforestation

Each year, 50 million acres (20 million hectares) of tropical rainforests are being felled by loggers. Trees remove carbon dioxide from the atmosphere and are vital to the prevention of soil erosion.

Vanishing Wilderness and Endangered Species

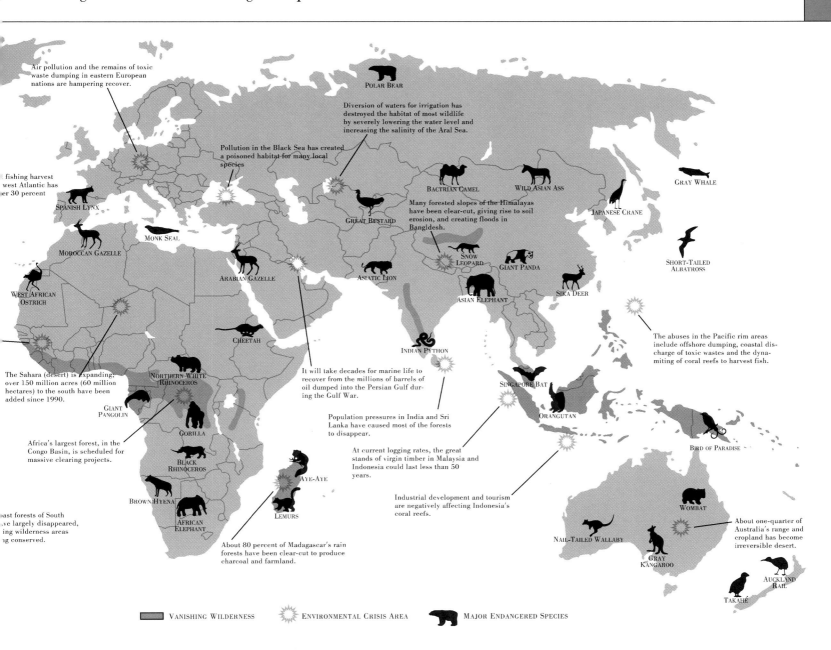

Air pollution and the remains of toxic waste dumping in eastern European nations are hampering recover.

POLAR BEAR

Diversion of waters for irrigation has destroyed the habitat of most wildlife by severely lowering the water level and increasing the salinity of the Aral Sea.

Pollution in the Black Sea has created a poisoned habitat for many local species

fishing harvest west Atlantic has er 30 percent

SPANISH LYNX

MONK SEAL

MOROCCAN GAZELLE

WEST AFRICAN OSTRICH

ARABIAN GAZELLE

The Sahara (desert) is expanding; over 150 million acres (60 million hectares) to the south have been added since 1990.

GIANT PANGOLIN

NORTHERN WHITE RHINOCEROS

Africa's largest forest, in the Congo Basin, is scheduled for massive clearing projects.

GORILLA

BLACK RHINOCEROS

BROWN HYENA

ast forests of South ve largely disappeared, ing wilderness areas ng conserved.

AFRICAN ELEPHANT

About 80 percent of Madagascar's rain forests have been clear-cut to produce charcoal and farmland.

AYE-AYE

LEMURS

CHEETAH

BACTRIAN CAMEL

WILD ASIAN ASS

GRAY WHALE

GREAT BUSTARD

Many forested slopes of the Himalayas have been clear-cut, giving rise to soil erosion, and creating floods in Bangldesh.

JAPANESE CRANE

SNOW LEOPARD

GIANT PANDA

SHORT-TAILED ALBATROSS

ASIATIC LION

SIKA DEER

ASIAN ELEPHANT

INDIAN PYTHON

It will take decades for marine life to recover from the millions of barrels of oil dumped into the Persian Gulf during the Gulf War.

Population pressures in India and Sri Lanka have caused most of the forests to disappear.

At current logging rates, the great stands of virgin timber in Malaysia and Indonesia could last less than 50 years.

Industrial development and tourism are negatively affecting Indonesia's coral reefs.

SINGAPORE BAT

ORANGUTAN

The abuses in the Pacific rim areas include offshore dumping, coastal discharge of toxic wastes and the dynamiting of coral reefs to harvest fish.

BIRD OF PARADISE

WOMBAT

NAIL-TAILED WALLABY

GRAY KANGAROO

About one-quarter of Australia's range and cropland has become irreversible desert.

AUCKLAND RAIL

TAKAHÉ

▬ VANISHING WILDERNESS ✺ ENVIRONMENTAL CRISIS AREA 🐻 MAJOR ENDANGERED SPECIES

Extinction
Biologists estimate that over 50,000 plant and animal species inhabiting the world's rain forests are disappearing each year due to pollution, unchecked hunting and the destruction of natural habitats.

Air Pollution
Billions of tons of industrial emissions and toxic pollutants are released into the air each year, depleting our ozone layer, killing our forests and lakes with acid rain and threatening our health.

Water Pollution
Only 3 percent of the earth's water is fresh. Pollution from cities, farms and factories has made much of it unfit to drink. In the developing world, most sewage flows untreated into lakes and rivers.

Ozone Depletion
The layer of ozone in the stratosphere shields earth from harmful ultraviolet radiation. But man-made gases are destroying this vital barrier, increasing the risk of skin cancer and eye disease.

Population

■ **Population Distribution** ■ **Population Density**

⊕ POPULATION DISTRIBUTION

This map provides a dramatic perspective by illuminating populated areas with one point of light for each city over 50,000 residents. Over 675 million people live in cities with populations in excess of 500,000. According to the latest census data, there are 11,650 people per square mile (4,500 per sq km) in London. In New York, there are 32,250 (12,450). Hong Kong has over 18,000 people per square mile (7,000 per sq km), and the Tokyo-Yokohama agglomeration includes over 14,250 (5,500). During the last decade, the movement to the cities has accelerated dramatically, particularly in developing nations. In Lagos, Nigeria, where there are over 28,500 people per square mile (11,000 per sq km), most live in shantytowns. In São Paulo, Brazil, 2,000 buses arrive each day, bringing field hands, farm workers and their families in search of a better life. Tokyo, Mexico and Mumbai are the world's largest urban agglomerations. By 2015, the United Nations predicts that 30 of the 40 largest urban agglomerations will be located in less-industrialized nations.

⊕ POPULATION DENSITY PER SQUARE MILE (SQ. KM.)

Legend:
- 1,000 - 5,000 (390 - 2,000)
- 500 - 1,000 (195 - 390)
- 100 - 500 (39 - 195)
- 30 - 100 (12 - 39)
- UNDER 30 (UNDER 12)

Source: U.S. Bureau of the Census, International

➤ AGE DISTRIBUTION

BOTSWANA

AGE	MALE	FEMALE

85+
80-84
75-79
70-74
65-69
60-64
55-59
50-54
45-49
40-44
35-39
30-34
25-29
20-24
15-19
10-14
5-9
0-4

% 8 6 4 2 0 2 4 6 8

(Percent of Total Population Male or Female)

UNITED STATES

AGE	MALE	FEMALE

85+
80-84
75-79
70-74
65-69
60-64
55-59
50-54
45-49
40-44
35-39
30-34
25-29
20-24
15-19
10-14
5-9
0-4

% 8 6 4 2 0 2 4 6 8

(Percent of Total Population Male or Female)

SWEDEN

AGE	MALE	FEMALE

85+
80-84
75-79
70-74
65-69
60-64
55-59
50-54
45-49
40-44
35-39
30-34
25-29
20-24
15-19
10-14
5-9
0-4

% 8 6 4 2 0 2 4 6 8

(Percent of Total Population Male or Female)

Source: U.S. Bureau of the Census, International Database

➤ URBAN & RURAL POPULATION COMPONENTS

WORLD'S LARGEST URBAN AREAS

MILLIONS OF INHABITANTS

Tokyo, Japan 26.5

Mexico, Mexico 18.1

Mumbai (Bombay), India 18.1

São Paulo, Brazil 17.7

New York, U.S. 16.6

Lagos, Nigeria 13.4

Los Angeles, U.S. 13.1

Kolkata, India 12.9

Shanghai, China 12.9

Buenos Aires, Argentina 12.5

Dhaka, Bangladesh 12.3

Jakarta, Indonesia 11.0

Osaka, Japan 11

Beijing, China 10.8

Rio de Janeiro, Brazil 10.5

URBAN & RURAL POPULATION COMPONENTS

SELECTED COUNTRIES

☐ URBAN   ☐ RURAL

Uruguay 87% / 13%

Australia 85% / 15%

Japan 77% / 23%

United States 74% / 26%

Russia 73% / 27%

Hungary 62% / 38%

Iran 54% / 46%

Egypt 44% / 56%

Philippines 37% / 63%

Portugal 30% / 70%

China 26% / 74%

Maldives 20% / 80%

Bangladesh 15% / 85%

Nepal 6% / 94%

➤ ANNUAL RATE OF POPULATION (NATURAL) INCREASE

■ 3.5 PERCENT OR MORE
■ 2.6 TO 3.4 PERCENT
■ 1.8 TO 2.5 PERCENT
■ .09 TO 1.7 PERCENT
■ .01 TO .08 PERCENT
☐ 0.0 OR DECREASE

Source: U.S. Bureau of the Census, International Database

Languages and Religions

■ Religions ■ Language Families

⊕ RELIGIONS

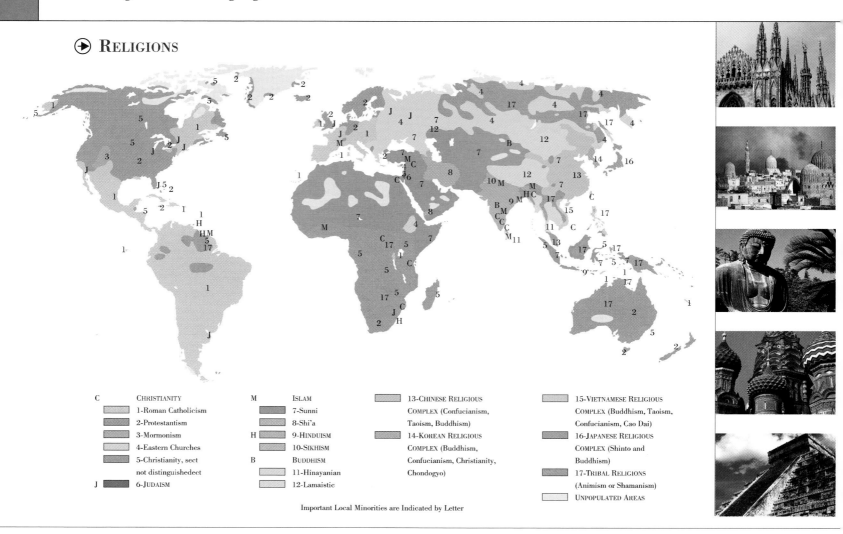

C CHRISTIANITY	**M** ISLAM	**13**-CHINESE RELIGIOUS COMPLEX (Confucianism, Taoism, Buddhism)	**15**-VIETNAMESE RELIGIOUS COMPLEX (Buddhism, Taoism, Confucianism, Cao Dai)
1-Roman Catholicism	**7**-Sunni		
2-Protestantism	**8**-Shi'a		**16**-JAPANESE RELIGIOUS COMPLEX (Shinto and Buddhism)
3-Mormonism	**H** **9**-HINDUISM	**14**-KOREAN RELIGIOUS COMPLEX (Buddhism, Confucianism, Christianity, Chondogyo)	
4-Eastern Churches	**10**-SIKHISM		**17**-TRIBAL RELIGIONS (Animism or Shamanism)
5-Christianity, sect not distinguishedect	**B** BUDDHISM		
6-JUDAISM	**11**-Hinayanian		UNPOPULATED AREAS
J	**12**-Lamaistic		

Important Local Minorities are Indicated by Letter

⊕ LANGUAGE FAMILIES

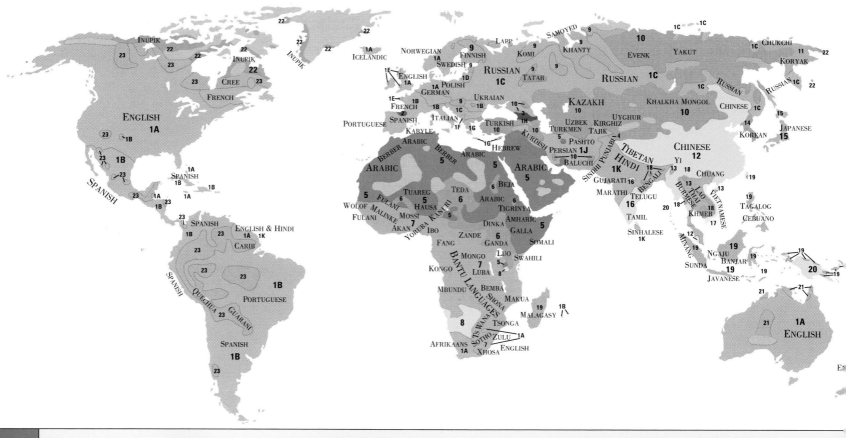

➤ THE INDO-EUROPEAN LANGUAGE TREE

The most well-established family tree is Indo-European. Spoken by more than 2.5 billion people, it contains dozens of languages. Some linguists theorize that all people – and all languages – are descended from a tiny population that lived in Africa some 200,000 years ago.

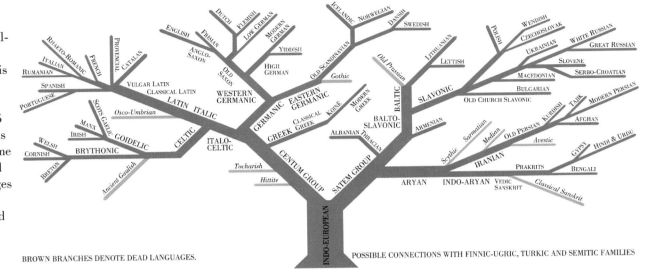

BROWN BRANCHES DENOTE DEAD LANGUAGES.

POSSIBLE CONNECTIONS WITH FINNIC-UGRIC, TURKIC AND SEMITIC FAMILIES

➤ LANGUAGES OF EUROPE

INDO-EUROPEAN FAMILY
- GERMANIC SUBFAMILY
- ROMANCE SUBFAMILY
- CELTIC SUBFAMILY
- SLAVIC SUBFAMILY
- BALTIC SUBFAMILY
- GREEK
- ALBANIAN

URALIC FAMILY
- FINNIC SUBFAMILY
- UGRIC SUBFAMILY
- SAMOYED

ALTAIC FAMILY
- TURKIC SUBFAMILY

AFRO-ASIATIC FAMILY
- MALTESE
- BASQUE

➤ Pictures on the left:

1. Milan Cathedral, Italy
2. City of the Dead, Cairo, Egypt
3. Buddha Statue, Japan
4. St. Basil's Cathedral, Moscow
5. Temple, Mexico

1-INDO-EUROPEAN	9-URALIC
1A-GERMANIC	10-ALTAIC
1B-ROMANCE	11-PALEO-SIBERIAN
1C-SLAVIC	FAMILIES
1D-BALTIC	12-SINO-TIBETAN
1E-CELTIC	13-THAI-KADAI
1F-ALBANIAN	14-KOREAN
1G-GREEK	15-JAPANESE
1H-ARMENIAN	16-DRAVIDIAN
1J-IRANIAN	17-VIETNAMESE
1K-INDO-ARYAN	18-AUSTRO-ASIATIC
2-BASQUE	19-AUSTRONESIAN
3-CAUCASIAN FAMILIES	20-PAPUAN
4-BURUSHASKI	21-AUSTRALIAN
5-AFRO-ASIATIC	22-ESKIMO-ALEUT
(HAMITO-SEMITIC)	23-AMERICAN INDIAN
6-NILO-SAHARAN	FAMILIES
7-NIGER-CONGO	UNPOPULATED AREAS
8-KHOISAN	

NOTE: Names may vary, depending on source.

Standards of Living

⊕ LITERATE PERCENT OF POPULATION

90 AND ABOVE	50-69	0-29
70-89	30-49	DATA NOT AVAILABLE

⊕ YEARS OF LIFE EXPECTANCY (MEN AND WOMEN)

80 AND ABOVE	60-69	LESS THAN 50
70-79	50-59	

⊕ INFANT DEATHS PER 1,000 LIVE BIRTH

OVER 120	51-100	0-10
101-120	11-50	

UNITED STATES
The United States a
developed countries
committed greater r
to both public and p
education. This has
their populations de
skills that are neces
more complex, tech
competitive societie

LATIN AMERICA
The gulf between rich and poor contin-
ues to widen, despite efforts to reform
oppressive governments, increase literacy and relieve overburdened cities.

SOUTH AMERICA
Political unrest, rising inflation and
slow economic growth continue to
thwart efforts to bring unity and pros-
perity to the nations of South America.

⊕ GROSS DOMESTIC PRODUCT GROWTH RATES

BEST GROWTH RATES		WORST GROWTH RATES	
EQUATORIAL GUINEA	20	ARGENTINA	-14.7
EAST TIMOR	18	ZIMBABWE	-12.1
ARMENIA	12.7	MADAGASCAR	-11.9
CHAD	11.3	URUGUAY	-10.5
LIECHTENSTEIN	11	SOLOMON ISLANDS	-10
KAZAKHSTAN	9.5	VENEZUELA	-8.9
ANGOLA	9	LIBERIA	-5
CHINA	8	PAPUA NEW GUINEA	-3.3
MOZAMBIQUE	8	IRAQ	-3
TURKEY	7.8	PARAGUAY	-2.5
BHUTAN	7.7	KUWAIT	-2
SAN MARINO	7.5	SAINT KITTS AND NEVIS	-1.9
LITHUANIA	6.7	CÔTE D'IVOIRE	-1.7
IRAN	6.5	HAITI	-1.5
SOUTH KOREA	6.2	ISRAEL	-1.1
AZERBAIJAN	6.1	BARBADOS	-1
BOTSWANA	6	NEPAL	-0.6
TURKMENISTAN	6	KYRGYSTAN	-0.5
VIETNAM	6	ST. VINCENT/GRENADINES	-0.5
GHANA	5.8	VANUATU	-0.3

Source: CIA World Factbook

■ **Gross National Product**   ■ **Number of Television Sets**

⊕ GROSS NATIONAL PRODUCT PER CAPITA IN DOLLARS

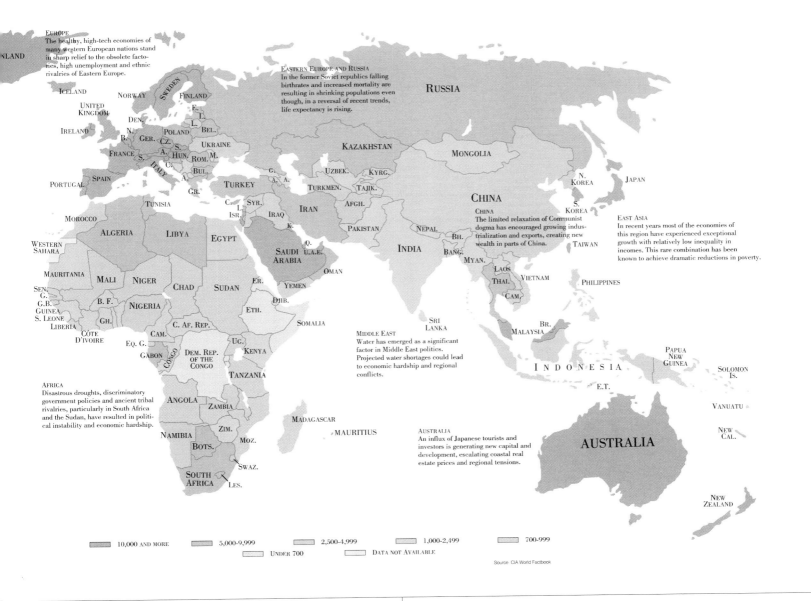

EUROPE
The healthy, high-tech economies of many western European nations stand in sharp relief to the obsolete factories, high unemployment and ethnic rivalries of Eastern Europe.

EASTERN EUROPE AND RUSSIA
In the former Soviet republics falling birthrates and increased mortality are resulting in shrinking populations even though, in a reversal of recent trends, life expectancy is rising.

CHINA
The limited relaxation of Communist dogma has encouraged growing industrialization and exports, creating new wealth in parts of China.

EAST ASIA
In recent years most of the economies of this region have experienced exceptional growth with relatively low inequality in incomes. This rare combination has been known to achieve dramatic reductions in poverty.

MIDDLE EAST
Water has emerged as a significant factor in Middle East politics. Projected water shortages could lead to economic hardship and regional conflicts.

AFRICA
Disastrous droughts, discriminatory government policies and ancient tribal rivalries, particularly in South Africa and the Sudan, have resulted in political instability and economic hardship.

AUSTRALIA
An influx of Japanese tourists and investors is generating new capital and development, escalating coastal real estate prices and regional tensions.

10,000 AND MORE   5,000-9,999   2,500-4,999   1,000-2,499   700-999
UNDER 700   DATA NOT AVAILABLE

Source: CIA World Factbook

⊕ TOTAL GROSS DOMESTIC PRODUCT
BILLIONS OF DOLLARS

USA 10,383
JAPAN 3993
GERMANY 1984
UNITED KINGDOM 1566
CHINA 1434
FRANCE 1431
ITALY 1184
CANADA 714
SPAIN 653
MEXICO 637
INDIA 510
S. KOREA 477
BRAZIL 452

Source: The World Bank

⊕ TELEVISION SETS PER 1,000 PEOPLE

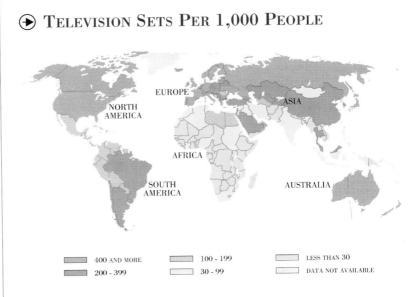

400 AND MORE   100 - 199   LESS THAN 30
200 - 399   30 - 99   DATA NOT AVAILABLE

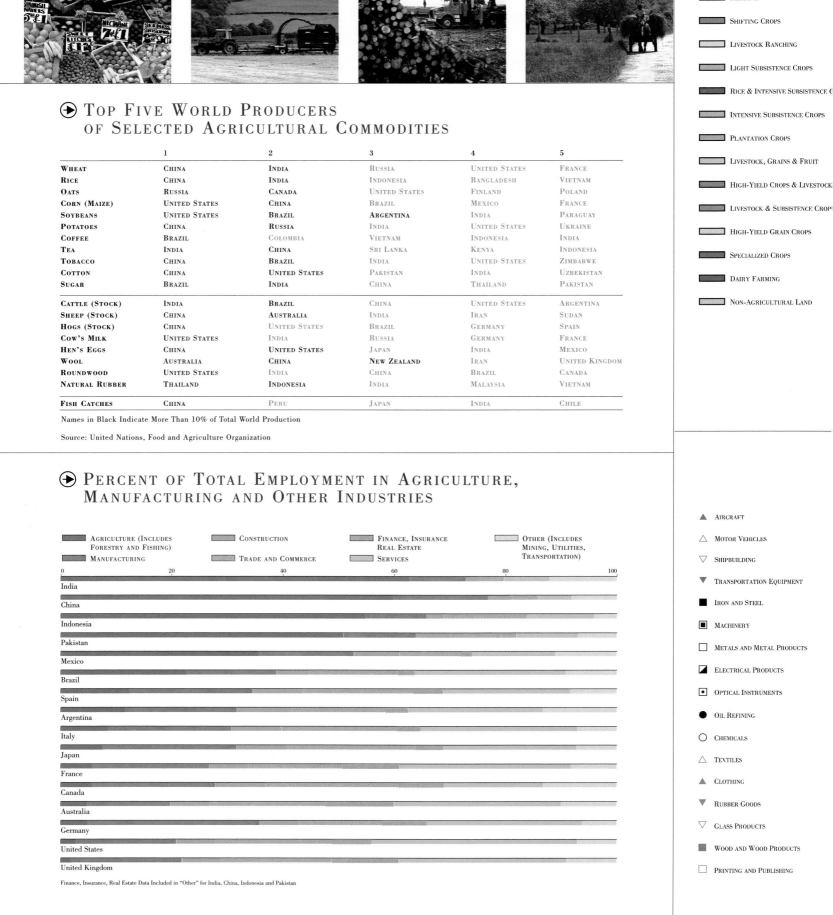

➤ TOP FIVE WORLD PRODUCERS OF SELECTED AGRICULTURAL COMMODITIES

	1	2	3	4	5
WHEAT	CHINA	INDIA	RUSSIA	UNITED STATES	FRANCE
RICE	CHINA	INDIA	INDONESIA	BANGLADESH	VIETNAM
OATS	RUSSIA	CANADA	UNITED STATES	FINLAND	POLAND
CORN (MAIZE)	UNITED STATES	CHINA	BRAZIL	MEXICO	FRANCE
SOYBEANS	UNITED STATES	BRAZIL	ARGENTINA	INDIA	PARAGUAY
POTATOES	CHINA	RUSSIA	INDIA	UNITED STATES	UKRAINE
COFFEE	BRAZIL	COLOMBIA	VIETNAM	INDONESIA	INDIA
TEA	INDIA	CHINA	SRI LANKA	KENYA	INDONESIA
TOBACCO	CHINA	BRAZIL	INDIA	UNITED STATES	ZIMBABWE
COTTON	CHINA	UNITED STATES	PAKISTAN	INDIA	UZBEKISTAN
SUGAR	BRAZIL	INDIA	CHINA	THAILAND	PAKISTAN
CATTLE (STOCK)	INDIA	BRAZIL	CHINA	UNITED STATES	ARGENTINA
SHEEP (STOCK)	CHINA	AUSTRALIA	INDIA	IRAN	SUDAN
HOGS (STOCK)	CHINA	UNITED STATES	BRAZIL	GERMANY	SPAIN
COW'S MILK	UNITED STATES	INDIA	RUSSIA	GERMANY	FRANCE
HEN'S EGGS	CHINA	UNITED STATES	JAPAN	INDIA	MEXICO
WOOL	AUSTRALIA	CHINA	NEW ZEALAND	IRAN	UNITED KINGDOM
ROUNDWOOD	UNITED STATES	INDIA	CHINA	BRAZIL	CANADA
NATURAL RUBBER	THAILAND	INDONESIA	INDIA	MALAYSIA	VIETNAM
FISH CATCHES	CHINA	PERU	JAPAN	INDIA	CHILE

Names in Black Indicate More Than 10% of Total World Production

Source: United Nations, Food and Agriculture Organization

➤ PERCENT OF TOTAL EMPLOYMENT IN AGRICULTURE, MANUFACTURING AND OTHER INDUSTRIES

Legend:
- AGRICULTURE (INCLUDES FORESTRY AND FISHING)
- MANUFACTURING
- CONSTRUCTION
- TRADE AND COMMERCE
- FINANCE, INSURANCE REAL ESTATE
- SERVICES
- OTHER (INCLUDES MINING, UTILITIES, TRANSPORTATION)

Scale: 0   20   40   60   80   100

India
China
Indonesia
Pakistan
Mexico
Brazil
Spain
Argentina
Italy
Japan
France
Canada
Australia
Germany
United States
United Kingdom

Finance, Insurance, Real Estate Data Included in "Other" for India, China, Indonesia and Pakistan

Map Legend (Agriculture)
- HERDING
- SHIFTING CROPS
- LIVESTOCK RANCHING
- LIGHT SUBSISTENCE CROPS
- RICE & INTENSIVE SUBSISTENCE C
- INTENSIVE SUBSISTENCE CROPS
- PLANTATION CROPS
- LIVESTOCK, GRAINS & FRUIT
- HIGH-YIELD CROPS & LIVESTOCK
- LIVESTOCK & SUBSISTENCE CROP
- HIGH-YIELD GRAIN CROPS
- SPECIALIZED CROPS
- DAIRY FARMING
- NON-AGRICULTURAL LAND

Map Legend (Manufacturing)
- ▲ AIRCRAFT
- △ MOTOR VEHICLES
- ▽ SHIPBUILDING
- ▼ TRANSPORTATION EQUIPMENT
- ■ IRON AND STEEL
- ▣ MACHINERY
- □ METALS AND METAL PRODUCTS
- ◪ ELECTRICAL PRODUCTS
- ⊡ OPTICAL INSTRUMENTS
- ● OIL REFINING
- ○ CHEMICALS
- △ TEXTILES
- ▲ CLOTHING
- ▼ RUBBER GOODS
- ▽ GLASS PRODUCTS
- ■ WOOD AND WOOD PRODUCTS
- □ PRINTING AND PUBLISHING

➤ AGRICULTURAL REGIONS

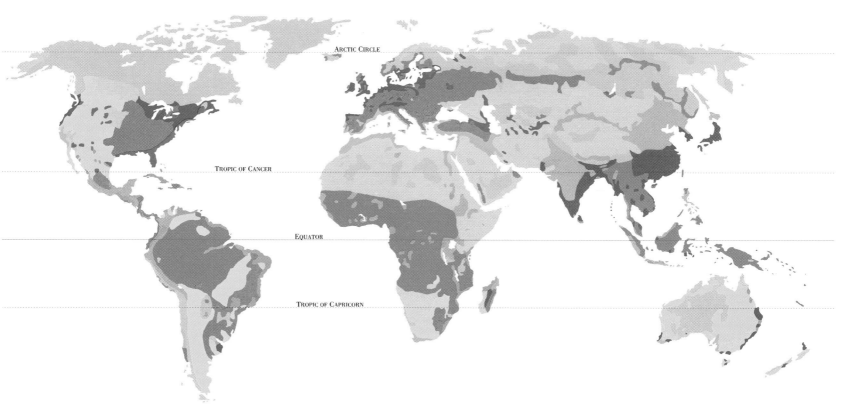

ARCTIC CIRCLE

TROPIC OF CANCER

EQUATOR

TROPIC OF CAPRICORN

➤ MANUFACTURING REGIONS

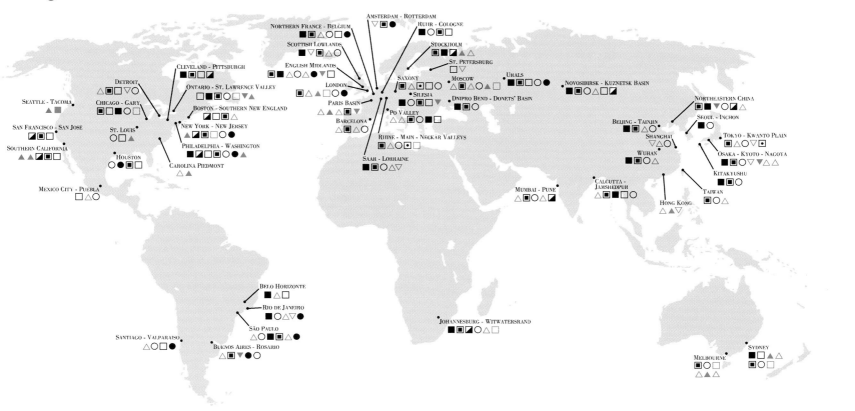

Energy and Resources

■ Mineral Fuels   ■ Metals and Nonmetals   ■ Top Producers of Selectd Mineral Commodities

⊕ MINERAL FUELS

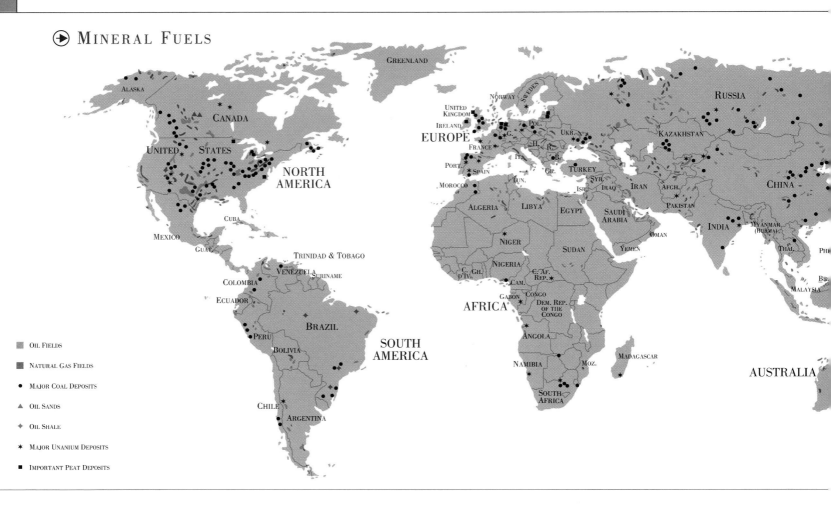

■ OIL FIELDS

■ NATURAL GAS FIELDS

● MAJOR COAL DEPOSITS

▲ OIL SANDS

◆ OIL SHALE

✱ MAJOR URANIUM DEPOSITS

■ IMPORTANT PEAT DEPOSITS

⊕ METALS AND NONMETALS

IRON AND FERROALLOY METALS

1	COBALT	5	MOLYBDENUM
2	CHROMIUM	6	NICKEL
3	IRON ORE	7	VANADIUM
4	MANGANESE	8	TUNGSTEN

OTHER METALS

1	SILVER	7	PLATINUM
2	BAUXITE	8	ANTIMONY
3	GOLD	9	TIN
4	COPPER	10	TITANIUM
5	MERCURY	11	ZINC
6	LEAD		

NONMETALS

1	ASBESTOS	10	MICA
2	BORAX	11	NITRATES
3	DIAMONDS	12	OPALS
4	EMERALDS	13	PHOSPHATES
5	FLOURSPAR	14	PEARLS
6	GRAPHITE	15	RUBIES
7	IODINE	16	SULFUR
8	JADE	17	SAPPHIRES
9	POTASH		

⊕ TOP FIVE WORLD PRODUCERS OF SELECTED MINERAL COMMODITIES

MINERAL FUELS	1	2	3	4	5
CRUDE OIL	SAUDI ARABIA	RUSSIA	UNITED STATES	IRAN	CHINA
GASOLINE	UNITED STATES	JAPAN	CHINA	CANADA	RUSSIA
NATURAL GAS	RUSSIA	UNITED STATES	CANADA	UNITED KINGDOM	NETHERLANDS
HARD COAL	CHINA	UNITED STATES	INDIA	AUSTRALIA	SOUTH AFRICA
URANIUM-BEARING ORES	CANADA	AUSTRALIA	NIGER	RUSSIA	KAZAKHSTAN

METALS					
CHROMITE	SOUTH AFRICA	KAZAKHSTAN	INDIA	ZIMBABWE	TURKEY
IRON ORE	CHINA	BRAZIL	AUSTRALIA	RUSSIA	INDIA
MANGANESE ORE	SOUTH AFRICA	GABON	AUSTRALIA	BRAZIL	CHINA
MINE NICKEL	RUSSIA	AUSTRALIA	CANADA	INDONESIA	NEW CALEDONIA
MINE SILVER	MEXICO	PERU	CHINA	AUSTRALIA	UNITED STATES
BAUXITE	AUSTRALIA	GUINEA	BRAZIL	JAMAICA	CHINA
ALUMINUM	CHINA	RUSSIA	CANADA	UNITED STATES	AUSTRALIA
MINE GOLD	SOUTH AFRICA	AUSTRALIA	UNITED STATES	CHINA	RUSSIA
MINE COPPER	CHILE	INDONESIA	UNITED STATES	AUSTRALIA	RUSSIA
MINE LEAD	AUSTRALIA	CHINA	UNITED STATES	PERU	MEXICO
MINE TIN	CHINA	PERU	INDONESIA	BRAZIL	BOLIVIA
MINE ZINC	CHINA	AUSTRALIA	PERU	CANADA	UNITED STATES

NONMETALS					
NATURAL DIAMOND	AUSTRALIA	DEM. REP. OF THE CONGO	RUSSIA	BOTSWANA	SOUTH AFRICA
POTASH	CANADA	RUSSIA	BELARUS	GERMANY	ISRAEL
PHOSPHATE ROCK	UNITED STATES	CHINA	MOROCCO	RUSSIA	TUNISIA
SULFUR (ALL FORMS)	UNITED STATES	CANADA	RUSSIA	CHINA	JAPAN

Names in Black Indicate More Than 10% of Total World Production

Source: U.S. Geological Survey, Mineral Commodity Summary; Handbook of International Economic Statistics

⊕ COMMERCIAL ENERGY PRODUCTION/CONSUMPTION

PERCENTAGE OF WORLD TOTAL

▭ PRODUCTION   ▬ CONSUMPTION

United States 18.8% / 26%

Russia 11% / 7%

China 8.3% / 8.7%

Saudi Arabia 5.3% / 1.1%

Canada 4.1% / 2.9%

United Kingdom 3.2% / 2.7%

India 2.8% / 3.6%

Iran 2.7% / 1.2%

Mexico 2.5% / 1.6%

Australia 2.4% / 1.3%

Norway 2.4% / 0.3%

Indonesia 2.3% / 1.1%

Venezuela 2.3% / 0.6%

Germany 1.4% / 3.7%

Source: United Nations

⊕ NATIONS WITH HIGHEST PERCENTAGE OF NUCLEAR POWER PRODUCTION

▬ NUCLEAR   ▭ THERMAL   ▬ HYDROELECTRIC

Belgium 98% / 1% / 1%

France 75% / 11% / 14%

South Korea 71% / 21% / 8%

Japan 65% / 9% / 26%

Finland 58% / 42%

Sweden 43% / 57%

Spain 41% / 40% / 19%

Switzerland 39% / 61%

Germany 26% / 71% / 3%

Hungary 22% / 78%

Ukraine 21% / 77% / 2%

Bulgaria 17% / 80% / 3%

United Kingdom 11% / 88% / 1%

United States 10% / 86% / 4%

PAPUA NEW GUINEA

NEW ZEALAND

Transportation and Trade

➤ WORLD EXPORTS BY REGION

PERCENT (BY VALUE) OF TOTAL EXPORTS

- To European Community
- To United States
- To Asia (excluding Japan)
- To Japan
- To European Free Trade Assn.
- To Canada
- To Latin America
- To Africa
- To Others

EUROPEAN COMMUNITY
| 25 | 20 | 17 | 8 | 5 | 5 | 20 |

UNITED STATES
| 24 | 20 | 20 | 15 | 12 | 9 |

ASIA (EXCLUDING JAPAN)
| 33 | 25 | 22 | 20 |

JAPAN
| 37 | 29 | 19 | 4 | 11 |

EUROPEAN FREE TRADE ASSN.
| 68 | 9 | 7 | 16 |

CANADA
| 76 | 8 | 6 | 5 | 5 |

LATIN AMERICA
| 43 | 30 | 8 | 7 | 12 |

AFRICA
| 62 | 20 | 6 | 12 |

AUSTRALIA AND NEW ZEALAND
| 35 | 28 | 13 | 11 | 13 |

➤ TRADE BALANCES OF LEADING EXPORT NATIONS

VALUE IN BILLIONS OF DOLLARS

■ ANNUAL EXPORTS ■ ANNUAL IMPORTS (DATA BASED ON AVERAGE OVER A 3-YEAR PERIOD)

United States 468 / 596
Germany 402 / 363
Japan 365 / 249
France 244 / 240
United Kingdom 192 / 215
Italy 179 / 175
Canada 140 / 131
Belgium 117 / 120
China 99 / 100
Taiwan 87 / 78
South Korea 85 / 88
Spain 69 / 95
Sweden 55 / 48

Mexico 46 / 64
Australia 45 / 44
Russia 43 / 33
Saudi Arabia 43 / 27
Brazil 39 / 26
Indonesia 36 / 28
Thailand 35 / 44
South Africa 24 / 19
India 22 / 24
Iran 16 / 21
Turkey 15 / 24
Venezuela 15 / 10
Argentina 14 / 17

⊕ Highways and Airports

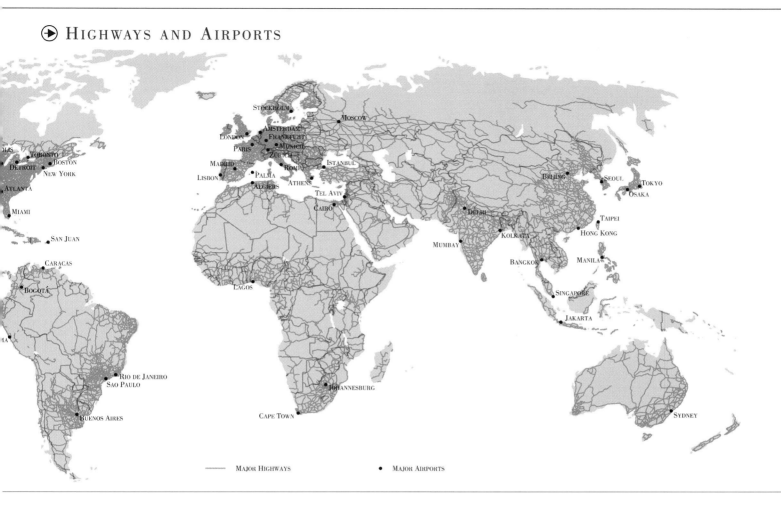

—— Major Highways   • Major Airports

⊕ Railroads, Waterways, Seaport, and Shipping Routes

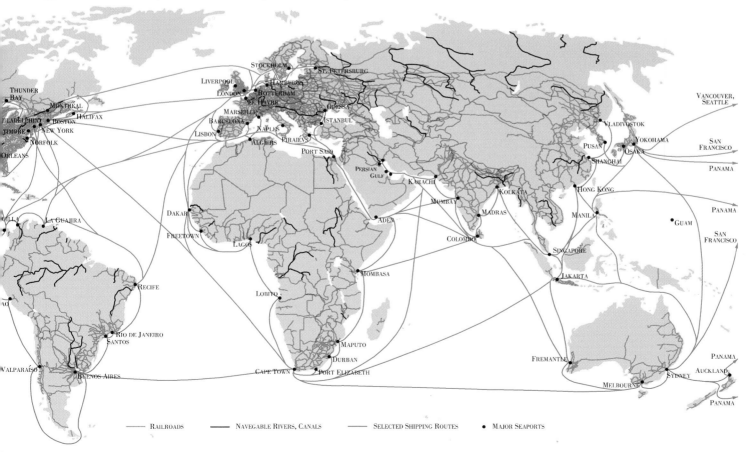

—— Railroads   —— Navegable Rivers, Canals   —— Selected Shipping Routes   • Major Seaports

Global Politics

⊕ INTERNATIONAL RELATIONSHIPS

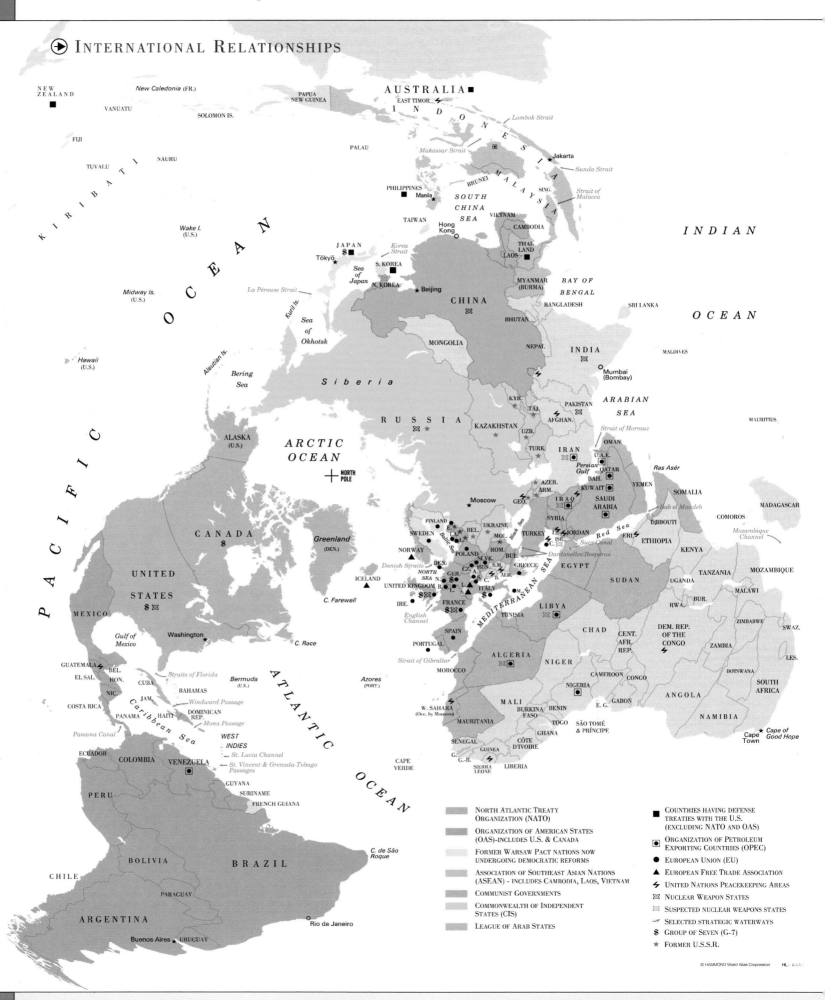

	NORTH ATLANTIC TREATY ORGANIZATION (NATO)	■ COUNTRIES HAVING DEFENSE TREATIES WITH THE U.S. (EXCLUDING NATO AND OAS)
	ORGANIZATION OF AMERICAN STATES (OAS)-INCLUDES U.S. & CANADA	⊙ ORGANIZATION OF PETROLEUM EXPORTING COUNTRIES (OPEC)
	FORMER WARSAW PACT NATIONS NOW UNDERGOING DEMOCRATIC REFORMS	● EUROPEAN UNION (EU)
	ASSOCIATION OF SOUTHEAST ASIAN NATIONS (ASEAN) - INCLUDES CAMBODIA, LAOS, VIETNAM	▲ EUROPEAN FREE TRADE ASSOCIATION
	COMMUNIST GOVERNMENTS	⚡ UNITED NATIONS PEACEKEEPING AREAS
	COMMONWEALTH OF INDEPENDENT STATES (CIS)	⌧ NUCLEAR WEAPON STATES
	LEAGUE OF ARAB STATES	⌧ SUSPECTED NUCLEAR WEAPONS STATES
		⌁ SELECTED STRATEGIC WATERWAYS
		$ GROUP OF SEVEN (G-7)
		★ FORMER U.S.S.R.

© HAMMOND World Atlas Corporation   HL - AAA

36

Regional Maps

 **Europe
and Northern Asia**

Asia

Australia and Pacific

**Africa,
Polar Regions**

North America

South America

Europe - Physical

AREA OF OPTIMIZATION
The red band which surrounds these physical and political maps defines the "Area of Optimization." Within this bounding curve is the most accurate conformal map that can be made of the region. Outside the optimized area, distortion increases rapidly, and tears or other irregularities in the grid may occur.

SCALE 1:21,000,000   OPTIMAL CONFORMAL PROJECTION

MILES 0   300   600   900
KILOMETERS 0   300   600   900

POPULATION OF CITIES AND TOWNS
▣ OVER 3,000,000   ◉ 500,000 - 999,999   ○ UNDER 100,000
▣ 1,000,000 - 2,999,999   ◉ 100,000 - 499,999

Europe - Political

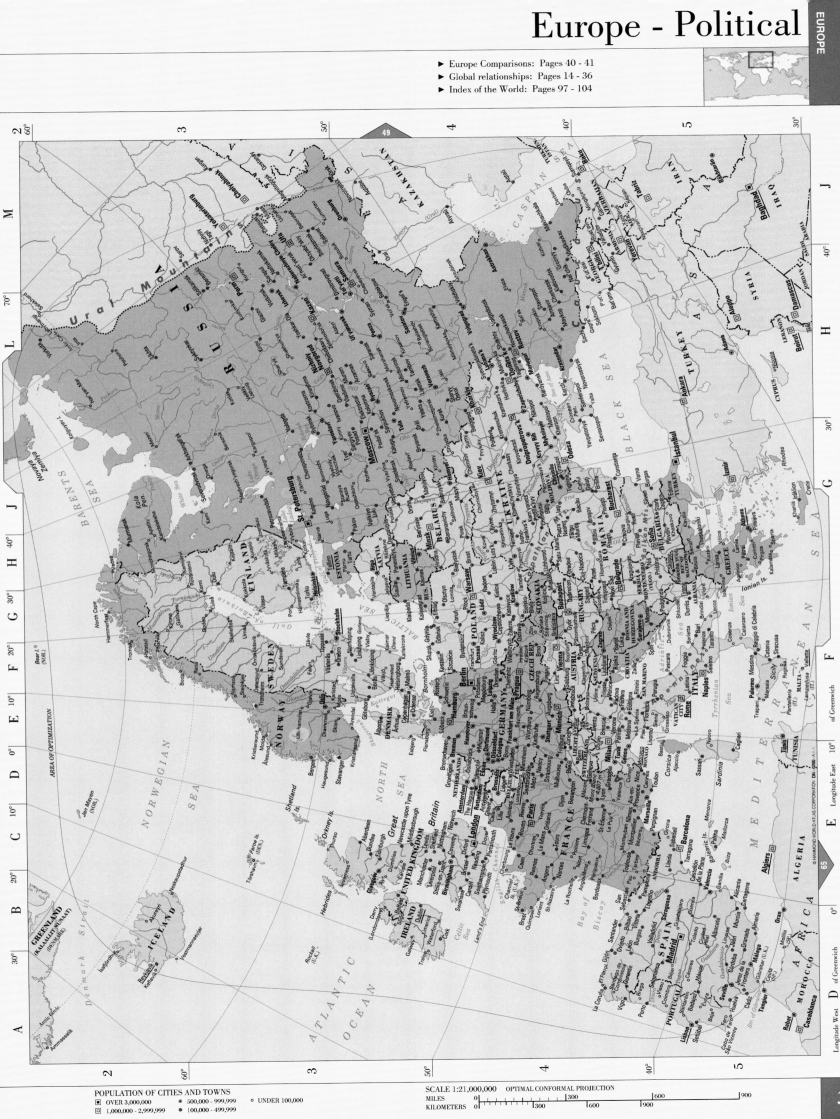

POPULATION OF CITIES AND TOWNS

◉ OVER 3,000,000   ● 500,000 - 999,999   ○ UNDER 100,000
◉ 1,000,000 - 2,999,999   ● 100,000 - 499,999

SCALE 1:21,000,000   OPTIMAL CONFORMAL PROJECTION

MILES   0   300   600   900
KILOMETERS   0   300   600   900

3

Europe - Comparisons

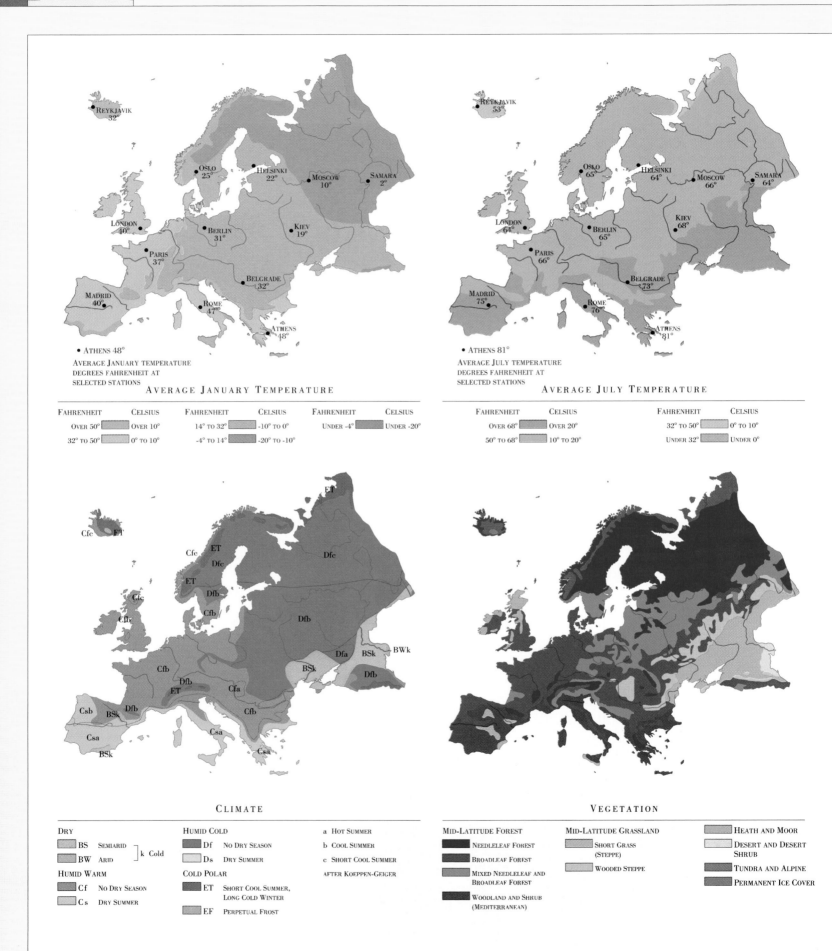

AVERAGE JANUARY TEMPERATURE

REYKJAVIK 32°
OSLO 25°
HELSINKI 22°
MOSCOW 10°
SAMARA 2°
LONDON 40°
BERLIN 31°
KIEV 19°
PARIS 37°
BELGRADE 32°
MADRID 40°
ROME 47°
ATHENS 48°

• ATHENS 48°
AVERAGE JANUARY TEMPERATURE
DEGREES FAHRENHEIT AT
SELECTED STATIONS

FAHRENHEIT	CELSIUS	FAHRENHEIT	CELSIUS	FAHRENHEIT	CELSIUS
OVER 50°	OVER 10°	14° TO 32°	-10° TO 0°	UNDER -4°	UNDER -20°
32° TO 50°	0° TO 10°	-4° TO 14°	-20° TO -10°		

AVERAGE JULY TEMPERATURE

REYKJAVIK 53°
OSLO 65°
HELSINKI 64°
MOSCOW 66°
SAMARA 64°
LONDON 64°
BERLIN 65°
KIEV 68°
PARIS 66°
BELGRADE 73°
MADRID 75°
ROME 76°
ATHENS 81°

• ATHENS 81°
AVERAGE JULY TEMPERATURE
DEGREES FAHRENHEIT AT
SELECTED STATIONS

FAHRENHEIT	CELSIUS	FAHRENHEIT	CELSIUS
OVER 68°	OVER 20°	32° TO 50°	0° TO 10°
50° TO 68°	10° TO 20°	UNDER 32°	UNDER 0°

CLIMATE

DRY
BS SEMIARID ⎤
BW ARID ⎦ k Cold

HUMID WARM
Cf NO DRY SEASON
Cs DRY SUMMER

HUMID COLD
Df NO DRY SEASON
Ds DRY SUMMER

COLD POLAR
ET SHORT COOL SUMMER, LONG COLD WINTER
EF PERPETUAL FROST

a HOT SUMMER
b COOL SUMMER
c SHORT COOL SUMMER

AFTER KOEPPEN-GEIGER

VEGETATION

MID-LATITUDE FOREST
NEEDLELEAF FOREST
BROADLEAF FOREST
MIXED NEEDLELEAF AND BROADLEAF FOREST
WOODLAND AND SHRUB (MEDITERRANEAN)

MID-LATITUDE GRASSLAND
SHORT GRASS (STEPPE)
WOODED STEPPE

HEATH AND MOOR
DESERT AND DESERT SHRUB
TUNDRA AND ALPINE
PERMANENT ICE COVER

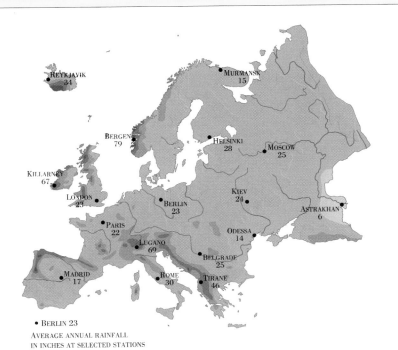

• BERLIN 23
AVERAGE ANNUAL RAINFALL
IN INCHES AT SELECTED STATIONS

AVERAGE ANNUAL RAINFALL

INCHES	CM	INCHES	CM	INCHES	CM
OVER 80	OVER 200	40 TO 60	100 TO 150	10 TO 20	25 TO 50
60 TO 80	150 TO 200	20 TO 40	50 TO 100	UNDER 10	UNDER 25

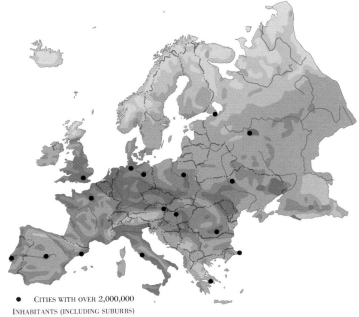

• CITIES WITH OVER 2,000,000
INHABITANTS (INCLUDING SUBURBS)

POPULATION DISTRIBUTION

DENSITY PER		SQ. MI.	SQ. KM.	SQ. MI.	SQ. KM.
SQ. MI.	SQ. KM.	130 TO 260	50 TO 100	3 TO 25	1 TO 10
OVER 260	OVER 100	25 TO 130	10 TO 50	UNDER 3	UNDER 1

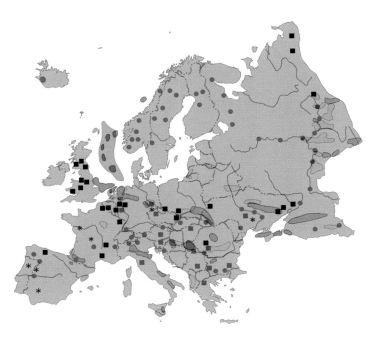

ENERGY SOURCES

▨ OIL REGION	■ COAL	● HYDROELECTRICITY
▨ NATURAL GAS REGION	▪ LIGNITE	✶ URANIUM

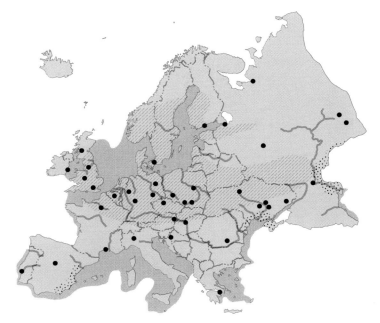

ENVIRONMENTAL CONCERNS

～ POLLUTED RIVERS	AREAS SUBJECT TO DEFORESTATION	⬛ EXTENT OF ACID RAIN
EXTENT OF COASTAL POLLUTION	AREAS SUBJECT TO DESERTIFICATION	● URBAN AREAS WITH SEVERE AIR POLLUTION

Below Sea Sea Lev. Level	200 700	500 1,600	1,000 3,300	1,500 5,000	2,000 6,500	4,000 13,000	6,000 m. 19,700 ft.

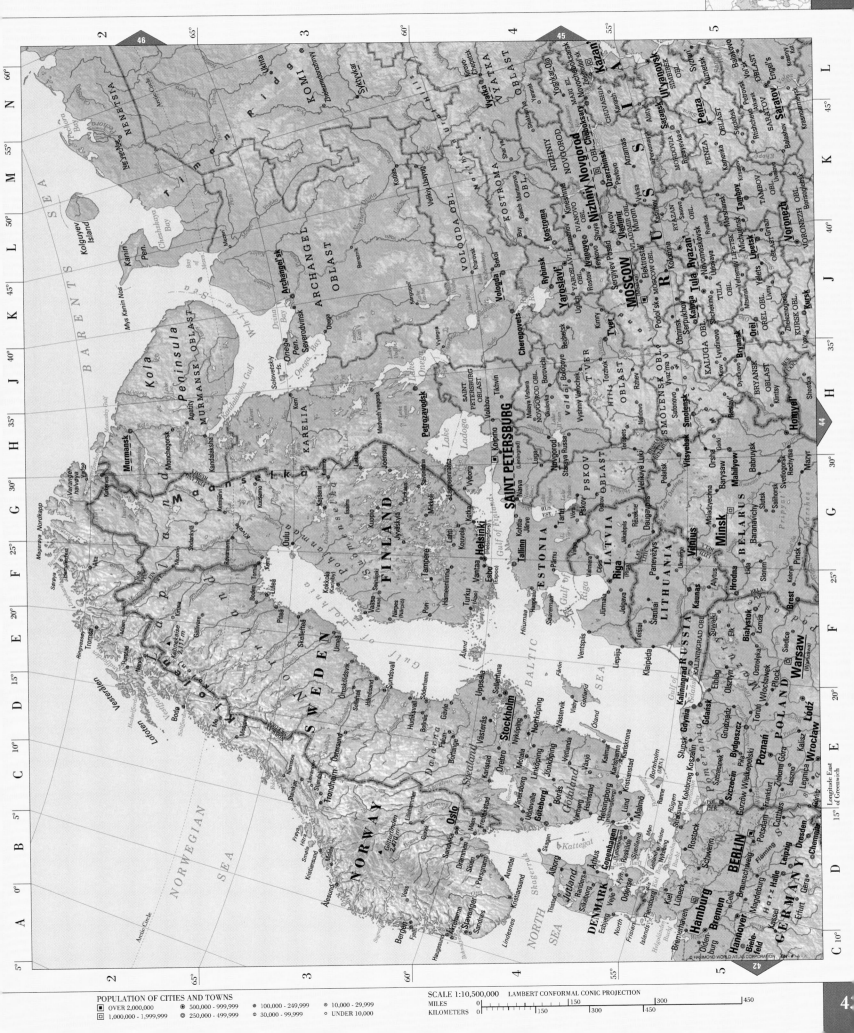

Northern Europe

POPULATION OF CITIES AND TOWNS

■ OVER 2,000,000	● 500,000 - 999,999	● 100,000 - 249,999	○ 10,000 - 29,999
▣ 1,000,000 - 1,999,999	● 250,000 - 499,999	○ 30,000 - 99,999	○ UNDER 10,000

SCALE 1:10,500,000   LAMBERT CONFORMAL CONIC PROJECTION

MILES 0   150   300   450

KILOMETERS 0   150   300   450

4

© HAMMOND WORLD ATLAS CORPORATION

South Central Europe

© HAMMOND WORLD ATLAS CORPORATION

Below Sea	200	500	1,000	1,500	2,000	4,000	6,000 m.
Sea Lev. Level	700	1,600	3,300	5,000	6,500	13,000	19,700 ft.

► Europe Comparisons: Pages 40 - 41
► Global relationships: Pages 14 - 36
► Index of the World: Pages 97 - 104

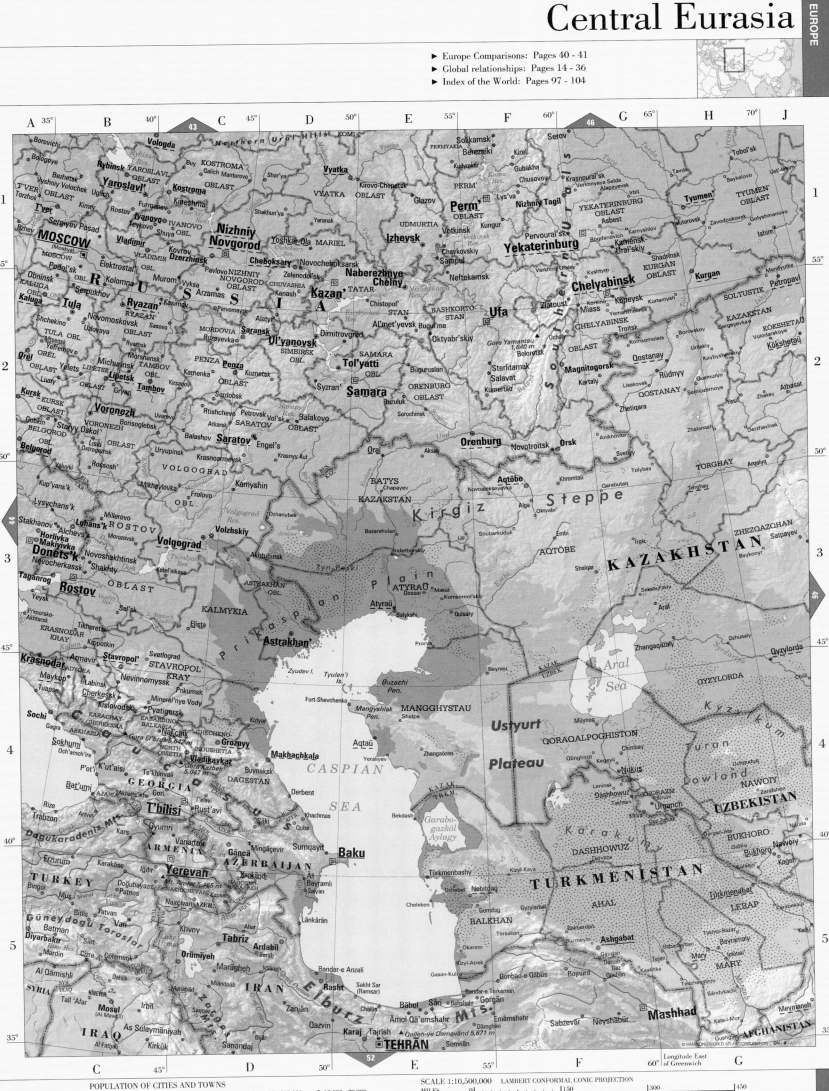

POPULATION OF CITIES AND TOWNS

■ OVER 2,000,000	● 500,000 - 999,999	● 100,000 - 249,999	○ 10,000 - 29,999
□ 1,000,000 - 1,999,999	● 250,000 - 499,999	○ 30,000 - 99,999	○ UNDER 10,000

SCALE 1:10,500,000   LAMBERT CONFORMAL CONIC PROJECTION

MILES   0   150   300   450

KILOMETERS   0   150   300   450

© HAMMOND WORLD ATLAS CORPORATION

4

Below Sea	200	500	1,000	1,500	2,000	4,000	6,000 m.
Sea Lev. Level	700	1,600	3,300	5,000	6,500	13,000	19,700 ft.

RUSSIA
(Administrative divisions are named only when they differ from their respective capitals.)

1. RESPUBLIKA ADYGEYA
2. RESPUBLIKA KARACHAYEVO-CHERKESIYA
3. RESPUBLIKA KABARDINO-BALKARIYA
4. RESPUBLIKA SEVERNAYA OSETIYA-ALANIYA
5. RESPUBLIKA INGUSHETIYA
6. RESPUBLIKA CHECHNYA
7. RESPUBLIKA DAGESTAN
8. RESPUBLIKA MORDOVIYA
9. RESPUBLIKA CHUVASHIYA
10. RESPUBLIKA MARIY-EL
11. RESPUBLIKA TATARSTAN
12. RESPUBLIKA BASHKORTOSTAN
13. RESPUBLIKA UDMURTIYA
14. KOMI-PERMYATSKIY AVTONOMNYY OKRUG
15. RESPUBLIKA KHAKASIYA
16. UST'-ORDYNSKIY BURYATSKIY AVT. OKRUG
17. AGINSKIY BURYATSKIY AVT. OKRUG

© HAMMOND WORLD ATLAS CORPORATION CN-1029-A·A·A

POPULATION OF CITIES AND TOWNS

■ OVER 2,000,000	● 500,000 - 999,999	○ 50,000 - 99,999
◻ 1,000,000 - 1,999,999	⊕ 100,000 - 499,999	· UNDER 50,000

SCALE 1:21,000,000   OPTIMAL CONFORMAL PROJECTION

MILES 0 ___ 300 ___ 600 ___ 900
KILOMETERS 0 ___ 300 ___ 600 ___ 900

Asia-Physical

► Asia Comparisons: Pages 50 - 51
► Global relationships: Pages 14 - 36
► Index of the World: Pages 97 - 104

ASIA

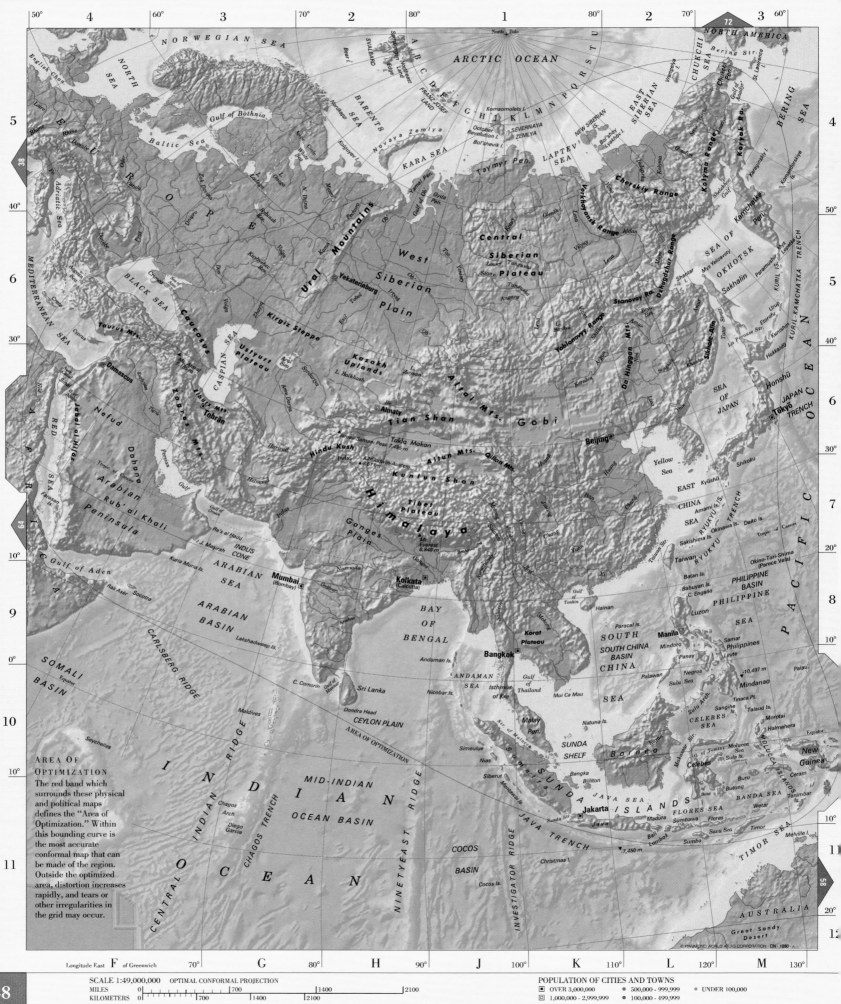

AREA OF OPTIMIZATION

The red band which surrounds these physical and political maps defines the "Area of Optimization." Within this bounding curve is the most accurate conformal map that can be made of the region. Outside the optimized area, distortion increases rapidly, and tears or other irregularities in the grid may occur.

Longitude East F of Greenwich

48

SCALE 1:49,000,000   OPTIMAL CONFORMAL PROJECTION

MILES   0   700   1400   2100

KILOMETERS   0   700   1400   2100

POPULATION OF CITIES AND TOWNS

■ OVER 3,000,000	● 500,000 - 999,999	○ UNDER 100,000
▣ 1,000,000 - 2,999,999	◉ 100,000 - 499,999	

© RAND MCNALLY WORLD ATLAS CORPORATION   CN-1030-A

► Asia Comparisons: Pages 50 - 51
► Global relationships: Pages 14 - 36
► Index of the World: Pages 97 - 104

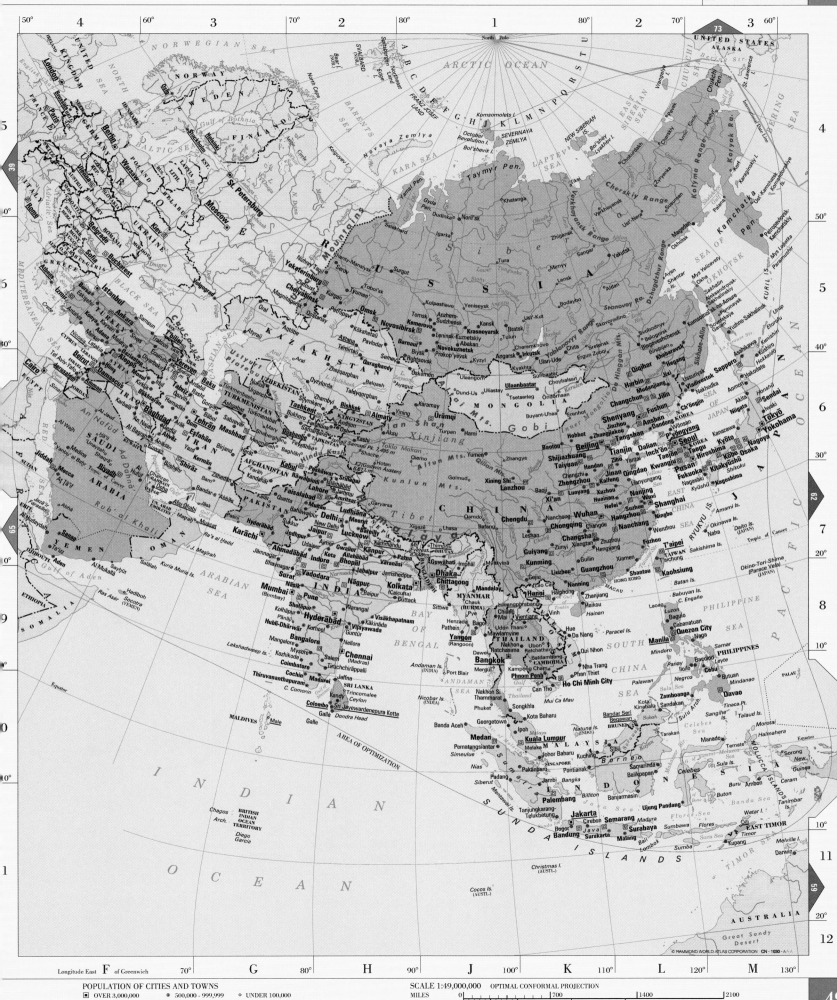

POPULATION OF CITIES AND TOWNS

■ OVER 3,000,000   ● 500,000 - 999,999   ○ UNDER 100,000
▣ 1,000,000 - 2,999,999   ⊙ 100,000 - 499,999

SCALE 1:49,000,000   OPTIMAL CONFORMAL PROJECTION

MILES   0   700   1400   2100

KILOMETERS   0   700   1400   2100

Longitude East F of Greenwich

© HAMMOND WORLD ATLAS CORPORATION   CN - 1030 - A-A-A

Asia - Comparisons

▶ Asia Physical / Political: Pages 48 - 49
▶ Global Relationships: Pages 14 - 36
▶ Index of the World: Pages 97 - 104

Average January Temperature

• TOKYO 38°
AVERAGE JANUARY TEMPERATURE
DEGREES FAHRENHEIT AT
SELECTED STATIONS

ANKARA 32°
YEKATERINBURG 7°
VERKHOYANSK -59°
ASTANA 1°
IRKUTSK -6°
TASHKENT 29°
RIYADH 58°
BEIJING 23°
TOKYO 38°
NEW DELHI 57°
DHAKA 67°
CHONGQING 47°
MUMBAI 75°
MANILA 78°
JAKARTA 79°

AVERAGE JANUARY TEMPERATURE

FAHRENHEIT	CELSIUS	FAHRENHEIT	CELSIUS	FAHRENHEIT	CELSIUS
OVER 68°	OVER 20°	14° TO 32°	-10° TO 0°	-40° TO -22°	-40° TO -30°
50° TO 68°	10° TO 20°	-4° TO 14°	-20° TO -10°	UNDER -40°	UNDER -40°
32° TO 50°	0° TO 10°	-22° TO -4°	-30° TO -20°		

Average July Temperature

• TOKYO 77°
AVERAGE JULY TEMPERATURE
DEGREES FAHRENHEIT AT
SELECTED STATIONS

ANKARA 73°
YEKATERINBURG 61°
VERKHOYANSK 56°
ASTANA 70°
IRKUTSK 60°
TASHKENT 78°
RIYADH 93°
BEIJING 79°
TOKYO 77°
NEW DELHI 88°
DHAKA 84°
CHONGQING 85°
MUMBAI 82°
MANILA 82°
JAKARTA 79°

AVERAGE JULY TEMPERATURE

FAHRENHEIT	CELSIUS	FAHRENHEIT	CELSIUS	FAHRENHEIT	CELSIUS
OVER 86°	OVER 30°	50° TO 68°	10° TO 20°	UNDER 32°	UNDER 0°
68° TO 86°	20° TO 30°	32° TO 50°	0° TO 10°		

Climate

Csa, Dsa, BSh, BWk, BWh, BWk, Dfb, BSk, BSh, Cwa, Aw, Am, Am, Aw, Am, Af, Af, Am, Aw, ET, Dwd, Dfd, Dwd, Dfc, Dfc, Dwe, Dfc, Dwb, Dfb, BWk, Dwa, E, ET, BSk, Cfa, Dwb, Cfa, Cwa, Af Cfa

CLIMATE

HUMID TROPICAL
- Af NO DRY SEASON
- Am SHORT DRY SEASON
- Aw DRY WINTER

DRY
- BS SEMIARID   } h HOT
- BW ARID   k COLD

AFTER KOEPPEN-GEIGER

HUMID WARM
- Cf NO DRY SEASON
- Cw DRY WINTER
- Cs DRY SUMMER

HUMID COLD
- Df NO DRY SEASON
- Dw DRY WINTER
- Ds DRY SUMMER

COLD POLAR
- ET SHORT COOL SUMMER, LONG COLD WINTER
- E   COLD AND UNCLASSIFIED HIGHLANDS

a HOT SUMMER
b COOL SUMMER
c SHORT COOL SUMMER
d VERY COLD WINTER

Vegetation

VEGETATION

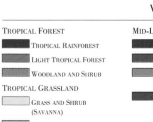

TROPICAL FOREST
- TROPICAL RAINFOREST
- LIGHT TROPICAL FOREST
- WOODLAND AND SHRUB

TROPICAL GRASSLAND
- GRASS AND SHRUB (SAVANNA)
- WOODED SAVANNA

MID-LATITUDE FOREST
- NEEDLELEAF FOREST
- BROADLEAF FOREST
- MIXED NEEDLELEAF AND BROADLEAF FOREST
- WOODLAND AND SHRUB (MEDITERRANEAN)

MID-LATITUDE GRASSLAND
- SHORT GRASS (STEPPE)
- WOODED STEPPE
- DESERT AND DESERT SHRUB
- TUNDRA AND ALPINE
- UNCLASSIFIED HIGHLANDS

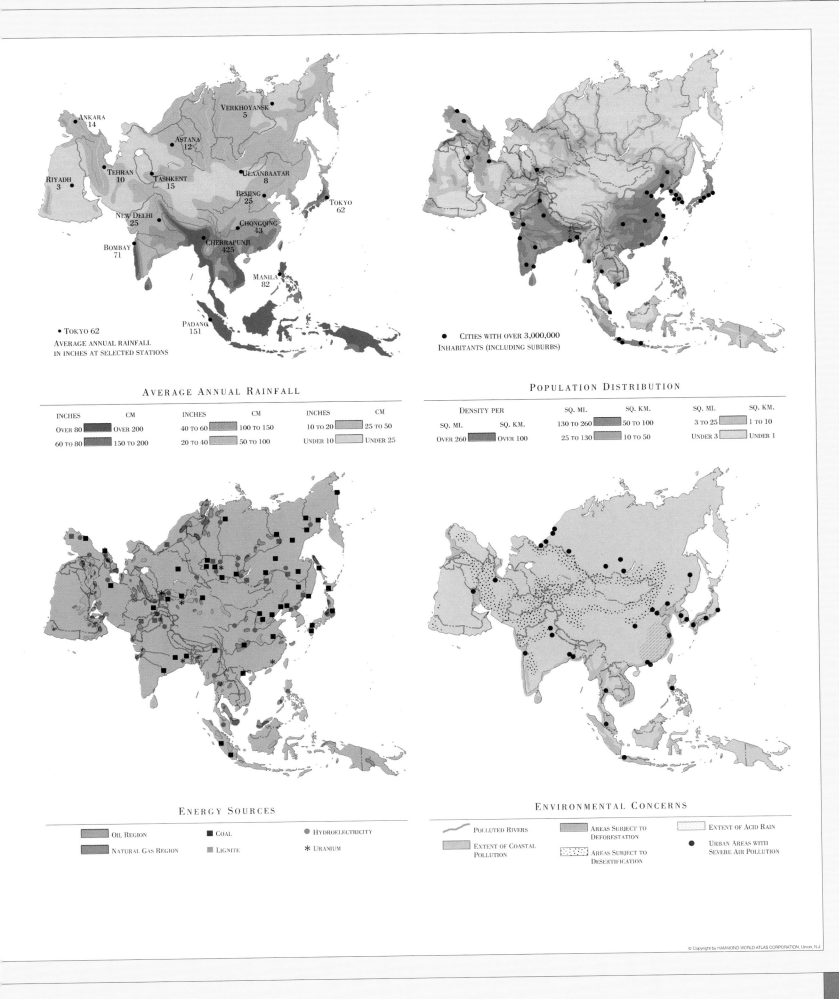

AVERAGE ANNUAL RAINFALL

ANKARA 14
VERKHOYANSK 5
ASTANA 12
TEHRAN 10
TASHKENT 15
ULAANBAATAR 8
RIYADH 3
BEIJING 25
TOKYO 62
NEW DELHI 25
CHONGQING 43
BOMBAY 71
CHERRAPUNJI 425
MANILA 82
PADANG 151

● TOKYO 62
AVERAGE ANNUAL RAINFALL
IN INCHES AT SELECTED STATIONS

INCHES	CM	INCHES	CM	INCHES	CM
OVER 80	OVER 200	40 TO 60	100 TO 150	10 TO 20	25 TO 50
60 TO 80	150 TO 200	20 TO 40	50 TO 100	UNDER 10	UNDER 25

POPULATION DISTRIBUTION

● CITIES WITH OVER 3,000,000
INHABITANTS (INCLUDING SUBURBS)

DENSITY PER		SQ. MI.	SQ. KM.	SQ. MI.	SQ. KM.
SQ. MI.	SQ. KM.	130 TO 260	50 TO 100	3 TO 25	1 TO 10
OVER 260	OVER 100	25 TO 130	10 TO 50	UNDER 3	UNDER 1

ENERGY SOURCES

OIL REGION ■ COAL ● HYDROELECTRICITY
NATURAL GAS REGION ■ LIGNITE ✳ URANIUM

ENVIRONMENTAL CONCERNS

POLLUTED RIVERS
EXTENT OF COASTAL POLLUTION
AREAS SUBJECT TO DEFORESTATION
AREAS SUBJECT TO DESERTIFICATION
EXTENT OF ACID RAIN
● URBAN AREAS WITH SEVERE AIR POLLUTION

Southwestern Asia

ASIA

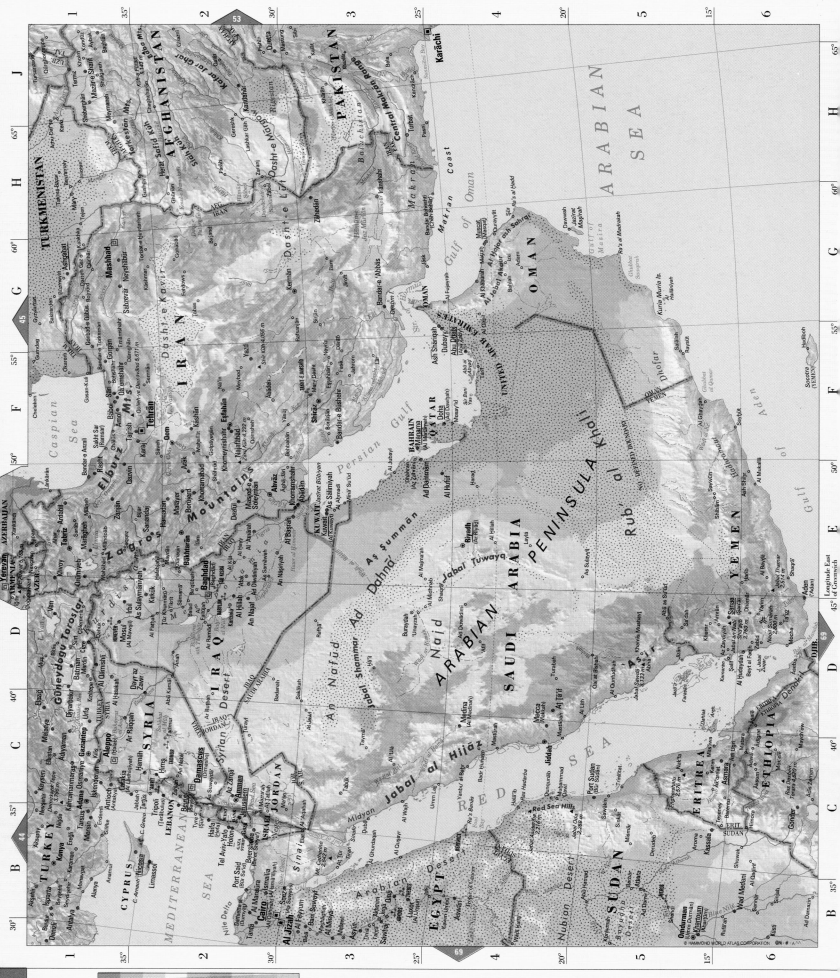

Below Sea   200   500   1,000   1,500   2,000   4,000   6,000 m.
Sea Lev. Level 700   1,600 3,300   5,000   6,500 13,000 19,700 ft.

Indian Subcontinent

► Asia Comparisons: Pages 50 - 51
► Global relationships: Pages 14 - 36
► Index of the World: Pages 97 - 104

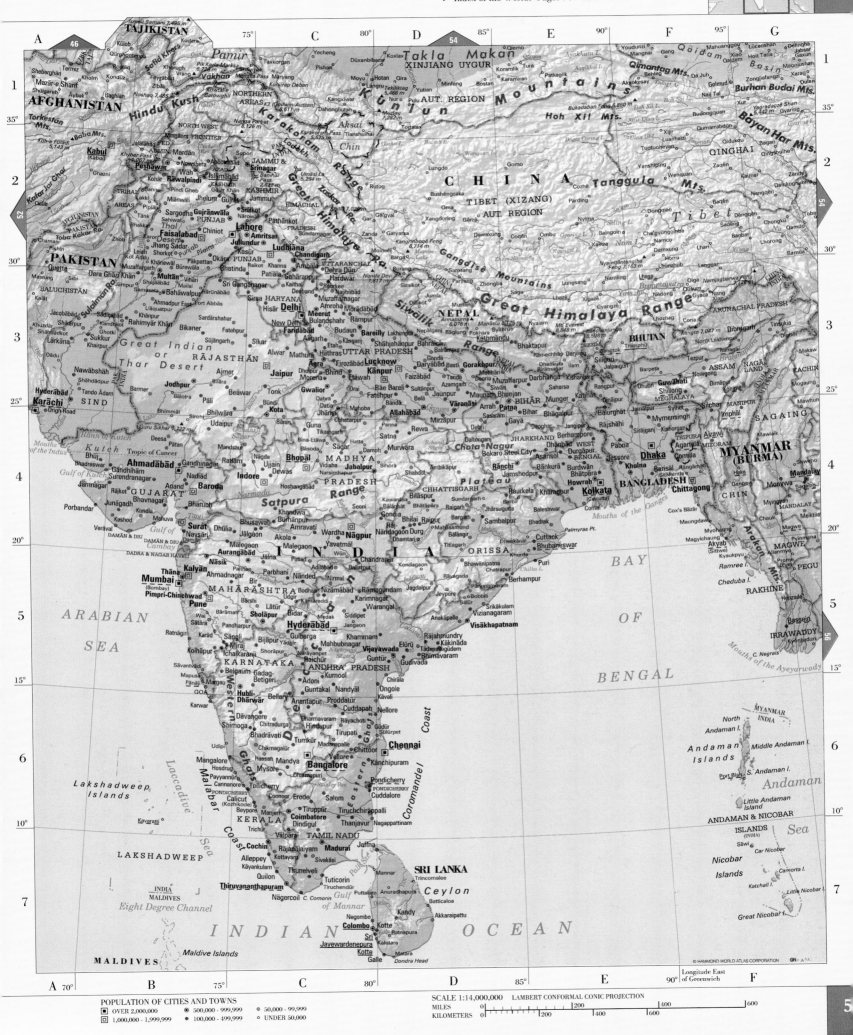

POPULATION OF CITIES AND TOWNS

■ OVER 2,000,000	● 500,000 - 999,999	• 50,000 - 99,999
▣ 1,000,000 - 1,999,999	⊙ 100,000 - 499,999	∘ UNDER 50,000

SCALE 1:14,000,000   LAMBERT CONFORMAL CONIC PROJECTION

MILES 0   200   400   600

KILOMETERS 0   200   400   600

Below Sea		200	500	1,000	1,500	2,000	4,000	6,000 m.
Sea Lev. Level		700	1,600	3,300	5,000	6,500	13,000	19,700 ft.

Eastern Asia

ASIA

► Asia Comparisons: Pages 50 - 51
► Global relationships: Pages 14 - 36
► Index of the World: Pages 97 -104

POPULATION OF CITIES AND TOWNS
SCALE 1:14,000,000   LAMBERT CONFORMAL CONIC PROJECTION

55

Below Sea | 200 | 500 | 1,000 | 1,500 | 2,000 | 4,000 | 6,000 m.
Sea Lev. Level | 700 | 1,600 | 3,300 | 5,000 | 6,500 | 13,000 | 19,700 ft.

PHILIPPINE SEA

PACIFIC

OCEAN

NORTHERN

MARIANAS

(U.S.)

PHILIPPINES

Luzon

Manila
Quezon City

Mindoro

Samar

Panay
Cebu
Bohol
Negros

Mindanao

CELEBES

SEA

Talaud
Is.

Sangihe
Is.

Halmahera

Minahasa

PALAU

CAROLINE ISLANDS

FEDERATED STATES OF MICRONESIA

BANDA   SEA

Ceram Sea

Buru   Ceram

New Guinea

Irian Jaya

Maoke Mountains

BISMARCK ARCH.

Bismarck Sea

Arafura

Sea

PAPUA

NEW GUINEA

EAST TIMOR

Timor

Timor   Sea

Gulf of
Papua

© HAMMOND WORLD ATLAS CORPORATION

POPULATION OF CITIES AND TOWNS

■ OVER 2,000,000   ● 500,000 - 999,999   ○ 50,000 - 99,999
□ 1,000,000 - 1,999,999   ● 100,000 - 499,999   ○ UNDER 50,000

SCALE 1:14,000,000   LAMBERT CONFORMAL CONIC PROJECTION

MILES
KILOMETERS

Australia, New Zealand - Physical

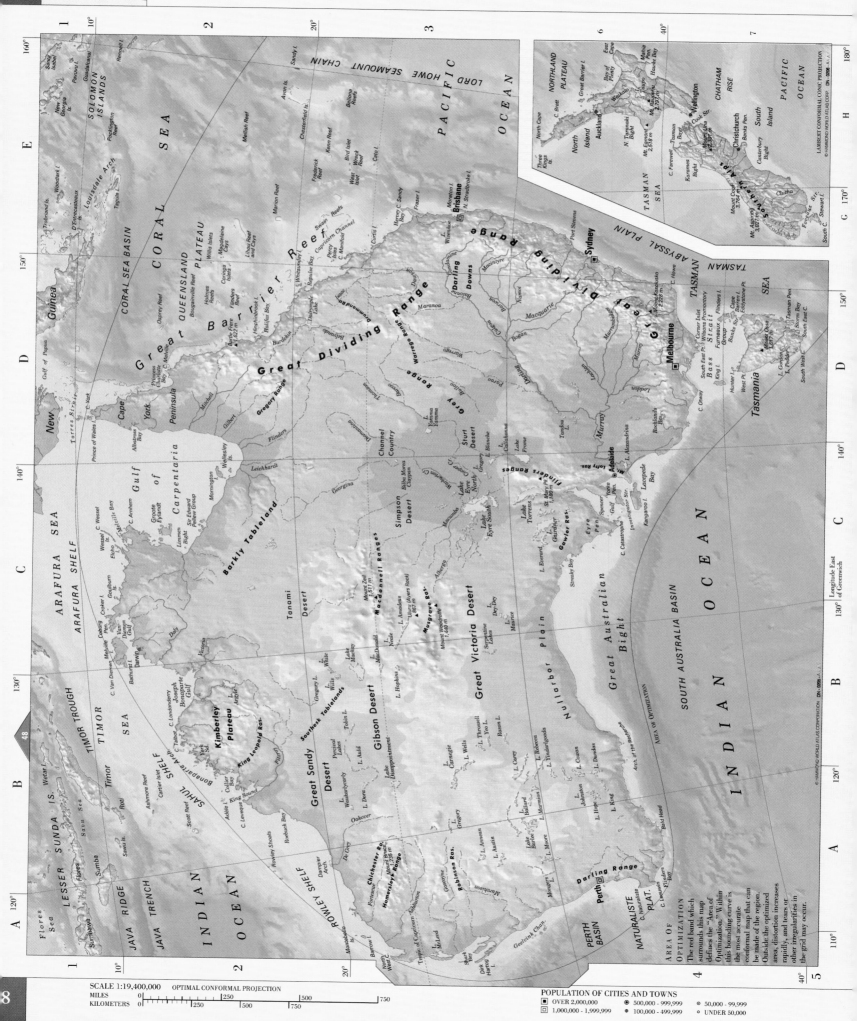

SCALE 1:19,400,000   OPTIMAL CONFORMAL PROJECTION

| MILES | 0 | 250 | 500 | 750 |
| KILOMETERS | 0 | 250 | 500 | 750 |

POPULATION OF CITIES AND TOWNS

■ OVER 2,000,000	● 500,000 - 999,999	⊙ 50,000 - 99,999
▣ 1,000,000 - 1,999,999	⊛ 100,000 - 499,999	○ UNDER 50,000

Australia, New Zealand - Political

► Australia Comparisons: Pages 60 - 61
► Global relationships: Pages 14 - 36
► Index of the World: Pages 97 - 104

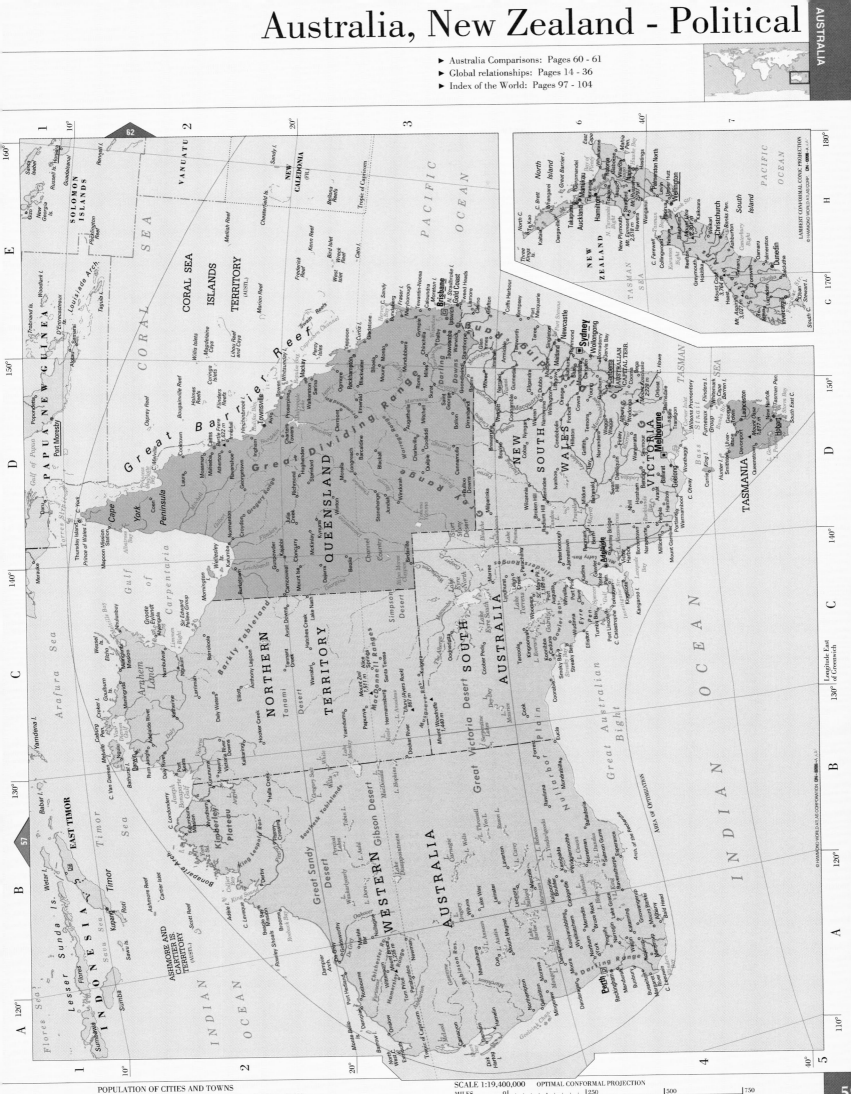

POPULATION OF CITIES AND TOWNS

- ■ OVER 2,000,000
- ⊡ 1,000,000 - 1,999,999
- ⦿ 500,000 - 999,999
- ⊕ 100,000 - 499,999
- ⊛ 50,000 - 99,999
- ○ UNDER 50,000

SCALE 1:19,400,000   OPTIMAL CONFORMAL PROJECTION

MILES   0   250   500   750
KILOMETERS   0   250   500   750

Australia, New Zealand - Comparisons

► Australia Physical / Political: Pages 58 - 59
► Global Relationships: Pages 14 - 36
► Index of the World: Pages 97 - 104

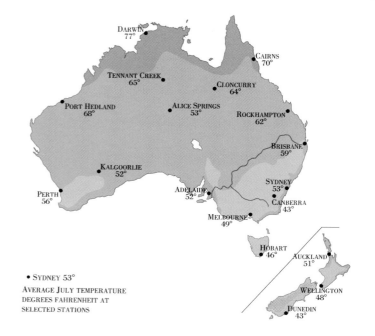

● SYDNEY 72°
AVERAGE JANUARY TEMPERATURE
DEGREES FAHRENHEIT AT
SELECTED STATIONS

● SYDNEY 53°
AVERAGE JULY TEMPERATURE
DEGREES FAHRENHEIT AT
SELECTED STATIONS

AVERAGE JANUARY TEMPERATURE

FAHRENHEIT	CELSIUS	FAHRENHEIT	CELSIUS	FAHRENHEIT	CELSIUS
OVER 86°	OVER 30°	50° TO 68°	10° TO 20°	UNDER 32°	UNDER 0°
68° TO 86°	20° TO 30°	32° TO 50°	0° TO 10°		

AVERAGE JULY TEMPERATURE

FAHRENHEIT	CELSIUS	FAHRENHEIT	CELSIUS
OVER 68°	OVER 20°	32° TO 50°	0° TO 10°
50° TO 68°	10° TO 20°	UNDER 32°	UNDER 0°

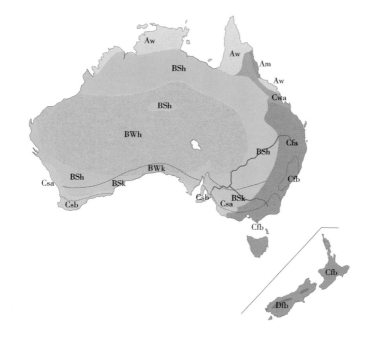

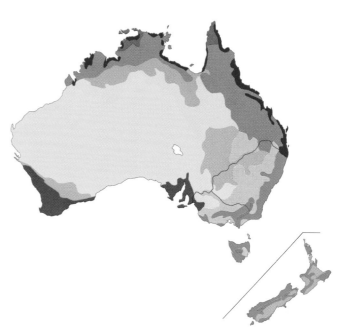

CLIMATE

HUMID TROPICAL
- Am SHORT DRY SEASON
- Aw DRY WINTER

DRY
- BS SEMIARID ⎤ h HOT
- BW ARID ⎦ k COLD

HUMID WARM
- Cf NO DRY SEASON
- Cw DRY WINTER
- Cs DRY SUMMER

HUMID COLD
- Df NO DRY SEASON
- a HOT SUMMER
- b COOL SUMMER

AFTER KOEPPEN-GEIGER

VEGETATION

TROPICAL FOREST
- TROPICAL RAINFOREST
- LIGHT TROPICAL FOREST
- WOODLAND AND SHRUB

TROPICAL GRASSLAND
- GRASS AND SHRUB (SAVANNA)
- WOODED SAVANNA

MID-LATITUDE FOREST
- MIXED NEEDLELEAF AND BROADLEAF FOREST
- MIXED WOODLAND
- WOODLAND AND SHRUB (MEDITERRANEAN)

- MID-LATITUDE GRASSLAND
- SCRUB AND FERNLANDS
- DESERT AND DESERT SHRUB
- ALPINE

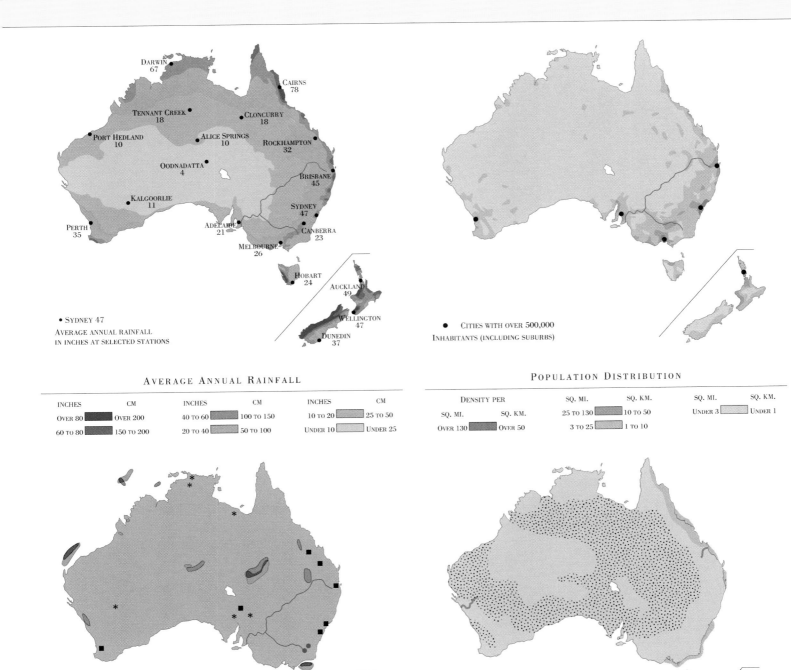

Average Annual Rainfall

DARWIN 67
CAIRNS 78
TENNANT CREEK 18
CLONCURRY 18
PORT HEDLAND 10
ALICE SPRINGS 10
ROCKHAMPTON 32
OODNADATTA 4
BRISBANE 45
KALGOORLIE 11
SYDNEY 47
PERTH 35
ADELAIDE 21
CANBERRA 23
MELBOURNE 26
HOBART 24
AUCKLAND 49
WELLINGTON 47
DUNEDIN 37

• SYDNEY 47
AVERAGE ANNUAL RAINFALL
IN INCHES AT SELECTED STATIONS

INCHES	CM	INCHES	CM	INCHES	CM
OVER 80	OVER 200	40 TO 60	100 TO 150	10 TO 20	25 TO 50
60 TO 80	150 TO 200	20 TO 40	50 TO 100	UNDER 10	UNDER 25

Population Distribution

• CITIES WITH OVER 500,000
INHABITANTS (INCLUDING SUBURBS)

DENSITY PER		SQ. MI.	SQ. KM.	SQ. MI.	SQ. KM.
SQ. MI.	SQ. KM.	25 TO 130	10 TO 50	UNDER 3	UNDER 1
OVER 130	OVER 50	3 TO 25	1 TO 10		

Energy Sources

OIL REGION	■ COAL	● HYDROELECTRICITY
NATURAL GAS REGION	■ LIGNITE	* URANIUM

Environmental Concerns

POLLUTED RIVERS	AREAS SUBJECT TO DEFORESTATION	AREAS SUBJECT TO DESERTIFICATION
EXTENT OF COASTAL POLLUTION		

CHINA

Xiangtan Changsha Nanchang Jingdezhen Ningbo
Hengyang Zhuzhou Huangang Shan Wenzhou
2,158 m
Guilin Ji'an Deyun Shan Fuzhou
Tonggu Zhang Ganzhou 1,849 m
1,526 m Xiamen
Guangzhou Shantou Chaozhou **Taipei**
Macau **Kaohsiung** **Tainan**
HONG KONG **TAIWAN**

EAST CHINA SEA

Tokara Is. **Kyūshū**
Osumi I.
Naze Amami-O-Shima **JAPAN**
Okinawa I. Naha
Ishigaki Daito Is.
Sakishima Is.

Tori-Shima (JAPAN)

Mukoshima Is.
Ogasawara Chichishima Is.
BONIN IS. Hahashima Is.
(JAPAN)

Ritou VOLCANO IS. Iwo Jima
(JAPAN) Minamiiō

Minami-Tori-Shima (JAPAN)

Tropic of Cancer

SOUTH
CHINA
SEA

Luzon Strait

Ibayat I.
Batan Is.

Calayan I.
Babuyan Is.

Laoag
Vigan
Dagupan Baguio
Mt. Pinatubo Cabanatuan
1,759 m
Manila **Quezon City**

Batangas Lucena
Mindoro Naga Catanduanes I.
Legaspi

PHILIPPINES

Panay Iloilo Masbate Samar
Bacolod Leyte Tacloban
Cebu Bohol
Negros Butuan

PHILIPPINE SEA

Farallon de Pajaros
Maug Is. Asuncion

Agrihan
Pagan
Alamagan
Guguan
Sarigan
Anatahan Farallon de Medinilla
Saipan Saipan (Capitol Hill)
Aguijan Tinian
Rota

Hagåtña **Guam**
(U.S.)

NORTHERN
MARIANA
ISLANDS
(U.S.)

Enewetak Bikini Rongelap Bikar
Rongerik Utirik Ailuk
Wotho **MARSHALL**
ISLANDS
Ujelang Ujae Kwajalein Erikub Wotje
Lae Namu
Ailinglapalap Aur
Arno
Namorik Majuro Majuro
Jaluit Mili

PALAW

Quezon Palawan

Sulu Sea

Balabac Str.

Kudat **Zamboanga**
MALAYSIA Basilan
Sabah Sandakan
Tawau
Borneo

Celebes Sea

Bacolod Cagayan de Oro **Davao**
General Santos
Mindanao

Sulu Archipelago

Ulithi
Colonia Yap I.
Kayangel Ngulu
Is.
Koror Babelthuap
Sonsorol Is.

Faraulep West
Fayu Pikelot
Sorol Olimarao Lamotrek
Eauripik Woleai Ifalik Elato Puluwat
Satawan

Gaferut Namonuito
Hall Is.

CAROLINE ISLANDS Etal Lukunor
Satawan Nukuoro

Pulap Moen Oroluk Senyavin Is.
Chuuk Palikir
Ant Pohnpei
Mokil Pingelap
Ngatik Lelu Kosrae

Ebon

Makin
Butaritari
Abaiang Bikenibeu
Tarawa Maiana Abemama
Kuria Aranuka
Nonouti
Utiroa Beru Nikunau
Tabiteuea Onotoa Tamana
Arorae

GILBERT
ISLANDS

Banaba
Tabiang

FEDERATED STATES OF MICRONESIA

Kapingamarangi

NAURU

INDONESIA

Makassar Strait
Samarinda
Palu
Kendari
Buton
Mona

Gulf of Tomini
Gorontalo
Manado
Ternate
Morotai
Halmahera
Waigeo
Schouten Is.

Celebes
Sula Buru
Banda Sea
Ambon Ceram
Buru

Flores Sea
Flores Alor Is.
Sumbawa Ruteng Leti
Sumba Savu Sea Kupang

Kai Is. Aru Is.
Tanimbar Is.
Babar Is.
Wetar Timor
Dili Timor
EAST TIMOR

Sorong Manokwari
Misool Yapen
Obi Is. Fakfak
Ceram Waigeo

Sula Equator

Cenderawasih Bay
Puncak Jaya
5,030 m Jayapura
New Guinea
Maoke Mts.
Yos Sudarso
Merauke

Arafura Sea

Ninigo Atolls Admiralty
Islands Mussau
Manus Lorengau St. Matthias Group
Lyra Reef
Kavieng
Vanimo Altape New Ireland
Wewak Namatanai Nuguria Is.
Karkar I. Rabaul
Madang Umboi New
Mt. Wilhelm Kundiawa Britain Kimbe
4,509 m Goroka
Mt. Hagen Lae
Bulolo Wau

BISMARCK ARCHIPELAGO
Bismarck Sea

Nissan I.
Tauu Is.
Buka
Nukumanu
Atoll
Bougainville
Arawa Kieta
Shortland Is.
Choiseul

Ontong Java

PAPUA
NEW GUINEA
Gulf of Papua
Daru **Port Moresby**

Trobriand Is.
Popondetta D'Entrecasteaux
Is. Woodlark I.
Alotau Normanby I. Tagula I.
Samarai Rossel I.
Louisiade
Arch.

Kia Santa Isabel
Buala
Aula Malaita
New
Gizo **Georgia** **Honiara**
Guadalcanal
Kirakira San
Cristobal
Rennell I.

SOLOMON
ISLANDS

Reef Is. Duff Is.
Nendö Utupua
Vanikolo
Santa Cruz Is.

Torres Is.
Banks Is.

MELANESIA

TUVALU

Lolua Nanumea Niutao
Nanumanga

Nui Vaitupu
Nukufetau Funafuti
Niulakita

Nukulaelae

WALLIS AND
FUTUNA
(FR.) Futuna
Ahau
Rotuma I.

FIJI
Vanua
Levu
Yasawa
Group Lambasa
Lautoka Savusavu
Nadi **Suva**
Viti Levu Vunisea
Kandavu Moala
Group

VANUATU
Espiritu Santo Aoba Maewo
Tabwemasana 1,879 m Pentecost
Luganville Ambrym
Norsup Epi Shepherd
Malakula Is.
Port-Vila Efate
Erromango
Isangel Tanna
Anatom

NEW HEBRIDES

NEW
CALEDONIA
(FR.)
Chesterfield Is.

Koumac Hienghene
New We
Mont Panié 1,628 m Thio
Bourail Humboldt
Bellona Caledonia 1,618 m Ile des Pins
Reefs **Noumea**
LOYALTY IS.

CORAL
SEA

AUSTRALIA

Melville I.
Bonaparte Arch.
Cape **Darwin**
Pine Creek
Wyndham Katherine
Kimberley Daly Waters
Plateau
Broome Halls Creek

Cape
York
Peninsula Coen

Gulf of
Carpentaria

Normanton
Camooweal Cloncurry Hughenden
Tennant Creek
Mt. Bruce Alice Springs
1,235 m
Uluru (Ayers Rock)
867 m Birdsville
Musgrave Ranges

Cooktown

Cairns

Townsville

Bowen Mackay

Clermont Rockhampton
Emerald
Longreach Bundaberg
Barcaldine

Roma Gympie
Charleville Toowoomba Gold Coast
Cunnamulla Saint **Brisbane**
George

INDIAN
OCEAN

Port Hedland
Roebourne
Onslow Marble Bar
Exmouth

Great Sandy
Desert

Gibson Desert

Great Victoria Desert

Carnarvon
Wiluna
Meekatharra
Northampton
Geraldton

Leonora
Kalgoorlie-Boulder

Lake
Eyre
Oodnadatta
Coober Pedy
Marree

Tarcoola
Woomera

Port Augusta
Port Pirie Broken Hill
Whyalla Port
Streaky Bay Port Lincoln Pirie
Adelaide
Nullarbor Plain Murray Bridge

Great
Australian
Bight

Merredin **Perth**
Norseman Northam

Moree
Armidale
Tamworth
Bourke Port Macquarie
Cobar Dubbo
Nyngan Orange Newcastle
Lithgow
Cootamundra **Sydney**
Mildura Wagga Wagga **Wollongong**
Canberra
Murray Albury
Mt. Kosciusko
2,228 m

Great Dividing Range

Kingston Norfolk I.
(AUSTL.)

Lord Howe I.
(AUSTL.)

Raoul I.

Macauley I.
Curtis I.
KERMADEC IS.
(N.Z.)

Three
Kings Is.
North Cape

NEW
ZEALAND
Whangarei
Auckland North I.
Hamilton Manukau
Tauranga
Rotorua

TASMAN SEA

SOUTH

NORTH P

MICRONESIA
RALIK CHAIN
RATAK CHAIN

MELANESIA

POLYNESIA

International Date Line

Tropic of Capricorn

Longitude East of Greenwich

Below Sea 200 500 1,000 1,500 2,000 4,000 6,000 m.
Sea Lev. Level 700 1,600 3,300 5,000 6,500 13,000 19,700 ft.

2

► Australia Comparisons: Pages 60 - 61
► Global relationships: Pages 14 - 36
► Index of the World: Pages 97 - 104

H 170° J 160° K 150° L 140° M 130° N 120° P 110° Q

MEXICO

Hermosillo
Guaymas
Ciudad Obregón
Culiacán

Isla de Guadalupe (MEX.)

Baja California

Gulf of California

La Paz

Mazatlán

Cabo San Lucas

Islas de Revillagigedo (MEX.)

2

Pearl and Hermes Reef
Lisianski I.
Laysan I. · Maro Reef
HAWAII (U.S.)
French Frigate Shoals
Necker I.
Nihoa
Kauai
Niihau · Oahu
Honolulu · Molokai
Lanai · Maui
Hilo
Hawaii

Tropic of Cancer

20°

H A W A I I A N   I S L A N D S

P
o
l
y
n
e
s
i
a

3

P A C I F I C   O C E A N

Johnston Atoll (U.S.)

10°

Kingman Reef (U.S.)
Palmyra Atoll (U.S.)

4

Teraina (Washington I.)
· Tabuaeran (Fanning I.)
· Kiritimati (Christmas I.)

L i n e   I s l a n d s

M i c r o n e s i a

International Date Line

Equator

0°

Howland I. (U.S.)
Baker I. (U.S.)

Jarvis I. (U.S.)

K I R I B A T I
PHOENIX IS.
Abariringa (Canton I.)
McKean · Enderbury
Birnie · Rawaki (Phoenix I.)
Kanaroro
Gardner I. (Hull I.)
Orona · Manra (Sydney I.)

Malden I.

Starbuck I.

5

10°

Atafu
TOKELAU (N.Z.)
Nukunonu
Fakaofo
Swains I.

Rakahanga
Tongareva (Penrhyn)
Manihiki

Pukapuka
Nassau
NORTHERN COOK IS.
Suwarrow

Vostok I.

Flint I.

Caroline I.

Eiao
Nuku Hiva
Taiohae · Ua Huka
Hakahau · Hiva Oa
Ua Pou · Atuona
Tahuata
Fatu Hiva

MARQUESAS ISLANDS

P o l y n e s i a

SAMOA
Mt. Silisili 1,858 m
Asau · Apia
Savai'i · Upolu
AMERICAN SAMOA
Pago Pago
Manua Is.
Tutuila

Njuafo'ou
Niuatoputapu Group
Rose I.

COOK ISLANDS (N.Z.)

Bellingshausen

Palmerston Atoll

Îles Sous le Vent
Maupiti · Tupai
Bora Bora
Huahine
Raiatea · Uturoa · Tetiaroa
Moorea · Faaa
SOCIETY IS.
Papeete
Tahiti
Îles du Vent

Tikehau
Tiputa · Rangiroa · Mataiva
Makatea
Kaukura · Apataki
Toau
Fakarava
Anaa · Tahanea
Hikueru
Marokau
Otepa
Hao

Manihi
Ahe
Takaroa
Takapoto
Arutua

Disappointment Is.
Tepoto · Napuka
Pukapuka

Fangatau
Fakahina

Takaroa
Tatakoto
Amanu · Pukarua
Reao
Vahitahi · Nukutavake

6

Neiafu
Vava'u Group
Alofi
NIUE (N.Z.)
Pangai
Ha'apai Group
Nuku'alofa
'Eua

TONGA

Aitutaki Atoll
Amuri
Manuae Atoll
SOUTHERN COOK IS.
Mitiaro
Atiu · Mauke
Avarua
Rarotonga
Mangaia

Hereheretue

Duke of Gloucester Is.

Vanavaro
Tureia
Mururoa
Fangataufa

Actaeon Group
Marutea
Maria

Rikitea · Mangareva
Temoe

GAMBIER IS.

PITCAIRN ISLANDS (U.K.)
Oeno Atoll
Henderson I.
Adamstown · Pitcairn I.
Ducie I.

Tropic of Capricorn

20°

Maria
Rimatara
Rurutu
Tubuai · Mataura
Raivavae
Moerai
Taravai
TUBUAI ISLANDS (Austral Islands)

Morane

FRENCH POLYNESIA

7

P A C I F I C   O C E A N

Rapa
Marotiri Is. (Bass Is.)

Easter Island (Isla de Pascua) (CHILE)

International Date Line

30°

© HAMMOND WORLD ATLAS CORPORATION   CN · 65 · A A A

8

H 170° J 160° K 150° L 140° M 130° N 120° P 110° Q 100°
Longitude West of Greenwich

POPULATION OF CITIES AND TOWNS
■ OVER 3,000,000   ● 500,000 - 999,999   ○ UNDER 100,000
◙ 1,000,000 - 2,999,999   ● 100,000 - 499,999

SCALE 1:31,500,000   LAMBERT AZIMUTHAL EQUAL-AREA PROJECTION
MILES   0   400   800   1200
KILOMETERS   0   400   800   1200

Africa - Physical

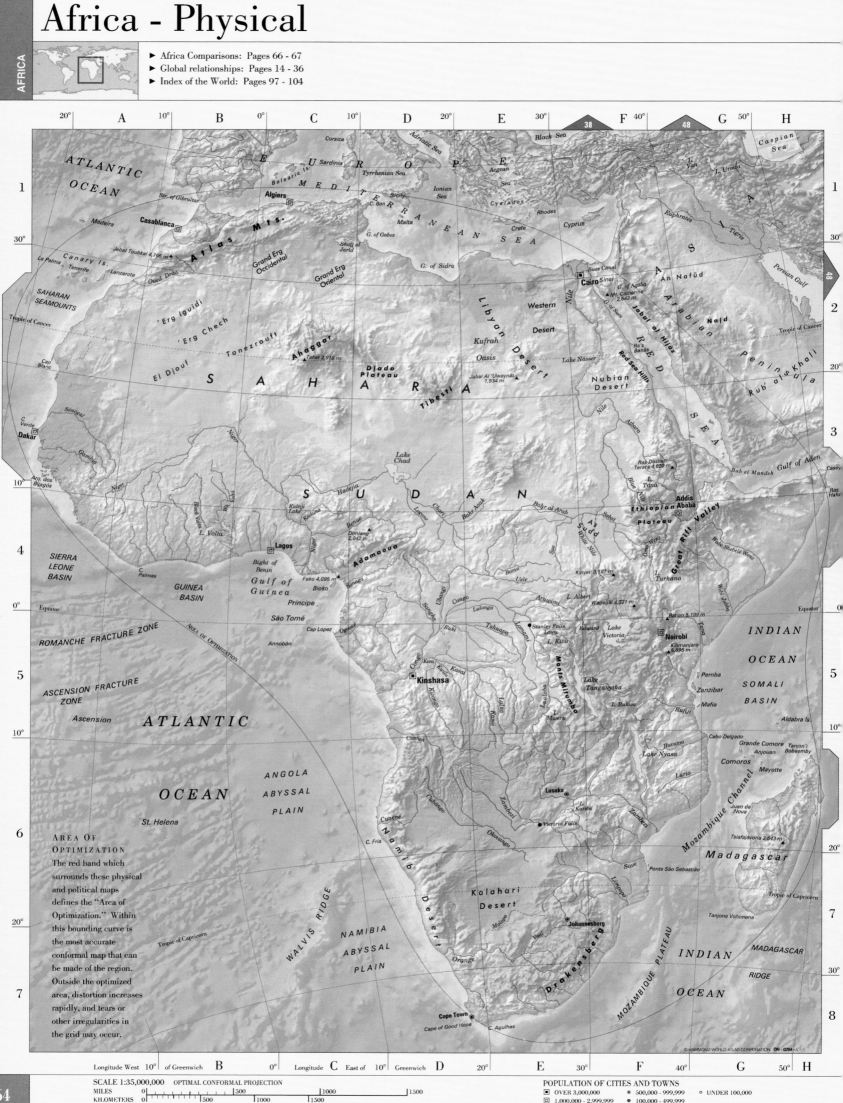

Area Of Optimization
The red band which surrounds these physical and political maps defines the "Area of Optimization." Within this bounding curve is the most accurate conformal map that can be made of the region. Outside the optimized area, distortion increases rapidly, and tears or other irregularities in the grid may occur.

SCALE 1:35,000,000   OPTIMAL CONFORMAL PROJECTION

MILES 0   500   1000   1500
KILOMETERS 0   500   1000   1500

POPULATION OF CITIES AND TOWNS
▣ OVER 3,000,000   ● 500,000 - 999,999   ○ UNDER 100,000
▣ 1,000,000 - 2,999,999   ● 100,000 - 499,999

© HAMMOND WORLD ATLAS CORPORATION   DN - 0204 - A

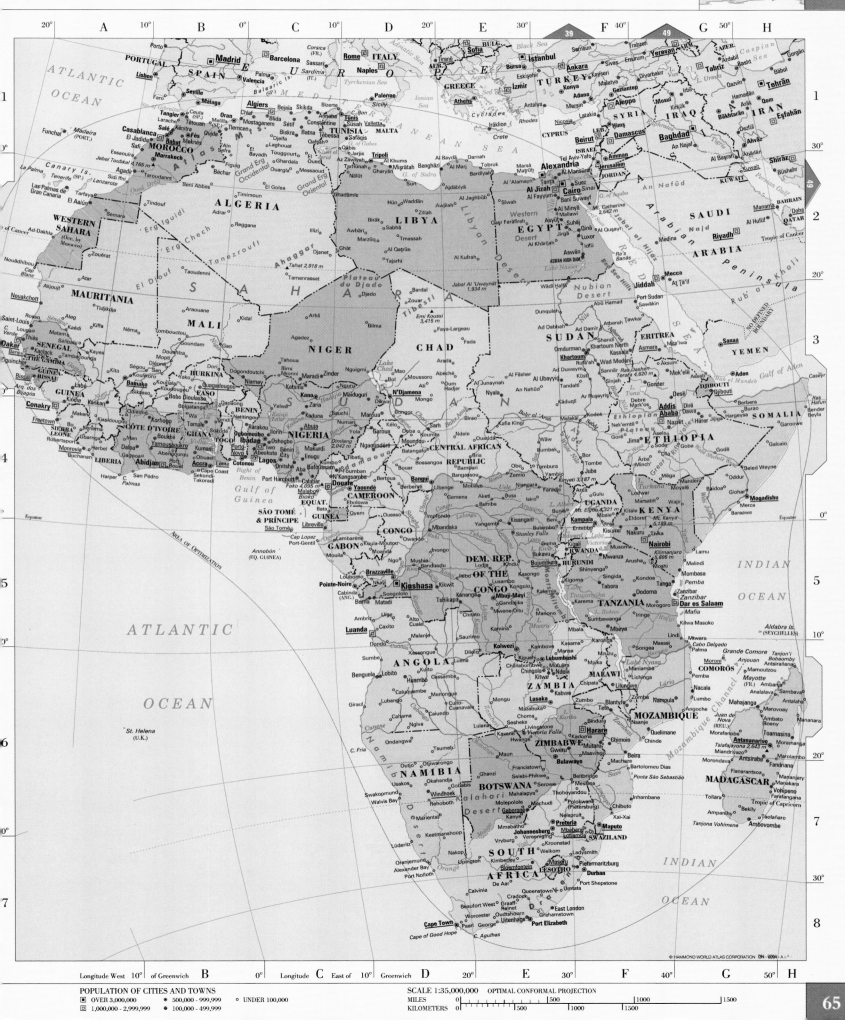

POPULATION OF CITIES AND TOWNS
☐ OVER 3,000,000 ● 500,000 - 999,999   ○ UNDER 100,000
☐ 1,000,000 - 2,999,999 ● 100,000 - 499,999

SCALE 1:35,000,000 OPTIMAL CONFORMAL PROJECTION
MILES 0   500   1000   1500
KILOMETERS 0   500   1000   1500

© HAMMOND WORLD ATLAS CORPORATION

Africa - Comparisons

AFRICA

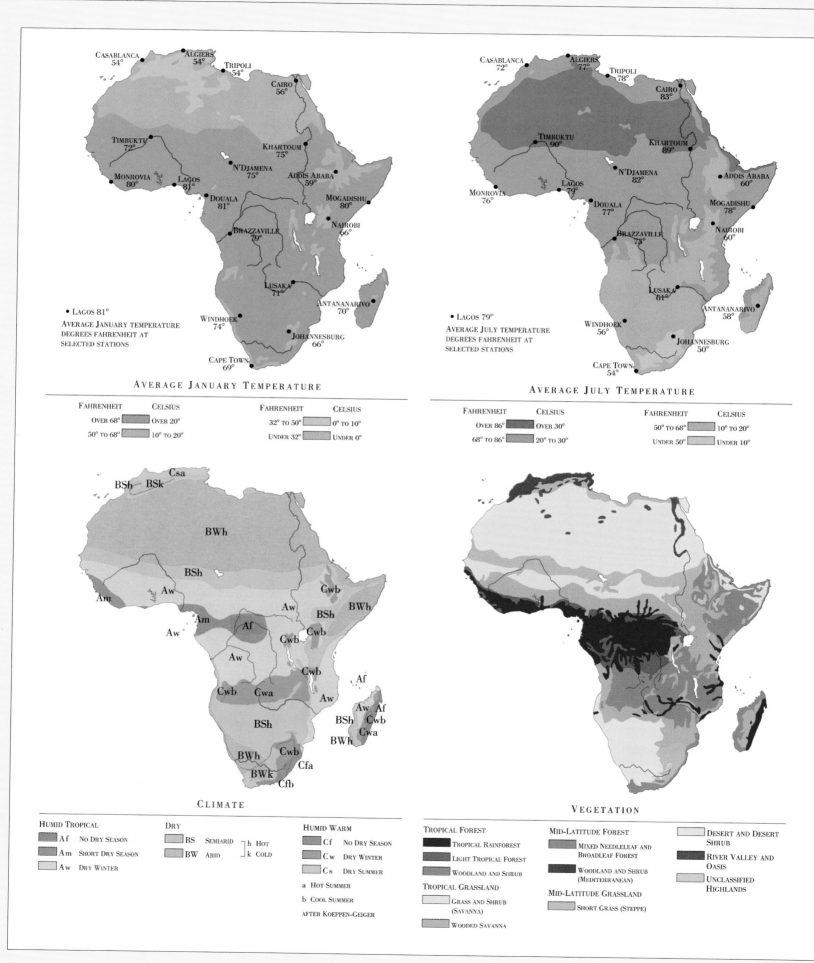

AVERAGE JANUARY TEMPERATURE

- Lagos 81°
AVERAGE JANUARY TEMPERATURE
DEGREES FAHRENHEIT AT
SELECTED STATIONS

FAHRENHEIT	CELSIUS		FAHRENHEIT	CELSIUS
OVER 68°	OVER 20°		32° TO 50°	0° TO 10°
50° TO 68°	10° TO 20°		UNDER 32°	UNDER 0°

AVERAGE JULY TEMPERATURE

- Lagos 79°
AVERAGE JULY TEMPERATURE
DEGREES FAHRENHEIT AT
SELECTED STATIONS

FAHRENHEIT	CELSIUS		FAHRENHEIT	CELSIUS
OVER 86°	OVER 30°		50° TO 68°	10° TO 20°
68° TO 86°	20° TO 30°		UNDER 50°	UNDER 10°

CLIMATE

HUMID TROPICAL
- Af NO DRY SEASON
- Am SHORT DRY SEASON
- Aw DRY WINTER

DRY
- BS SEMIARID
- BW ARID
  - h HOT
  - k COLD

HUMID WARM
- Cf NO DRY SEASON
- Cw DRY WINTER
- Cs DRY SUMMER

a HOT SUMMER
b COOL SUMMER

AFTER KOEPPEN-GEIGER

VEGETATION

TROPICAL FOREST
- TROPICAL RAINFOREST
- LIGHT TROPICAL FOREST
- WOODLAND AND SHRUB

TROPICAL GRASSLAND
- GRASS AND SHRUB (SAVANNA)
- WOODED SAVANNA

MID-LATITUDE FOREST
- MIXED NEEDLELEAF AND BROADLEAF FOREST
- WOODLAND AND SHRUB (MEDITERRANEAN)

MID-LATITUDE GRASSLAND
- SHORT GRASS (STEPPE)

- DESERT AND DESERT SHRUB
- RIVER VALLEY AND OASIS
- UNCLASSIFIED HIGHLANDS

Africa - Comparisons

► Africa Physical / Political: Pages 64 - 65
► Global Relationships: Pages 14 - 36
► Index of the World: Pages 97 - 104

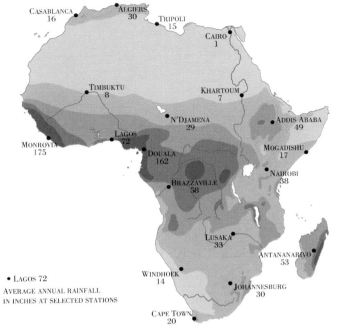

CASABLANCA 16
ALGIERS 30
TRIPOLI 15
CAIRO 1
TIMBUKTU 8
KHARTOUM 7
N'DJAMENA 29
ADDIS ABABA 49
LAGOS 72
MONROVIA 175
DOUALA 162
MOGADISHU 17
BRAZZAVILLE 58
NAIROBI 38
LUSAKA 33
ANTANANARIVO 53
WINDHOEK 14
JOHANNESBURG 30
CAPE TOWN 20

• LAGOS 72
AVERAGE ANNUAL RAINFALL
IN INCHES AT SELECTED STATIONS

AVERAGE ANNUAL RAINFALL

INCHES	CM	INCHES	CM	INCHES	CM
OVER 80	OVER 200	40 TO 60	100 TO 150	10 TO 20	25 TO 50
60 TO 80	150 TO 200	20 TO 40	50 TO 100	UNDER 10	UNDER 25

• CITIES WITH OVER 1,000,000
INHABITANTS (INCLUDING SUBURBS)

POPULATION DISTRIBUTION

DENSITY PER		SQ. MI.	SQ. KM.	SQ. MI.	SQ. KM.
SQ. MI.	SQ. KM.	130 TO 260	50 TO 100	3 TO 25	1 TO 10
OVER 260	OVER 100	25 TO 130	10 TO 50	UNDER 3	UNDER 1

ENERGY SOURCES

▨ OIL REGION	■ COAL	✳ URANIUM	
▨ NATURAL GAS REGION	● HYDROELECTRICITY		

ENVIRONMENTAL CONCERNS

～ POLLUTED RIVERS	AREAS SUBJECT TO DEFORESTATION	▨ EXTENT OF ACID RAIN
EXTENT OF COASTAL POLLUTION	AREAS SUBJECT TO DESERTIFICATION	

Below Sea | 200 | 500 | 1,000 | 1,500 | 2,000 | 4,000 | 6,000 m.
Sea Lev. Level | 700 | 1,600 | 3,300 | 5,000 | 6,500 | 13,000 | 19,700 ft.

POPULATION OF CITIES AND TOWNS

▣ OVER 2,000,000	◉ 500,000 - 999,999	○ 50,000 - 99,999
◻ 1,000,000 - 1,999,999	● 100,000 - 499,999	○ UNDER 50,000

SCALE 1:17,500,000   POLYCONIC PROJECTION

MILES 0 ___ 250 ___ 500 ___ 750

KILOMETERS 0 ___ 250 ___ 500 ___ 750

© HAMMOND WORLD ATLAS CORPORATION   CN - 2103 - A A A

Southern Africa

AFRICA

SCALE 1:17,500,000 POLYCONIC PROJECTION

MILES | 0 | 250 | 500 | 750
KILOMETERS | 0 | 250 | 500 | 750

POPULATION OF CITIES AND TOWNS
▫ OVER 2,000,000 ● 500,000 - 999,999 ○ 50,000 - 99,999
▫ 1,000,000 - 1,999,999 ● 100,000 - 499,999 ○ UNDER 50,000

© HAMMOND WORLD ATLAS CORPORATION CN - 2101 - A - A -

SAME SCALE AS MAIN MAP

© HAMMOND WAC CN - 2106 - A - A -

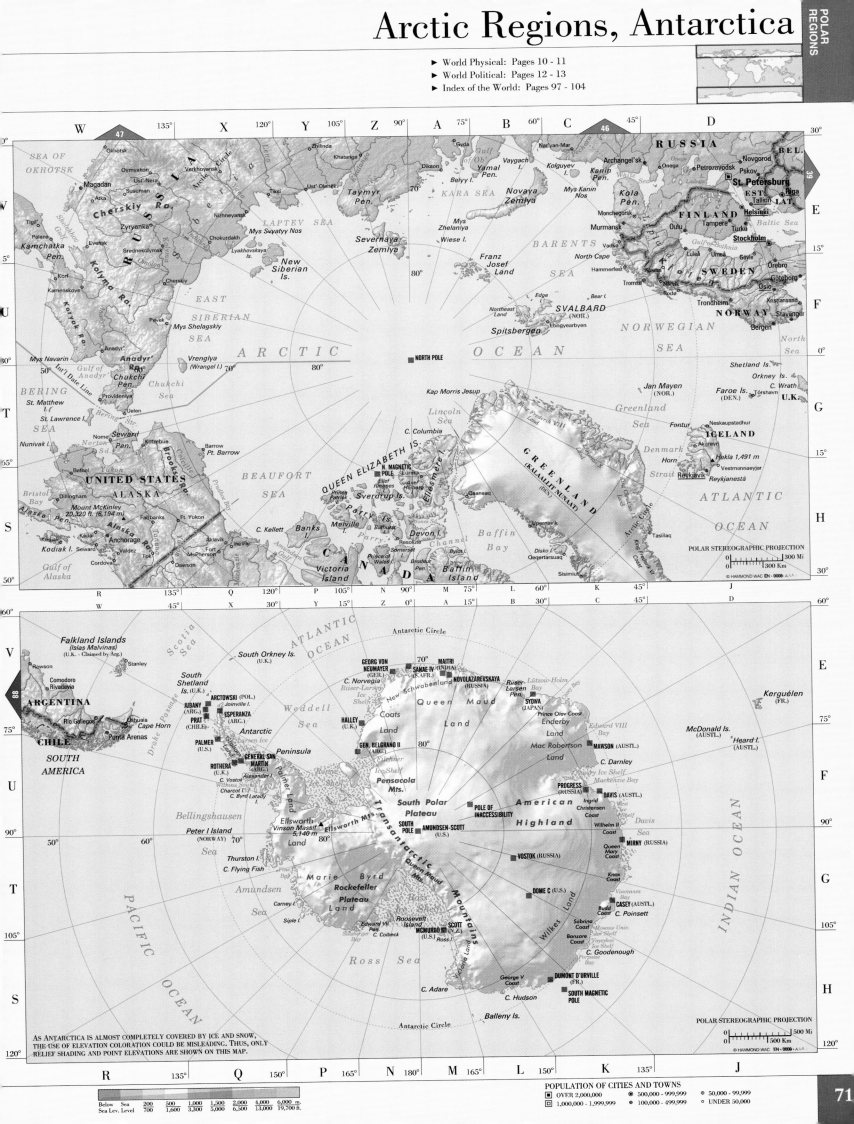

▶ World Physical: Pages 10 - 11
▶ World Political: Pages 12 - 13
▶ Index of the World: Pages 97 - 104

North America - Physical

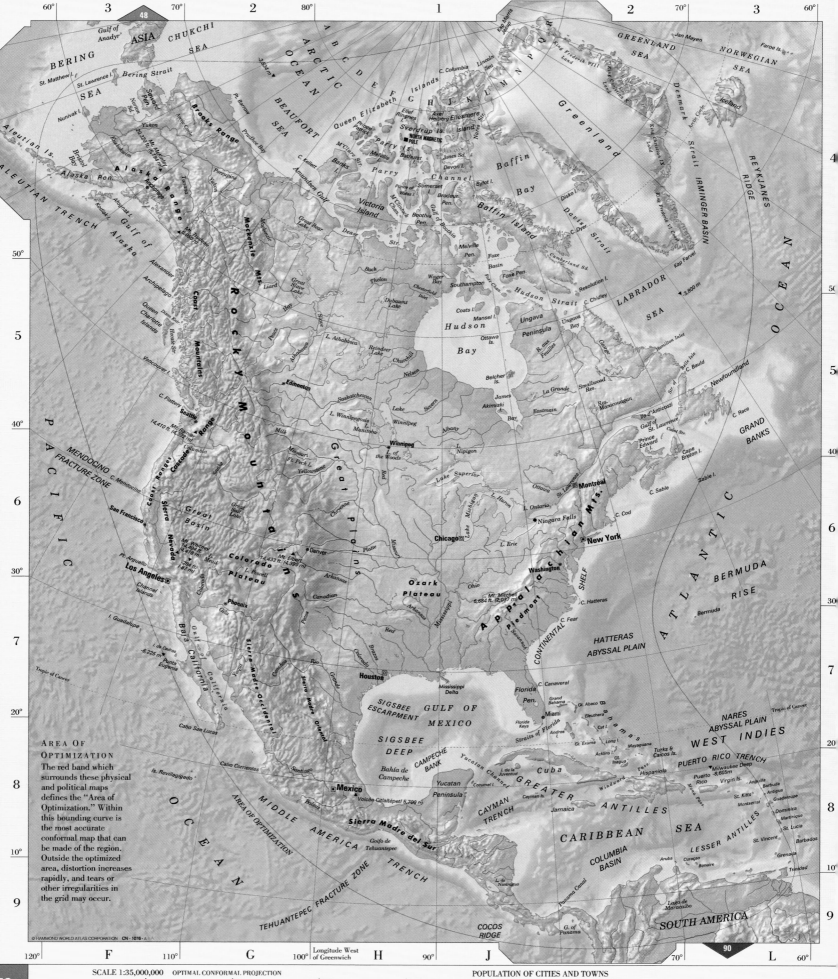

AREA OF OPTIMIZATION
The red band which surrounds these physical and political maps defines the "Area of Optimization." Within this bounding curve is the most accurate conformal map that can be made of the region. Outside the optimized area, distortion increases rapidly, and tears or other irregularities in the grid may occur.

SCALE 1:35,000,000   OPTIMAL CONFORMAL PROJECTION

MILES   0   500   1000   1500
KILOMETERS   0   500   1000   1500

POPULATION OF CITIES AND TOWNS
■ OVER 3,000,000   ● 500,000 - 999,999   ○ UNDER 100,000
◻ 1,000,000 - 2,999,999   □ 100,000 - 499,999

© HAMMOND WORLD ATLAS CORPORATION   CN - 1076 - A

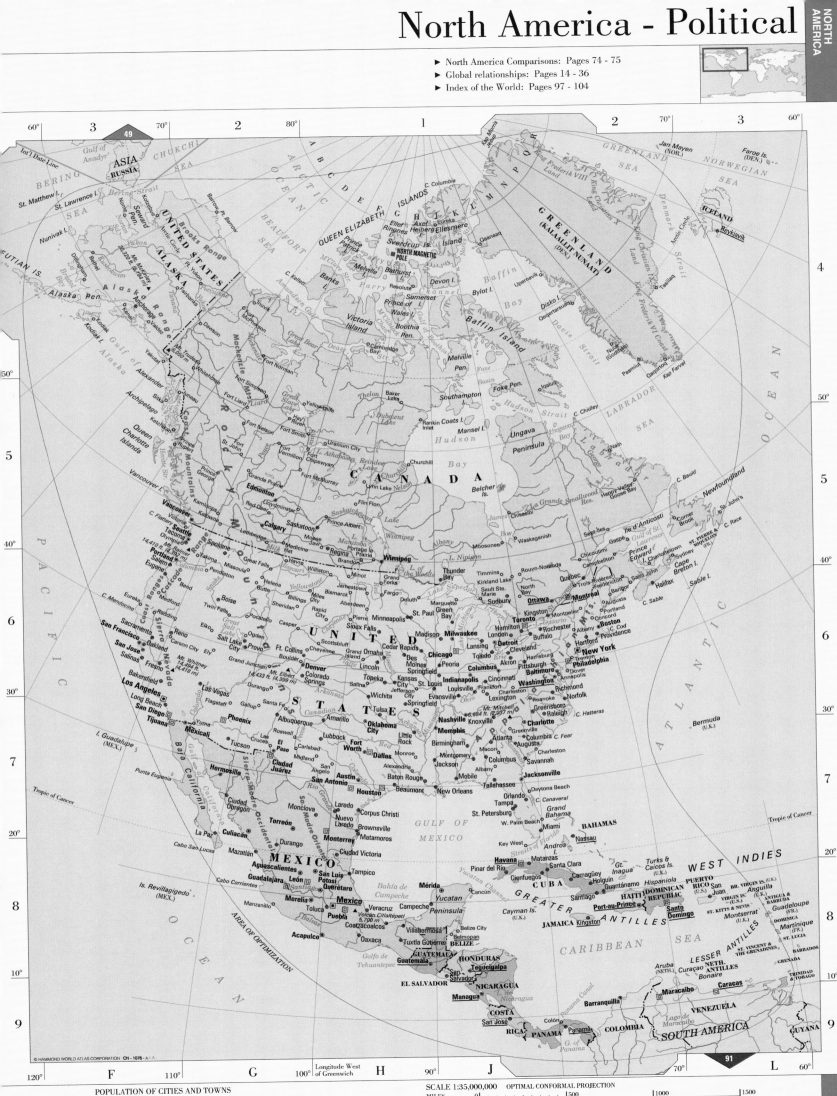

POPULATION OF CITIES AND TOWNS
- ■ OVER 3,000,000
- ■ 1,000,000 - 2,999,999
- ● 500,000 - 999,999
- ● 100,000 - 499,999
- ○ UNDER 100,000

SCALE 1:35,000,000   OPTIMAL CONFORMAL PROJECTION

MILES 0   500   1000   1500
KILOMETERS 0   500   1000   1500

North America - Comparisons

▶ North America Physical / Political: Pages 72 - 73
▶ Global Relationships: Pages 14 - 36
▶ Index of the World: Pages 97 - 104

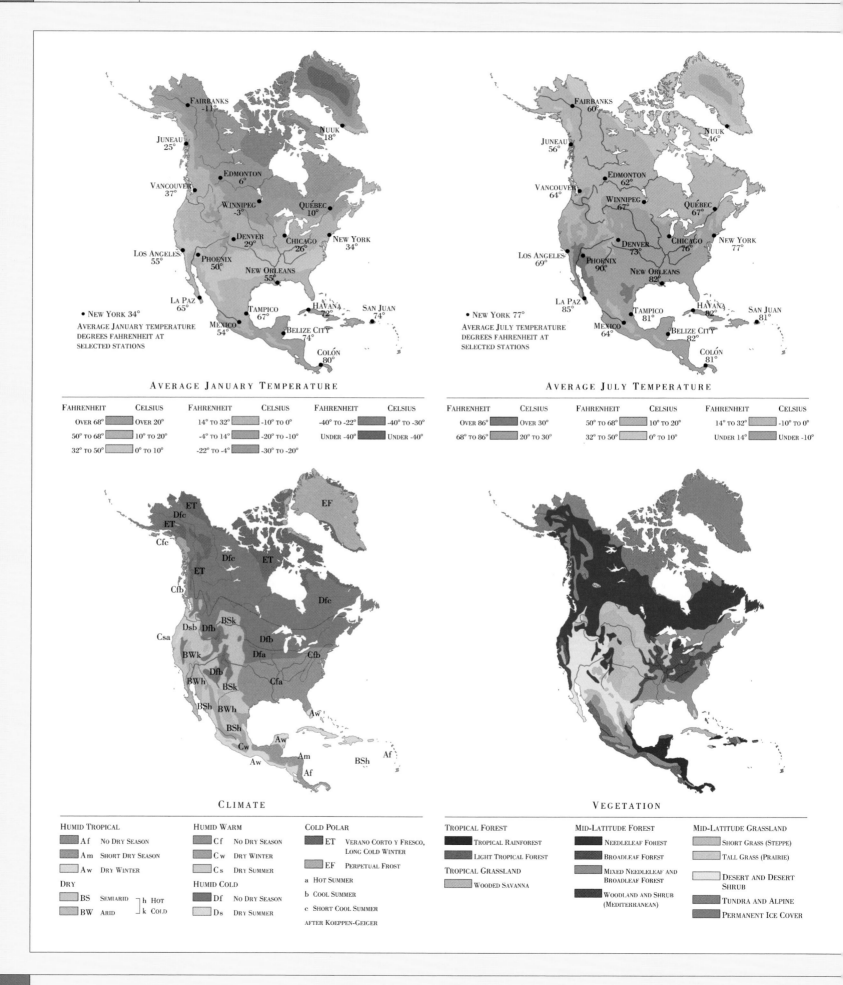

AVERAGE JANUARY TEMPERATURE

FAIRBANKS -11°
NUUK 18°
JUNEAU 25°
VANCOUVER 37°
EDMONTON 6°
WINNIPEG -3°
QUÉBEC 10°
DENVER 29°
CHICAGO 26°
NEW YORK 34°
LOS ANGELES 55°
PHOENIX 50°
NEW ORLEANS 55°
LA PAZ 65°
TAMPICO 67°
HAVANA 72°
SAN JUAN 74°
MEXICO 54°
BELIZE CITY 74°
COLÓN 80°

● NEW YORK 34°
AVERAGE JANUARY TEMPERATURE
DEGREES FAHRENHEIT AT
SELECTED STATIONS

FAHRENHEIT	CELSIUS	FAHRENHEIT	CELSIUS	FAHRENHEIT	CELSIUS
OVER 68°	OVER 20°	14° TO 32°	-10° TO 0°	-40° TO -22°	-40° TO -30°
50° TO 68°	10° TO 20°	-4° TO 14°	-20° TO -10°	UNDER -40°	UNDER -40°
32° TO 50°	0° TO 10°	-22° TO -4°	-30° TO -20°		

AVERAGE JULY TEMPERATURE

FAIRBANKS 60°
NUUK 46°
JUNEAU 56°
VANCOUVER 64°
EDMONTON 62°
WINNIPEG 67°
QUÉBEC 67°
DENVER 73°
CHICAGO 76°
NEW YORK 77°
LOS ANGELES 69°
PHOENIX 90°
NEW ORLEANS 82°
LA PAZ 85°
TAMPICO 81°
HAVANA 82°
SAN JUAN 81°
MEXICO 64°
BELIZE CITY 82°
COLÓN 81°

● NEW YORK 77°
AVERAGE JULY TEMPERATURE
DEGREES FAHRENHEIT AT
SELECTED STATIONS

FAHRENHEIT	CELSIUS	FAHRENHEIT	CELSIUS	FAHRENHEIT	CELSIUS
OVER 86°	OVER 30°	50° TO 68°	10° TO 20°	14° TO 32°	-10° TO 0°
68° TO 86°	20° TO 30°	32° TO 50°	0° TO 10°	UNDER 14°	UNDER -10°

CLIMATE

HUMID TROPICAL		HUMID WARM		COLD POLAR	
Af	NO DRY SEASON	Cf	NO DRY SEASON	ET	VERANO CORTO Y FRESCO, LONG COLD WINTER
Am	SHORT DRY SEASON	Cw	DRY WINTER	EF	PERPETUAL FROST
Aw	DRY WINTER	Cs	DRY SUMMER	a	HOT SUMMER

DRY		HUMID COLD	
BS	SEMIARID ⎤h HOT	Df	NO DRY SEASON
BW	ARID ⎦k COLD	Ds	DRY SUMMER

b COOL SUMMER
c SHORT COOL SUMMER

AFTER KOEPPEN-GEIGER

VEGETATION

TROPICAL FOREST	MID-LATITUDE FOREST	MID-LATITUDE GRASSLAND
TROPICAL RAINFOREST	NEEDLELEAF FOREST	SHORT GRASS (STEPPE)
LIGHT TROPICAL FOREST	BROADLEAF FOREST	TALL GRASS (PRAIRIE)
TROPICAL GRASSLAND	MIXED NEEDLELEAF AND BROADLEAF FOREST	DESERT AND DESERT SHRUB
WOODED SAVANNA	WOODLAND AND SHRUB (MEDITERRANEAN)	TUNDRA AND ALPINE
		PERMANENT ICE COVER

North America - Comparisons

NORTH AMERICA

▶ North America Physical / Political: Pages 72 - 73
▶ Global Relationships: Pages 14 - 36
▶ Index of the World: Pages 97 - 104

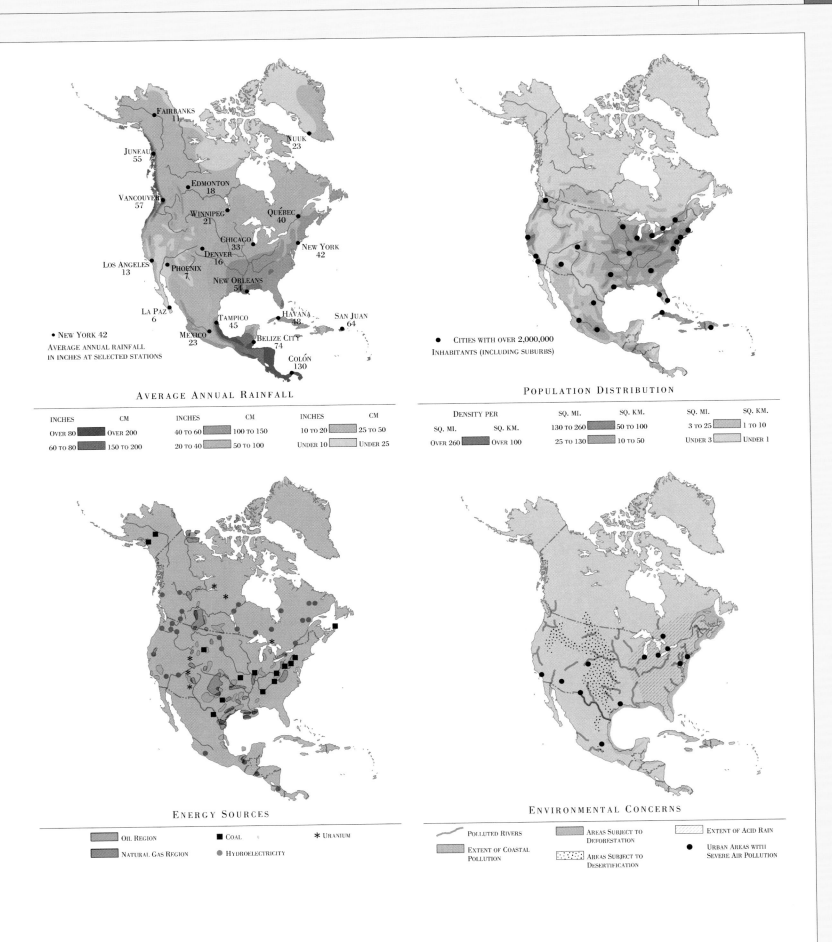

FAIRBANKS
11

NUUK
23

JUNEAU
55

EDMONTON
18

VANCOUVER
57

WINNIPEG
21

QUÉBEC
40

CHICAGO
33

NEW YORK
42

DENVER
16

LOS ANGELES
13

PHOENIX
7

NEW ORLEANS
54

LA PAZ
6

TAMPICO
45

HAVANA
48

SAN JUAN
64

● NEW YORK 42
AVERAGE ANNUAL RAINFALL
IN INCHES AT SELECTED STATIONS

MEXICO
23

BELIZE CITY
74

COLÓN
130

AVERAGE ANNUAL RAINFALL

INCHES	CM	INCHES	CM	INCHES	CM
OVER 80	OVER 200	40 TO 60	100 TO 150	10 TO 20	25 TO 50
60 TO 80	150 TO 200	20 TO 40	50 TO 100	UNDER 10	UNDER 25

● CITIES WITH OVER 2,000,000
INHABITANTS (INCLUDING SUBURBS)

POPULATION DISTRIBUTION

DENSITY PER		SQ. MI.	SQ. KM.	SQ. MI.	SQ. KM.
SQ. MI.	SQ. KM.	130 TO 260	50 TO 100	3 TO 25	1 TO 10
OVER 260	OVER 100	25 TO 130	10 TO 50	UNDER 3	UNDER 1

ENERGY SOURCES

OIL REGION	■ COAL	✳ URANIUM
NATURAL GAS REGION	● HYDROELECTRICITY	

ENVIRONMENTAL CONCERNS

POLLUTED RIVERS	AREAS SUBJECT TO DEFORESTATION	EXTENT OF ACID RAIN
EXTENT OF COASTAL POLLUTION	AREAS SUBJECT TO DESERTIFICATION	● URBAN AREAS WITH SEVERE AIR POLLUTION

A · 150° · B · 78 · 110° · F · 100° · G · 90

BEAUFORT SEA

Banks Island

AULAVIK NP

Prince Albert Peninsula

Victoria Island

Prince of Wales Island

Somerset Island

Amundsen Gulf

Coronation Gulf

Boothia Peninsula

ALASKA
UNITED STATES

Anchorage

Alaska Ra.

MT. McKINLEY 20,320 ft. (6,194 m)

Gulf of Alaska

YUKON TERRITORY

Whitehorse

NORTHWEST TERRITORIES

Great Slave Lake

Yellowknife

Great Bear Lake

NUNAVUT

Baker Lake

Whale Cove

PACIFIC OCEAN

Alexander Archipelago

Queen Charlotte Islands

Hecate Strait

Queen Charlotte Sound

BRITISH COLUMBIA

Rocky Mountains

Coast Mountains

Caribou Mtns.

WOOD BUFFALO NATIONAL PARK

Fort Smith

Fort Chipewyan

Lake Athabasca

Uranium City

Fond du Lac

Churchill

WAPUSK NP

C. Tatnam

York Factory

Gillam

Vancouver Island

Vancouver

Victoria

Prince George

ALBERTA

Edmonton

JASPER NAT'L PARK

BANFF NAT'L PARK

Calgary

Red Deer

MT. COLUMBIA 12,294 ft. (3,747 m)
MT. ROBSON 12,972 ft. (3,954 m)

SASKATCHEWAN

PRINCE ALBERT NAT'L PARK

Prince Albert

Saskatoon

Regina

Saskatchewan

Reindeer Lake

La Ronge

MANITOBA

Lake Winnipeg

RIDING MTN. NP

Lake Winnipegosis

Lake Manitoba

The Pas

Thompson

Flin Flon

Winnipeg

Brandon

Seattle
Tacoma
WASHINGTON

MT. RAINIER 14,410 ft. (4,392 m)

Spokane

NORTH CASCADES NP

OLYMPIC NP

Portland
Salem
OREGON

CRATER LAKE NP

REDWOOD NP

CALIFORNIA

Sacramento
San Francisco
San Jose

NEVADA

Reno
Carson City

Great Basin

MT. SHASTA 14,162 ft. (4,317 m)

LASSEN VOLCANIC NP

YOSEMITE NP

Salt Lake City
Provo
Orem

UTAH

Columbia Plateau

IDAHO
Boise

Twin Falls

GRAND TETON NAT'L PARK
YELLOWSTONE NAT'L PARK

GANNETT PK. 13,804 ft. (4,207 m)

WYOMING

Casper

Cheyenne

UNITED STATES

MONTANA

Helena
Great Falls
Butte
Billings

GLACIER NAT'L PARK

Missoula

NORTH DAKOTA

Bismarck
Fargo

THEODORE ROOSEVELT NAT'L PARK

BADLANDS NAT'L PARK

SOUTH DAKOTA

Rapid City
Pierre
Sioux Falls

HARNEY PK. 7,242 ft. (2,207 m)

MINNESOTA

Minneapolis
Saint Paul
Duluth

VOYAGEURS NP

ISLE ROYALE NP

Thunder Bay

WISCONSIN

Eau Claire

Lake of the Woods

NEBRASKA

IOWA

D · 120° · E · 78 · 110° · F · 100° · Longitude West of Greenwich · G · 90°

Below Sea Level | Sea Level | 200 | 500 | 1,000 | 1,500 | 2,000 | 4,000 | 6,000 m.
700 | 1,600 | 3,300 | 5,000 | 6,500 | 13,000 | 19,700 ft.

Canada

► North America Comparisons: Pages 74 - 75
► Global relationships: Pages 14 - 36
► Index of the World: Pages 97 - 104

POPULATION OF CITIES AND TOWNS

Symbol	Population
■	OVER 2,000,000
◙	1,000,000 - 1,999,999
●	500,000 - 999,999
⊙	100,000 - 499,999
∘	50,000 - 99,999
○	UNDER 50,000

SCALE 1:14,000,000 LAMBERT CONFORMAL CONIC PROJECTION

MILES 0 — 200 — 400 — 600
KILOMETERS 0 — 200 — 400 — 600

© HAMMOND WORLD ATLAS CORPORATION

Below Sea | 200 | 500 | 1,000 | 1,500 | 2,000 | 4,000 | 6,000 m.
Sea Lev. Level | 700 | 1,600 | 3,300 | 5,000 | 6,500 | 13,000 | 19,700 ft.

► North America Comparisons: Pages 74 - 75
► Global relationships: Pages 14 - 36
► Index of the World: Pages 97 - 104

POPULATION OF CITIES AND TOWNS

- ■ OVER 2,000,000
- ◻ 1,000,000 - 1,999,999
- ● 500,000 - 999,999
- ◉ 100,000 - 499,999
- ● 50,000 - 99,999
- ○ UNDER 50,000

SCALE 1:14,000,000   LAMBERT CONFORMAL CONIC PROJECTION

MILES 0   200   400   600

KILOMETERS 0   200   400   600

© HAMMOND WORLD ATLAS CORPORATION

CN - 1079 - A A A

Below Sea 200 500 1,000 1,500 2,000 4,000 6,000 m
Sea Lev. Level 700 1,600 3,300 5,000 6,500 13,000 19,700 ft.

Longitude West of Greenwich

► North America Comparisons: Pages 74 - 75
► Global relationships: Pages 14 - 36
► Index of the World: Pages 97 - 104

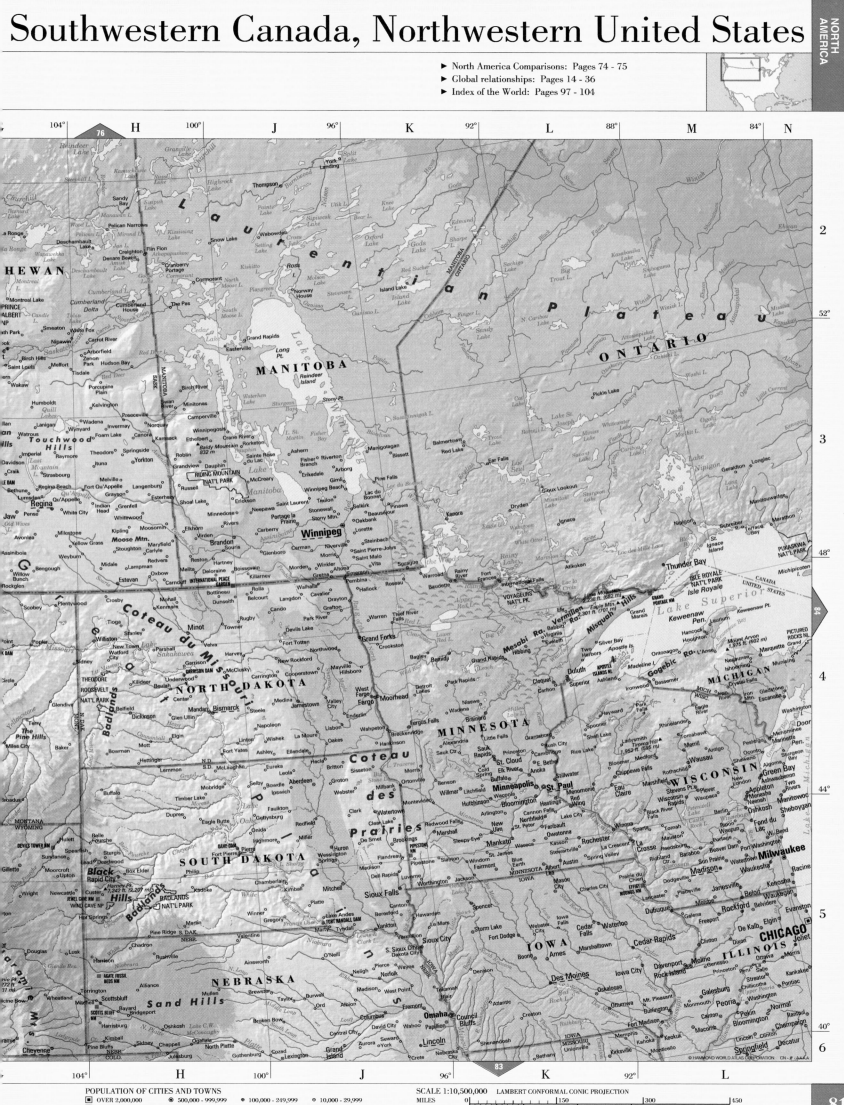

POPULATION OF CITIES AND TOWNS

■ OVER 2,000,000	● 500,000 - 999,999
▣ 1,000,000 - 1,999,999	● 250,000 - 499,999

● 100,000 - 249,999	○ 10,000 - 29,999
● 30,000 - 99,999	○ UNDER 10,000

SCALE 1:10,500,000   LAMBERT CONFORMAL CONIC PROJECTION

MILES   0   150   300   450
KILOMETERS 0   150   300   450

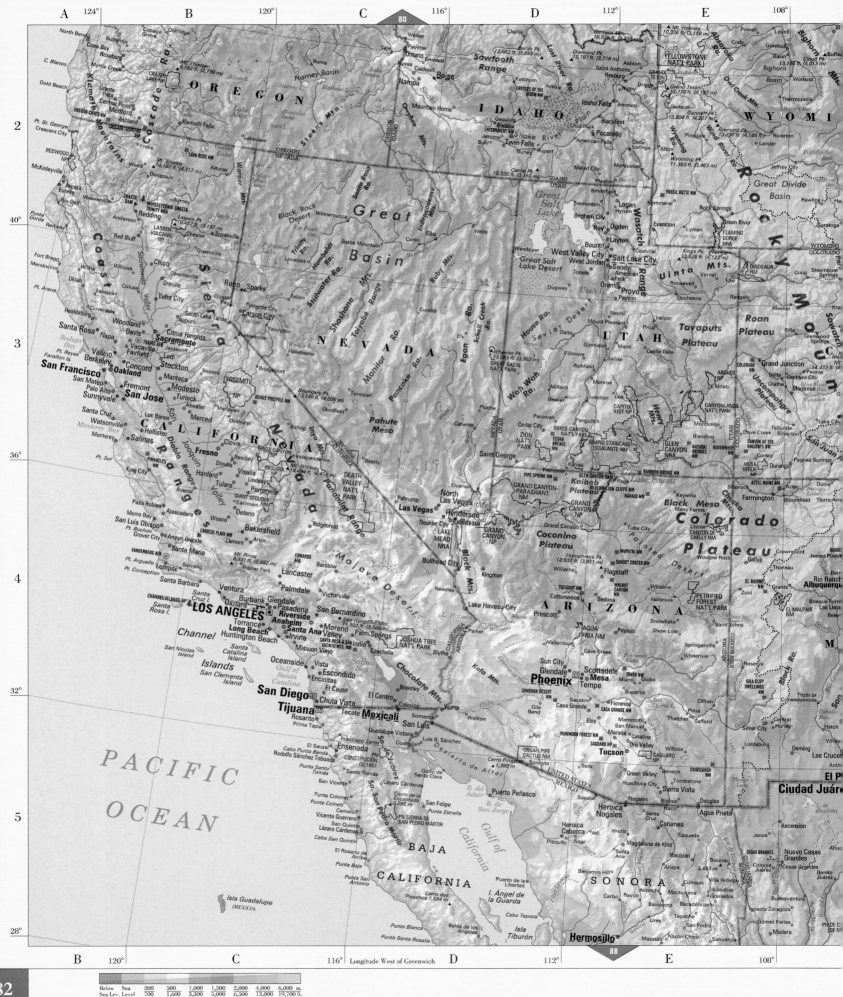

	Below Sea	200	500	1,000	1,500	2,000	4,000	6,000 m.
	Sea Lev. Level	700	1,600	3,300	5,000	6,500	13,000	19,700 ft.

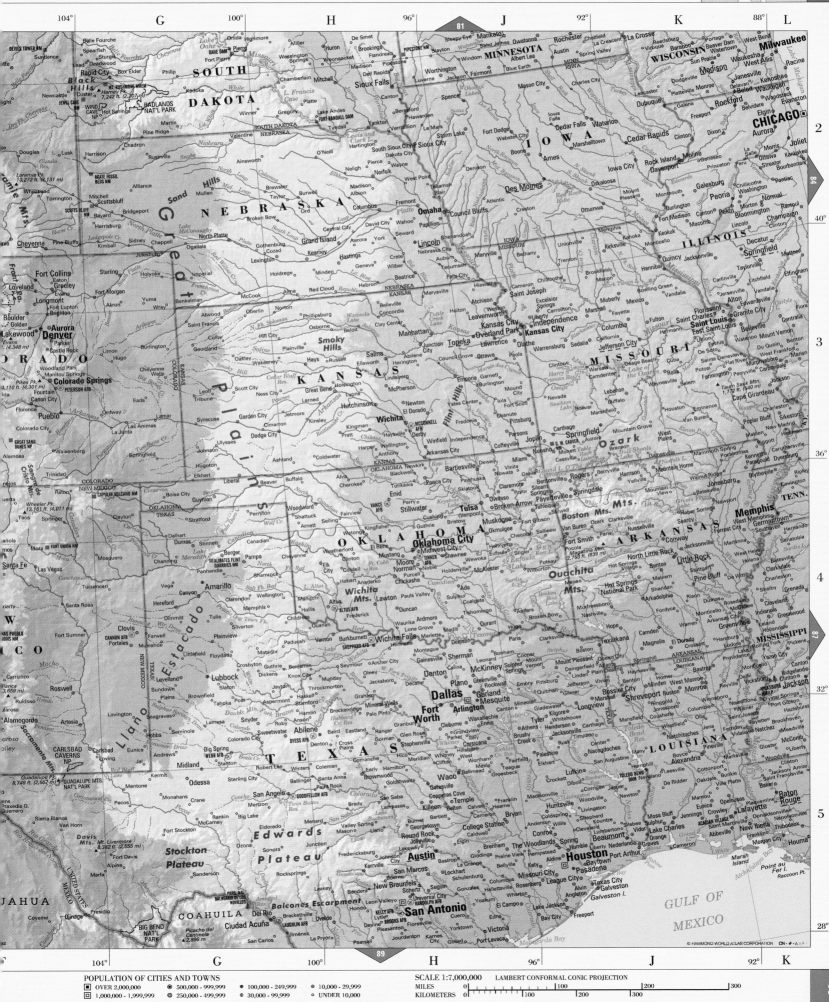

POPULATION OF CITIES AND TOWNS

| ■ | OVER 2,000,000 | ● | 500,000 - 999,999 | ● | 100,000 - 249,999 | ○ | 10,000 - 29,999 |
| □ | 1,000,000 - 1,999,999 | ◉ | 250,000 - 499,999 | ● | 30,000 - 99,999 | ○ | UNDER 10,000 |

SCALE 1:7,000,000   LAMBERT CONFORMAL CONIC PROJECTION

MILES 0 ___ 100 ___ 200 ___ 300

KILOMETERS 0 ___ 100 ___ 200 ___ 300

© HAMMOND WORLD ATLAS CORPORATION   CN · ◆ · A·A

Southeastern Canada, Northeastern United States

Below Sea   200   500   1,000   1,500   2,000   4,000   6,000 m.
Sea Lev. Level   700   1,600   3,300   5,000   6,500   13,000   19,700 ft.

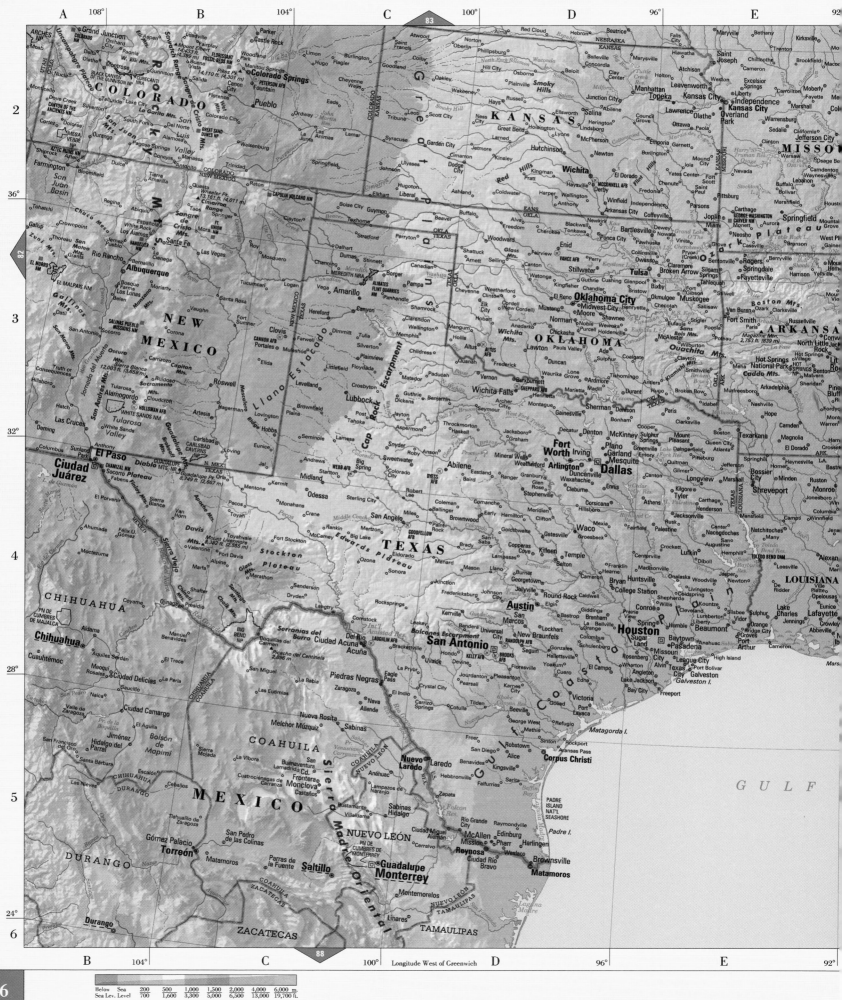

Below Sea   200   500   1,000   1,500   2,000   4,000 6,000 m.
Sea Lev. Level   700   1,600   3,300   5,000   6,500 13,000 19,700 ft.

► North America Comparisons: Pages 74 - 75
► Global relationships: Pages 14 - 36
► Index of the World: Pages 97 - 104

POPULATION OF CITIES AND TOWNS

☐ OVER 2,000,000   ● 500,000 - 999,999   ● 100,000 - 249,999   ● 10,000 - 29,999
☐ 1,000,000 - 1,999,999   ☐ 250,000 - 499,999   ● 30,000 - 99,999   ○ UNDER 10,000

SCALE 1:7,000,000   LAMBERT CONFORMAL CONIC PROJECTION

MILES 0   100   200   300
KILOMETERS 0   100   200   300

Middle America and Caribbean

► North America Comparisons: Pages 74 - 75
► Global relationships: Pages 14 - 36
► Index of the World: Pages 97 - 104

POPULATION OF CITIES AND TOWNS

■ OVER 2,000,000	● 500,000 - 999,999
▣ 1,000,000 - 1,999,999	● 250,000 - 499,999

● 100,000 - 249,999   ⊙ 10,000 - 29,999
● 30,000 - 99,999   ○ UNDER 10,000

	Below	Sea	200	500	1,000	1,500	2,000	4,000	6,000 m.
	Sea Lev.	Level	700	1,600	3,300	6,500	13,000	19,700 ft.

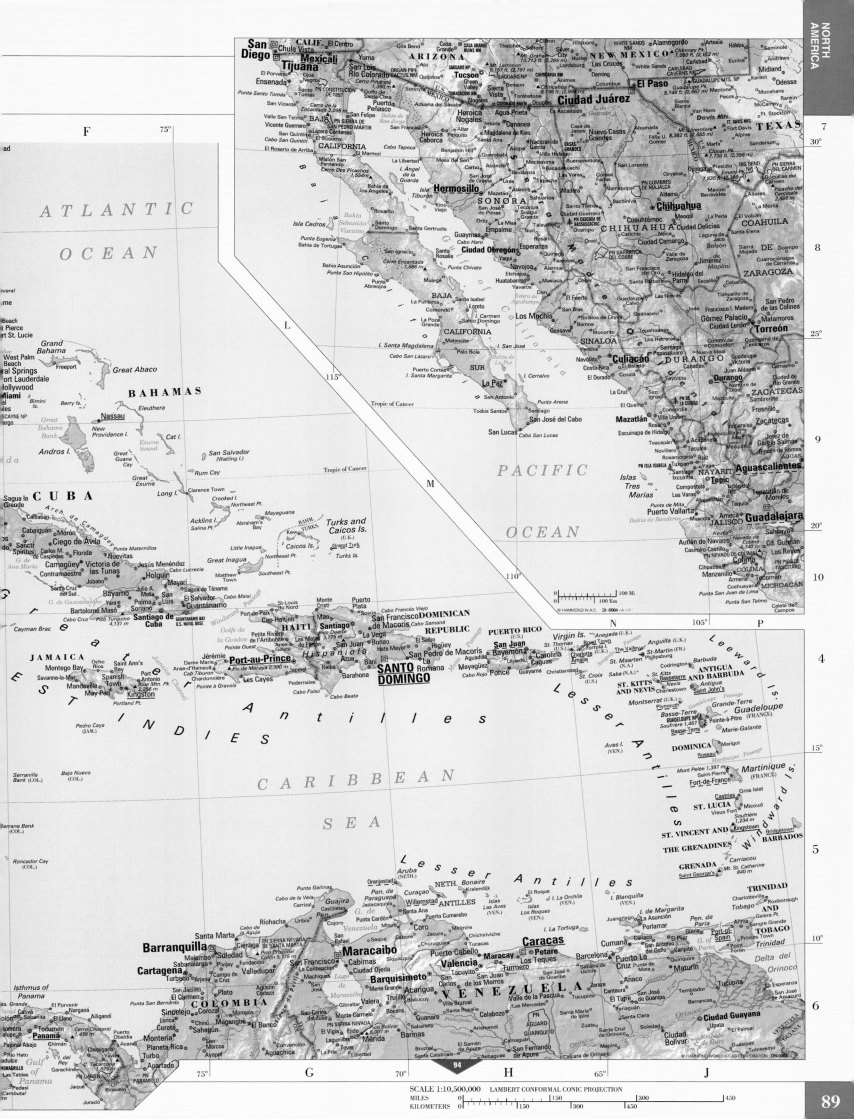

South America - Physical

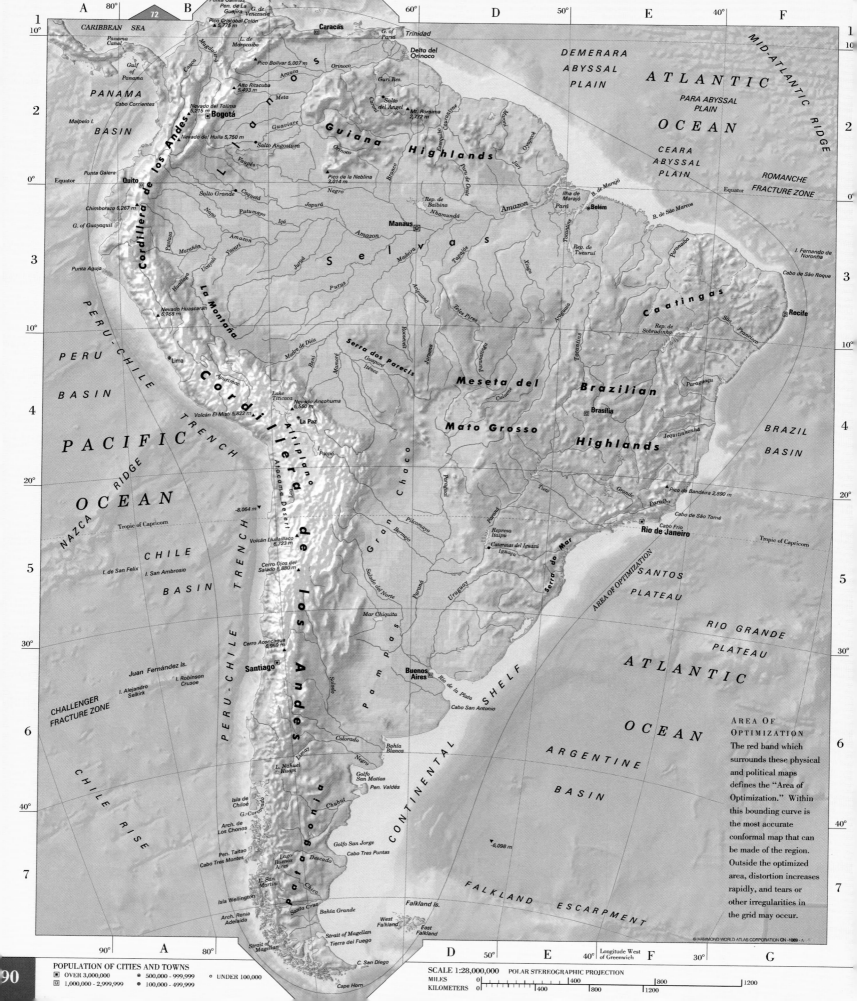

AREA OF OPTIMIZATION The red band which surrounds these physical and political maps defines the "Area of Optimization." Within this bounding curve is the most accurate conformal map that can be made of the region. Outside the optimized area, distortion increases rapidly, and tears or other irregularities in the grid may occur.

POPULATION OF CITIES AND TOWNS
■ OVER 3,000,000   ● 500,000 - 999,999   ○ UNDER 100,000
▣ 1,000,000 - 2,999,999   ● 100,000 - 499,999

SCALE 1:28,000,000   POLAR STEREOGRAPHIC PROJECTION
MILES   0   400   800   1200
KILOMETERS 0   400   800 1200

© HAMMOND WORLD ATLAS CORPORATION CN -1069 - A

South America - Political

► South America Comparisons: Pages 92 - 93
► Global relationships: Pages 14 - 36
► Index of the World: Pages 97 - 104

© HAMMOND WORLD ATLAS CORPORATION CN -1069 - AAA

POPULATION OF CITIES AND TOWNS

▣ OVER 3,000,000	● 500,000 - 999,999
■ 1,000,000 - 2,999,999	● 100,000 - 499,999
	○ UNDER 100,000

SCALE 1:28,000,000   POLAR STEREOGRAPHIC PROJECTION

MILES   0   400   800   1200

KILOMETERS   0   400   800   1200

South America - Comparisons

► South America Physical / Political: Pages 90 - 91
► Global Relationships: Pages 14 - 36
► Index of the World: Pages 97 - 104

SOUTH AMERICA

AVERAGE JANUARY TEMPERATURE

AVERAGE JULY TEMPERATURE

FAHRENHEIT	CELSIUS	FAHRENHEIT	CELSIUS	FAHRENHEIT	CELSIUS
OVER 86°	OVER 30°	50° TO 68°	10° TO 20°	UNDER 32°	UNDER 0°
68° TO 86°	20° TO 30°	32° TO 50°	0° TO 10°		

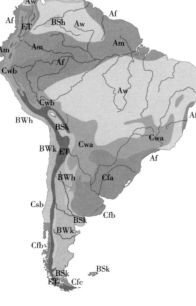

CLIMATE

HUMID TROPICAL
- Af NO DRY SEASON
- Am SHORT DRY SEASON
- Aw DRY WINTER

DRY
- BS SEMIARID ⎤h HOT
- BW ARID ⎦k COLD

HUMID WARM
- Cf NO DRY SEASON
- Cw DRY WINTER
- Cs DRY SUMMER

COLD POLAR
- ET SHORT COOL SUMMER, LONG COLD WINTER

a HOT SUMMER
b COOL SUMMER
c SHORT COOL SUMMER

AFTER KOEPPEN-GEIGER

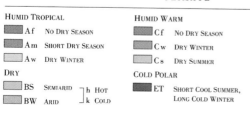

VEGETATION

TROPICAL FOREST
- TROPICAL RAINFOREST
- LIGHT TROPICAL FOREST
- WOODLAND AND SHRUB

TROPICAL GRASSLAND
- GRASS AND SHRUB (SAVANNA)
- WOODED SAVANNA

MID-LATITUDE FOREST
- NEEDLELEAF FOREST
- MIXED NEEDLELEAF AND BROADLEAF FOREST
- WOODLAND AND SHRUB (MEDITERRANEAN)

MID-LATITUDE GRASSLAND
- SHORT GRASS (STEPPE)
- TALL GRASS (PRAIRIE) AND WOODED STEPPE

- DESERT AND DESERT SHRUB
- TUNDRA AND ALPINE
- UNCLASSIFIED HIGHLANDS

► South America Physical / Political: Pages 90 - 91
► Global Relationships: Pages 14 - 36
► Index of the World: Pages 97 - 104

• MANAUS 71
AVERAGE ANNUAL RAINFALL
IN INCHES AT SELECTED STATIONS

• CITIES WITH OVER 1,000,000
INHABITANTS (INCLUDING SUBURBS)

AVERAGE ANNUAL RAINFALL

INCHES	CM	INCHES	CM	INCHES	CM
OVER 80	OVER 200	40 TO 60	100 TO 150	10 TO 20	25 TO 50
60 TO 80	150 TO 200	20 TO 40	50 TO 100	UNDER 10	UNDER 25

POPULATION DISTRIBUTION

DENSITY PER		SQ. MI.	SQ. KM.	SQ. MI.	SQ. KM.
SQ. MI.	SQ. KM.	130 TO 260	50 TO 100	3 TO 25	1 TO 10
OVER 260	OVER 100	25 TO 130	10 TO 50	UNDER 3	UNDER 1

ENERGY SOURCES

	OIL REGION	■ COAL	✳ URANIUM
	NATURAL GAS REGION	● HYDROELECTRICITY	

ENVIRONMENTAL CONCERNS

	POLLUTED RIVERS		AREAS SUBJECT TO DEFORESTATION		EXTENT OF ACID RAIN
	EXTENT OF COASTAL POLLUTION		AREAS SUBJECT TO DESERTIFICATION	●	URBAN AREAS WITH SEVERE AIR POLLUTION

CARIBBEAN SEA

SAINT VINCENT
AND THE GRENADINES

GRENADA

NETH. ANTILLES

TRINIDAD
AND
TOBAGO

VENEZUELA

COLOMBIA

Guiana Highla

GUYA

ECUADOR

PERU

BOLIVIA

PACIFIC

OCEAN

B R

CHILE

ARGENTINA

PARAGUA

Tropic of Capricorn

Longitude West of Greenwich

Below Sea   200   500   1,000 1,500 2,000 4,000 6,000 m.
Sea Lev. Level 700 1,600 3,300 5,000 6,500 13,000 19,700 ft.

► South America Comparisons: Pages 92 - 93
► Global relationships: Pages 14 - 36
► Index of the World: Pages 97 - 104

POPULATION OF CITIES AND TOWNS
- ■ OVER 2,000,000
- ◉ 500,000 - 999,999
- ○ 50,000 - 99,999
- ▣ 1,000,000 - 1,999,999
- ◎ 100,000 - 499,999
- ○ UNDER 50,000

SCALE 1:15,000,000   LAMBERT CONFORMAL CONIC PROJECTION
MILES   0 | 200 | 400 | 600
KILOMETERS   0 | 200 | 400 | 600

©HAMMOND WORLD ATLAS CORPORATION   CN - 2107 • A • A A

Southern South America

► South America Comparisons: Pages 92 - 93
► Global relationships: Pages 14 - 36
► Index of the World: Pages 97 - 104

POPULATION OF CITIES AND TOWNS

| ▣ OVER 2,000,000 | ● 500,000 - 999,999 | ○ 50,000 - 99,999 |
| ▢ 1,000,000 - 1,999,999 | ● 100,000 - 499,999 | ○ UNDER 50,000 |

SCALE 1:15,000,000 LAMBERT CONFORMAL CONIC PROJECTION

MILES   0   200   400   600
KILOMETERS   0   200   400   600

| Below Sea | 200 | 500 | 1,000 | 1,500 | 2,000 | 4,000 | 6,000 m. |
| Sea Lev. Level | 700 | 1,600 | 3,300 | 5,000 | 6,500 | 13,000 | 19,700 ft. |

Index of the World

This alphabetical list gives countries, cities, regions, political divisions, and physical features for the world. Latitude/longitude coordinates are given for each entry, where possible, followed by the page number for the map on which the entry appears to the best advantage. The entry may be located on other maps as well by the use of the coordinates given. Capitals are designated by asterisks (*).

INDEX ABBREVIATIONS

Afghan.	Afghanistan
Ala.	Alabama
Alg.	Algeria
Alta.	Alberta
Amer.	America
arch.	archipelago
Arg.	Argentina
Ariz.	Arizona
Ark.	Arkansas
Austl.	Australia
Azer.	Azerbaijan
Belg.	Belgium
Bots.	Botswana
Br. Col.	British Columbia
Calif.	California
Can.	Canada
CAfr.	Central African Republic
chan.	channel
Col.	Colombia
Colo.	Colorado
Conn.	Connecticut
C.R.	Costa Rica
Czech Rep.	Czech Republic
D.C.	District of Columbia
Del.	Delaware
Den.	Denmark
Dom. Rep.	Dominican Republic
D.R. Congo	Democratic Republic of the Congo
E.	East, Eastern
El Sal.	El Salvador
Eng.	England
Eq. Guin.	Equatorial Guinea
Falk. Is.	Falkland Islands
Fla.	Florida
Fr.	France, French
Ga.	Georgia
Ger.	Germany
Guat.	Guatemala
Ill.	Illinois
Ind.	Indiana
Indon.	Indonesia
isl., isls.	island, islands
Kans.	Kansas
Kazak.	Kazakhstan
Ky.	Kentucky
La.	Louisiana
Lux.	Luxembourg
Man.	Manitoba
Mart.	Martinique
Mass.	Massachusetts
Md.	Maryland
Mex.	Mexico
Mich.	Michigan
Minn.	Minnesota
Miss.	Mississippi
Mo.	Missouri
Mont.	Montana
Mor.	Morocco
Moz.	Mozambique
mt., mts.	mountain, mountains
N,. No.	North, Northern
Namb.	Namibia
Nat'l Pk	National Park
N.B.	New Brunswick
N.C.	North Carolina
N.D.	North Dakota
Neb.	Nebraska
Neth.	Netherlands
Neth. Ant.	Netherlands Antilles
Nev.	Nevada
New Cal.	New Caledonia
Newf.	Newfoundland and Labrador
N.H.	New Hampshire
Nic.	Nicaragua
N.J.	New Jersey
N. Korea	North Korea
N.M.	New Mexico
No. Ire.	Northern Ireland
N.S.	Nova Scotia
N.W. Terrs.	Northwest Territories (Canada)
N.Y.	New York
N.Z.	New Zealand
Nun.	Nunavut
Okla.	Oklahoma
Ont.	Ontario
Ore.	Oregon
Pa.	Pennsylvania
Pak.	Pakistan
P.E.I.	Prince Edward Island
pen.	peninsula
Phil.	Philippines
plat.	plateau
P.N.G.	Papua New Guinea
Port.	Portugal, Portuguese
P.R.	Puerto Rico
prom.	promontory
prov.	province, provincial
Qué.	Québec
Rep.	Republic
res.	reservoir
R.I.	Rhode Island
Rom.	Romania
S., So.	South, Southern
S. Afr.	South Africa
S. Ar.	Saudi Arabia
Sask.	Saskatchewan
S.C.	South Carolina
Scot.	Scotland
S.D.	South Dakota
Serb.	Serbia and Montenegro
S. Korea	South Korea
Sol. Is.	Solomon Islands
Sp.	Spain, Spanish
St. Ste.	Saint, Sainte
Switz.	Switzerland
Tajik.	Tajikistan
Tanz.	Tanzania
Tenn.	Tennessee
Terr.	Territory
Thai.	Thailand
Trkm.	Turkmenistan
U.K.	United Kingdom
Un.	United
U.S.	United States
Uzb.	Uzbekistan
Va.	Virginia
Ven.	Venezuela
Vt.	Vermont
W.	West, Western
Wash.	Washington
Wis.	Wisconsin
W. Va.	West Virginia
Wyo.	Wyoming
Zim.	Zimbabwe

A

NAME	POPULATION	LATITUDE	LONGITUDE	PAGE
Aberdeen, Scot.	219,120	57° 09′ N	02° 06′ W	42
Abidjan, Côte d'Ivoire	1,929,079	05 20 N	04 01 W	68
Abilene, Texas, U.S.	115,930	32 27 N	99 44 W	83
Abitibi (lake), Ont.,Qué., Can.		48 30 N	79 30 W	84
Abitibi (river), Ont., Can.		49 00 N	81 00 W	84
Abu Dhabi,* United Arab Emirates	398,695	24 28 N	54 22 E	52
Abuja,* Nigeria	305,900	67 20 N	09 05 E	68
Acadia Nat'l Pk., Maine, U.S.		44 30 N	68 30 W	85
Acapulco, Mex.	620,656	16 51 N	99 55 W	88
Accra,* Ghana	953,500	05 33 N	00 12 W	68
Aconcagua (mt.), Arg.,Chile		32 45 S	70 14 W	96
Adair, (cape), Nun., Can.		72 00 N	71 30 W	77
Adana, Turkey	916,150	37 00 N	35 15 E	44
Ad Dahna' (desert), S. Ar.		27 30 N	45 00 E	52
Addis Ababa,* Ethiopia	2,316,400	09 01 N	38 45 E	69
Adelaide, Austl.	995,955	34 55 S	138 37 E	59
Aden, Yemen	562,000	12 45 N	45 05 E	52
Adirondack (mts.), N.Y., U.S.		44 00 N	74 00 W	84
Admiralty (inlet), Nun., Can.		73 00 N	86 00 W	77
Adrar de Iforas (plat.), Alg.,Mali		20 00 N	02 00 E	68
Adriatic (sea), Europe		42 50 N	15 40 E	44
Aegean (sea), Greece,Turkey		40 23 N	25 00 E	44
Afghanistan	**29,547,078**	**34 00 N**	**65 00 E**	**49**
Africa (cont.)	875,027,307			65
Agra, India	1,259,979	27 10 N	78 08 E	53
Aguascalientes, Mex.	594,092	21 53 N	102 18 W	88
Agulhas (cape), S. Afr.		34 51 S	19 59 E	70
Ahaggar (mts.), Alg.		23 00 N	05 00 E	68
Ahmadabad, India	2,876,710	23 00 N	72 44 E	53
Ahvāz, Iran	804,980	31 19 N	48 42 E	52
Aklavik, N.W. Terrs., Can.	632	68 12 N	135 00 W	76
Akron, Ohio, U.S.	217,074	41 05 N	81 31 W	84
Alabama (state), U.S.	4,447,100	33 00 N	87 00 W	87
Åland (isls.), Finland		60 15 N	20 00 E	43
Alaska (gulf), Alaska, U.S.		59 00 N	145 00 W	78
Alaska (pen.), Alaska, U.S.		57 00 N	158 00 W	78
Alaska (range), Alaska, U.S.		63 00 N	151 00 W	78
Alaska (state), U.S.	626,932	65 00 N	154 00 W	78
Albania	**3,544,808**	**41 00 N**	**20 00 E**	**44**
Albany (river), On., Can.		52 16 N	81 30 W	77
Albany, Ga., U.S.	76,939	31 34 N	84 09 W	87
Albany,* N.Y., U.S.	95,658	42 39 N	73 45 W	84
Albert (lake), D.R. Congo,Uganda		01 45 N	31 00 E	69
Alberta (prov.), Can.	2,974,807	54 00 N	115 00 W	76
Albuquerque, N.M., U.S.	448,607	35 05 N	106 39 W	82
Aleppo, Syria	1,542,000	36 12 N	37 10 E	52
Aleutian (isls.), Alaska, U.S.		52 00 N	175 00 W	78
Alexandria, Egypt	3,380,000	31 12 N	29 55 E	69
Alexandria, La., U.S.	46,342	31 18 N	92 26 W	83
Alexandria, Va., U.S.	128,283	38 48 N	77 03 W	84
Algeria	**33,357,089**	**30 00 N**	**04 00 E**	**68**
Algiers,* Alg.	1,687,579	36 45 N	03 04 E	68
Alicante, Spain	274,964	38 21 N	00 29 W	42
Al Jīsah, Egypt	2,144,000	30 01 N	31 13 E	69
Allahabad, India	990,298	25 30 N	81 58 E	69
Allentown, Pa., U.S.	106,632	40 36 N	75 28 W	84
Almaty, Kazak.	1,176,000	43 15 N	76 57 E	54
Alps (mts.), Europe		46 40 N	10 00 E	42
Altai (mts.), China,Mongolia		47 00 N	92 00 E	54
Altun (mts.), China		37 30 N	88 00 E	54
Amarillo, Texas, U.S.	173,627	35 13 N	101 50 W	83
Amazon (river), Brazil,Peru		00 00	49 00 W	95
American Highland (upland), Antarctica		72 30 S	78 00 E	71
American Samoa, U.S.	68,688	14 20 S	170 00 W	63
Ames, Iowa, U.S.	50,731	42 01 N	93 37 W	81
Amherst, N.S., Can.	9,502	45 50 N	64 12 W	85
Amman,* Jordan	969,598	31 57 N	35 56 E	52
Amritsar, India	975,695	31 45 N	74 58 E	53
Amsterdam,* Neth.	713,407	52 20 N	04 50 E	42
Amu Darya (river), Trkm.,Uzb.		43 40 N	59 01 E	46
Amundsen (sea), Antarctica		72 00 S	109 00 W	71
Amur (river), China,Russia		52 56 N	141 10 E	55
Anadyr' (mts.), Russia		67 00 N	176 00 E	47
Anaheim, Calif., U.S.	328,014	33 50 N	117 55 E	82
Anatolia (region), Turkey		39 00 N	30 00 E	44
Anchorage, Alaska, U.S.	260,283	61 10 N	149 55 W	78
Andaman (isls.), India	305,000	12 00 N	92 45 E	53
Anderson, Ind., U.S.	59,734	40 06 N	85 40 W	84
Andes (mts.), S. America		27 00 S	69 00 W	91
Andorra	**69,865**	**42 34 N**	**01 35 E**	**42**
Andorra la Vella,* Andorra	16,151	01 32 N	42 30 E	42
Angara (river), Russia		56 05 N	101 48 E	47
Angola	**10,978,552**	**12 00 S**	**17 00 E**	**70**
Anguilla, U.K.	13,008	18 13 N	63 03 W	89
Ankara,* Turkey	2,559,471	39 55 N	32 52 E	44
Annapolis,* Md., U.S.	35,838	38 58 N	76 29 W	84
Ann Arbor, Mich., U.S.	114,024	42 17 N	83 44 W	84
Anshan, China	1,215,155	41 08 N	122 59 E	55
Antananarivo,* Madagascar	675,669	18 54 S	47 30 E	70
Antarctic (pen.), Antarctica		69 30 S	65 00 W	71
Antarctica (cont.)				71
Anticosti (isl.), Qué., Can.		49 30 N	63 00 W	85
Antigua and Barbuda	**68,320**	**17 05 N**	**61 48 W**	**89**
Antwerp, Belg.	467,518	51 20 N	04 25 E	42
Apennines (mts.), Italy		43 00 N	13 00 E	44
Apia,* Samoa	32,099	13 56 S	171 45 W	63
Appalachian (mts.), U.S.		40 00 N	78 00 W	79
Appleton, Wis., U.S.	70,087	44 15 N	88 25 W	84
Aqaba (gulf). S. Ar.,Egypt		29 30 N	35 05 E	52
Aqtōbe, Kazakhstan	264,000	50 17 N	57 10 E	45
Arafura (sea), Indon.		09 00 S	134 00 E	57
Arakan (mts.), Myanmar		19 00 N	94 00 E	53
Aral (sea) Kazak.,Uzb.		44 46 N	60 00 E	45
Ararat (mt.), Turkey		39 42 N	44 18 E	45
Aras (river), Azer.,Iran		39 56 N	48 20 E	45
Archangel'sk, Russia	409,886	64 34 N	40 32 E	43
Ardennes (region), Belg.		50 10 N	05 30 E	42
Arequipa, Peru	624,500	16 24 S	71 33 W	94
Argentina	**39,144,753**	**35 00 S**	**65 00 W**	**96**
Århus, Den.	209,404	56 11 N	10 15 E	43
Arizona (state), U.S.	5,130,632	34 00 N	112 00 W	82
Arkansas (river), U.S.		33 48 N	91 07 W	83
Arkansas (state), U.S.	2,673,400	34 45 N	92 30 W	83
Arlington, Texas, U.S.	332,969	32 44 N	97 06 W	83
Arlington, Va., U.S.	189,453	38 53 N	77 05 W	84
Armenia	**3,325,307**	**40 15 N**	**45 00 E**	**45**
Aruba (isl.) Neth.	71,218	12 30 N	69 58 W	89
Ascension (isl.), U.K.	1,117	07 57 S	14 22 W	12
Asheville, N.C., U.S.	68,889	35 36 N	82 33 W	87
Ashgabat,* Trkm.	407,000	37 57 N	58 23 E	45
Asia (cont.)	3,861,712,437			49
Asir (region), S. Ar.		18 00 N	42 00 E	52
Asmara,* Eritrea	435,000	15 20 N	38 57 E	69
Assiniboine, (riv.), Man.,Sask., Can.		51 30 N	99 00 W	83
Astana,* Kazakhstan	287,000	51 10 N	71 30 E	62
Astrakhan', Russia	507,710	46 21 N	48 03 E	69
Asunción,* Paraguay	546,637	25 16 S	57 40 W	96
Atacama (desert), Chile		24 00 S	70 00 W	96
Atatürk (res.), Turkey		37 30 N	38 30 E	44
Athabasca (lake), Alta.,Sask., Can.		59 20 N	109 00 W	76
Athabasca (river), Alta., Can.		58 30 N	111 00 W	76
Athens, Ga., U.S.	101,489	33 57 N	83 23 W	87
Athens,* Greece	772,072	37 59 N	23 44 E	44
Atlanta,* Ga., U.S.	416,474	33 45 N	84 24 W	87
Atlantic City, N.J., U.S.	40,517	39 21 N	74 27 W	84
Atlas (mts.), Alg.,Mor.		34 00 N	00 01 W	68
Attu (isl.), Alaska, U.S.		52 55 N	172 55 E	78
Auckland, N.Z.	367,737	36 53 S	174 45 E	61
Augsburg, Germany	254,867	48 20 N	10 53 E	42
Augusta, Ga., U.S.	199,775	33 28 N	81 58 W	87
Augusta,* Maine, U.S.	18,560	44 18 N	69 46 W	85
Aurora, Co., U.S.	276,393	39 44 N	104 50 W	83
Aurora, Ill., U.S.	142,990	41 45 N	88 19 W	84
Austin,* Texas, U.S.	656,562	30 16 N	97 44 W	86
Australia (cont.)	**19,913,144**	**25 00 S**	**135 00 E**	**59**
Australian Capital Terr., Austl.	311,947	35 18 S	149 07 E	59
Austria	**8,174,762**	**47 15 N**	**14 00 E**	**42**
Auyuittuq Nat'l Pk., Nun., Can.		67 00 N	66 00 W	77
Avalon (pen.), Newf., Can.		46 30 N	53 30 W	85
Axel Heiberg (isl.), Nun., Can		79 00 N	90 00 W	76
Ayeyarwady (river), Myanmar		23 19 N	96 00 E	53
Azerbaijan	**7,868,385**	**40 30 N**	**48 00 E**	**45**
Azores (isls.), Port.	237,315	38 30 N	28 00 W	12
Azov (sea), Russia, Ukraine		46 00 N	37 00 E	44

B

NAME	POPULATION	LATITUDE	LONGITUDE	PAGE
Back (river), Nun., Can.		66° 00′ N	96° 00′ W	76
Badlands Nat'l Pk., S.D., U.S.		43 00 N	102 00 W	81
Baffin (bay), Nun., Can.		74 00 N	68 00 W	77
Baffin (isl.), Nun., Can.		68 30 N	70 00 W	77
Baghdad,* Iraq	3,841,268	33 21 N	44 24 E	52
Bahamas, The	**299,697**	**24 00 N**	**76 00 W**	**89**
Bahrain	**677,886**	**26 00 N**	**50 40 E**	**52**
Baie-Comeau, Qué., Can.	23,079	49 12 N	68 12 W	85
Baja California (pen.), Mex.		28 00 N	114 00 W	89
Bakersfield, Calif., U.S.	247,057	35 22 N	119 01 W	82
Bākhtarān, Iran	665,636	34 19 N	47 04 E	52
Baku,* Azer.	1,725,500	40 23 N	49 51 E	45
Balaton (lake), Hungary		46 50 N	17 50 E	44
Balearic (isls.), Spain	841,669	39 30 N	03 00 E	42
Bali (isl.), Indon.	3,151,162	08 30 S	115 30 E	56
Balkan (mts.), Europe		43 15 N	23 00 E	44
Balkhash (lake), Kazak.		46 00 N	74 00 E	54
Baltic (sea), Europe		56 30 N	19 00 E	43
Baltimore, Md., U.S.	651,154	39 17 N	76 36 W	84
Bamako,* Mali	658,275	12 38 N	07 59 W	68
Banaba (isl.), Kiribati		00 52 S	169 35 E	62
Banda (sea), Indon.		06 00 S	128 00 E	57
Bandar Seri Begawan,* Brunei	45,867	04 55 N	114 55 E	56
Bandung, Indon.	2,026,366	06 56 S	107 36 E	56
Banff, Alta., Can.	7,135	51 10 N	115 34 W	80
Banff Nat'l Pk., Alta., Can.		51 30 N	115 45 W	80
Bangalore, India	4,292,223	12 59 N	77 28 E	53
Bangka (isl.), Indon.		02 22 S	106 08 E	56
Bangkok,* Thai.	5,876,000	13 45 N	100 30 E	56
Bangladesh	**141,340,476**	**23 30 N**	**90 00 E**	**53**
Bangor, Maine, U.S.	31,473	44 48 N	68 46 W	85
Bangui,* CAfr.	597,000	04 22 N	18 36 E	69
Bangweulu (lake), Zambia		11 00 S	29 45 E	70
Banjul,* Gambia	42,326	13 28 N	16 35 W	68
Banks (isl.) N.W. Terrs., Can.		73 00 N	122 00 W	76
Baotou, China	980,436	40 40 N	109 59 E	55
Barbados	**278,289**	**13 10 N**	**59 30 W**	**89**
Barcelona, Spain	1,630,867	41 38 N	02 10 E	42
Bareilly, India	699,839	28 21 N	79 25 E	53
Barents (sea), Russia		70 00 N	45 00 E	46
Bari, Italy	332,143	41 07 N	16 52 E	44
Barisan (mts.), Indon.		03 00 S	102 15 E	56
Barkly Tableland (plat.), Austl.		18 00 S	136 00 E	59
Baroda, India	1,306,035	22 18 N	73 12 E	53
Barquisimeto, Ven.	625,450	10 04 N	69 19 W	94
Barranquilla, Col.	1,000,283	10 59 N	74 50 W	94
Barrie, Ont., Can.	103,710	44 24 N	79 40 W	84
Barrow (strait), Nun., Can.		74 00 N	94 00 W	76
Basel, Switz.	174,007	47 35 N	07 32 E	42

Index of the World

NAME	POPULATION	LATITUDE	LONGITUDE	PAGE
Bass (strait), Austl.		40 15 S	146 00 E	59
Basseterre,* St. Kitts & Nevis	12,605	17 18 N	62 43 W	89
Bathurst, N.B., Can.	12,924	47 36 N	65 39 W	85
Bathurst (inlet), Nun., Can.		67 30 N	99 00 W	76
Baton Rouge,* La., U.S.	227,818	30 27 N	91 09 W	87
Battle Creek, Mich., U.S.	53,364	42 19 N	85 10 W	84
Baykal (lake), Russia		54 00 N	109 00 E	47
Beaufort (sea), Can., U.S.		71 00 N	140 00 W	76
Beaumont, Texas, U.S.	113,866	30 05 N	94 05 W	86
Beersheba, Israel	152,645	31 14 N	34 47 E	52
Beijing (Peking),* China	5,715,368	39 56 N	116 24 E	55
Beira, Moz.	397,368	19 50 S	34 50 E	70
Beirut,* Lebanon	1,000,000	33 55 N	35 30 E	52
Belarus	**10,310,520**	**53 00 N**	**28 00 E**	**43**
Belcher (isls.), Nun., Can.		56 00 N	79 30 W	77
Belém, Brazil	765,476	01 28 S	48 27 W	95
Belfast,* No. Ire.	279,237	54 35 N	05 55 W	42
Belgium	**10,348,276**	**50 45 N**	**04 30 E**	**42**
Belgrade,* Serb.	1,280,639	44 48 N	20 29 E	44
Belitung (isl.), Indon.		02 54 S	107 58 E	56
Belize	**272,945**	**17 00 N**	**88 45 W**	**88**
Belize City, Belize	49,050	17 30 N	88 12 W	88
Bell (pen.), Nun., Can.		64 00 N	80 30 W	77
Belle Isle (strait), Newf., Can.		51 30 N	56 30 W	77
Bellingham, Wash., U.S.	67,171	48 45 N	122 29 W	80
Bellingshausen (sea), Antarctica		69 00 S	81 00 E	71
Belmopan,* Belize	8,130	17 15 N	88 47 W	88
Belo Horizonte, Brazil	2,206,116	19 56 S	43 57 W	95
Bend, Ore., U.S.	52,029	44 03 N	121 19 W	80
Bengal (bay), Asia		18 00 N	90 00 E	53
Benghazi, Libya	446,000	32 07 N	20 03 E	69
Benin	**7,250,033**	**09 00 N**	**02 00 E**	**68**
Benin, Bight of (bay), Africa		05 00 N	04 00 E	68
Ben Nevis (mt.), Scot., U.K.		56 48 N	04 59 W	42
Bergen, Norway	209,375	60 25 N	05 20 E	43
Bering (sea), Russia,U.S.		55 00 N	180 00	47
Bering (strait), Russia,U.S.		67 00 N	170 00 W	78
Berkeley, Calif., U.S.	102,743	37 52 N	122 16 W	82
Berlin,* Germany	3,386,667	52 30 N	13 20 E	42
Bermuda, U.K.	64,935	32 20 N	64 40 W	73
Bern,* Switz.	127,469	47 00 N	07 30 E	42
Bethlehem, Pa., U.S.	71,329	40 37 N	75 22 W	84
Bhopāl, India	1,433,875	23 16 N	77 24 E	53
Bhutan	**2,185,569**	**27 15 N**	**90 00 E**	**53**
Bialystok, Poland	267,670	53 09 N	23 09 E	44
Bienville (lake), Qué., Can.		55 00 N	73 00 W	77
Bikini (isl.), Marshall Islands		11 37 N	165 33 E	62
Bilbao, Spain	371,876	43 16 N	03 05 W	42
Billings, Mont., U.S.	89,847	45 47 N	108 30 W	80
Biloxi, Miss., U.S.	50,644	30 23 N	88 52 W	87
Binghamton, N.Y., U.S.	47,380	42 06 N	75 55 W	84
Birmingham, Ala., U.S.	242,820	33 31 N	86 48 W	87
Birmingham, Eng., U.K.	965,928	52 30 N	01 55 W	42
Biscay (bay), Fr.		45 00 N	05 00 W	42
Bishkek,* Kyrgyzstan	627,800	42 54 N	74 36 E	54
Bismarck (arch.), P.N.G.		04 00 S	150 00 E	62
Bismarck,* N.D., U.S.	55,532	46 48 N	100 47 W	81
Bissau,* Guinea-Bissau	109,214	11 51 N	15 35 W	68
Bitterroot (mts.), Idaho,Mont., U.S.		46 30 N	114 25 W	80
Black (sea), Asia,Europe		42 30 N	35 00 E	44
Black Hills (mts.), S.D. U.S.		44 00 N	103 30 W	81
Blanc (mt.), Fr.,Italy		45 50 N	06 51 E	42
Blantyre, Malawi	478,155	15 49 S	35 00 E	70
Bloemfontein,* S. Afr.	111,698	29 07 S	26 14 E	70
Bloomington, Ill., U.S.	64,808	40 29 N	88 59 W	84
Bloomington, Ind., U.S.	69,291	39 10 N	86 31 W	84
Blue Nile (river), Egypt,Ethiopia		15 37 N	32 31 E	69
Boca Raton, Fla., U.S.	74,764	26 21 N	80 05 W	87
Bogotá,* Col.	5,698,566	04 36 N	74 05 W	94
Boise,* Idaho, U.S.	185,787	43 36 N	116 12 W	80
Bolivia	**8,724,156**	**16 00 S**	**64 00 W**	**94**
Bologna, Italy	379,964	44 30 N	11 20 E	42
Bonaire (isl.), Neth. Ant.	14,218	12 12 N	68 15 W	89
Bonifacio (strait), Fr.,Italy		41 18 N	09 15 E	42
Bonn, Germany	301,048	50 44 N	07 06 E	42
Boothia (gulf), Nun., Can.		70 00 N	91 00 W	76
Boothia (pen.), Nun., Can.		70 00 N	95 00 W	76
Bordeaux, Fr.	218,948	44 50 N	00 35 W	42
Borden (pen.), Nun., Can.		74 00 N	83 00 W	77
Borneo (isl.), Asia	16,254,358	00 00	113 00 E	56
Bornholm (isl.), Den.		55 10 N	15 00 E	43
Bosnia and Herzegovina	**4,007,608**	**44 00 N**	**18 00 E**	**44**
Bosporus (strait), Turkey		41 15 N	29 10 E	44
Boston,* Mass., U.S.	589,141	42 21 N	71 03 W	85
Bothnia (gulf), Finland,Sweden		62 00 N	20 00 E	43
Botou, China	65,535	38 05 N	116 30 E	55
Botswana	**1,561,973**	**22 00 S**	**24 00 E**	**70**
Bougainville (isl.), P.N.G.		06 10 S	155 15 E	62
Boulder, Colo., U.S.	94,673	40 01 N	105 16 W	83
Bouvet (isl.), Norway		54 26 S	03 24 E	12
Bozeman, Mont., U.S.	27,509	45 41 N	111 02 W	80
Bradford, Eng., U.K.	289,376	53 47 N	01 45 W	42
Brahmaputra (river), Bangladesh,India		29 30 N	95 00 E	53
Brăila, Rom.	235,243	45 15 N	27 58 E	44
Brampton, Ont., Can.	325,428	43 41 N	79 45 W	84
Brandon, Man., Can.	39,716	49 50 N	99 57 W	81
Brasília,* Brazil	1,492,542	15 47 S	47 55 W	95
Braşov, Romania	319,908	45 39 N	25 37 E	44
Bratislava,* Slovakia	442,197	48 09 N	17 07 E	44
Braunschweig, Germany	246,322	52 22 N	10 42 E	42
Brazil	**184,101,109**	**14 00 S**	**50 00 W**	**91**
Brazos (river), Texas, U.S.		28 57 N	95 18 W	86
Brazzaville,* Congo	937,500	04 17 S	15 14 E	70
Bremen, Germany	540,330	53 10 N	08 40 E	42
Brescia, Italy	194,697	45 30 N	10 15 E	42
Breton (cape), N.S., Can.		45 56 N	59 48 W	85
Bridgeport, Conn., U.S.	139,529	41 11 N	73 11 W	85
Bridgetown,* Barbados	6,700	13 06 N	59 37 W	89
Brisbane, Austl.	1,490,475	27 25 S	153 05 E	59
Bristol (bay), Alaska, U.S.		57 45 N	160 00 W	78
Bristol, Eng., U.K.	407,992	51 28 N	02 35 W	42
Britanny (region), Fr.		48 00 N	03 00 W	42
British Columbia (prov.), Can.	3,907,735	55 00 N	125 00 W	76
British Indian Ocean Terr., U.K.	3,200	06 00 S	72 00 E	13
Brno, Czech Rep.	379,185	49 10 N	16 30 E	42
Brockton, Mass., U.S.	94,304	42 05 N	71 01 W	85
Brockville, Ont., Can.	23,014	44 36 N	75 41 W	84
Brodeaur (pen.), Nun., Can.		73 00 N	89 30 W	76
Brooks (mts.), Alaska, U.S.		68 30 N	153 00 W	78
Brownsville, Texas, U.S.	139,722	25 54 N	97 30 W	86
Brunei	**365,251**	**04 30 N**	**115 00 E**	**56**
Brussels,* Belg.	954,045	50 50 N	04 22 E	42
Bryan, Texas, U.S.	65,660	30 40 N	96 22 W	86
Bucharest,* Rom.	2,037,278	44 25 N	26 06 E	44
Budapest,* Hungary	2,016,774	47 30 N	19 10 E	44
Buenos Aires,* Arg.	2,776,138	34 36 S	58 26 W	96
Buffalo, N.Y., U.S.	292,648	42 53 N	78 52 W	84
Bujumbura,* Burundi	235,440	03 23 S	29 22 E	70
Bulawayo, Zimbabwe	621,742	20 09 S	28 36 E	70
Bulgaria	**7,517,973**	**42 30 N**	**25 30 E**	**44**
Burbank, Calif., U.S.	100,316	34 11 N	118 18 W	82
Burgundy (region), Fr.		47 00 N	05 00 E	42
Burkina Faso	**13,574,820**	**12 00 N**	**01 30 W**	**68**
Burlington, Ont., Can.	150,836	43 19 N	79 47 W	84
Burlington, Vt., U.S.	38,889	44 28 N	73 12 W	85
Burma (Myanmar)	**42,720,196**	**20 00 N**	**96 00 E**	**49**
Bursa, Turkey	834,576	40 11 N	29 04 E	44
Burundi	**6,231,221**	**03 30 S**	**30 00 E**	**70**
Bydgoszcz, Poland	380,426	53 50 N	27 35 E	42
C				
Caatingas (region), Brazil		07° 00′ N	43° 00′ W	95
Cabonga (res.), Qué., Can.		47 30 N	76 30 W	84
Cádiz, Spain	155,438	36 32 N	06 18 W	42
Cagliari, Italy	162,993	39 13 N	09 07 E	42
Cairo,* Egypt	6,663,000	30 03 N	31 15 E	69
Calgary, Alta., Can.	878,866	51 03 N	114 05 W	80
Cali, Col.	1,624,937	03 28 N	76 30 W	94
California (gulf), Mex.		28 00 N	112 00 W	89
California (state), U.S.	33,871,648	37 00 N	120 00 W	82
Callao, Peru	515,200	12 03 S	77 10 W	94
Camagüey, Cuba	249,332	21 53 N	77 55 W	89
Cambodia	**13,363,421**	**12 00 N**	**105 00 E**	**56**
Cambridge, Ont., Can.	110,372	43 23 N	80 19 W	84
Cambridge, Mass., U.S.	101,355	43 22 N	71 06 W	85
Camden, N.J., U.S.	79,904	39 56 N	75 06 W	84
Cameroon	**16,063,678**	**05 00 N**	**13 00 E**	**68**
Campbell River, Br. Col., Can.	31,294	50 02 N	125 15 W	80
Campbellton, N.B., Can.	7,798	48 00 N	66 40 W	85
Campeche (bay), Mex.		20 00 N	93 00 W	88
Campinas, Brazil	748,076	22 54 S	47 05 W	95
Canada	**32,507,874**	**60 00 N**	**100 00 W**	**76**
Canadian (river), U.S.		35 28 N	95 04 W	83
Canary (isls.), Spain	1,694,477	28 00 N	16 00 W	68
Canaveral (cape), Fla., U.S.		28 27 N	80 31 W	87
Canberra,* Austl.	307,053	35 18 S	149 07 E	61
Caniapiscau (lake), Qué., Can.		54 00 N	70 00 W	77
Caniapiscau (river), Qué., Can.		55 00 N	69 30 W	77
Cannes, Fr.	68,214	43 33 N	07 01 E	42
Cantabrica (mts.), Spain		43 15 N	05 00 W	42
Canton (Guangzhou), China	2,891,643	23 07 N	113 15 E	55
Canton, Ohio, U.S.	80,806	40 48 N	81 22 W	84
Cape Breton (isl.), N.S., Can.		46 00 N	61 00 W	85
Cape Breton Highlands Nat'l Pk., N.S., Can.		47 00 N	61 00 W	85
Cape Town,* S. Afr.	987,007	33 57 S	18 28 E	70
Cape Verde	**415,294**	**16 00 N**	**24 00 W**	**12**
Cape York (pen.), Austl.		13 00 S	142 30 E	59
Caprivi Strip (region), Namibia		18 00 S	23 00 E	70
Caracas,* Ven.	1,822,465	10 30 N	66 55 W	94
Cardiff,* Wales	272,129	51 30 N	03 12 W	42
Caribbean (sea)		15 00 N	75 00 W	89
Caribou (mts.), Alta., Can.		59 00 N	115 00 W	76
Caroline (isls.), Micronesia		08 00 N	150 00 E	62
Carpathian (mts.), Europe		48 00 N	23 00 E	44
Carpentaria (gulf), Austl.		15 00 S	139 00 E	59
Carson City,* Nev., U.S.	52,457	39 10 N	119 46 W	82
Cartegena, Spain	576,307	37 36 N	00 59 W	42
Casablanca, Mor.	2,540,909	33 36 N	07 38 W	68
Cascades (mts.), U.S.		48 00 N	122 00 W	80
Casper, Wyo., U.S.	49,644	42 51 N	106 19 W	81
Caspian (sea)		42 00 N	50 00 E	44
Castries,* St. Lucia	12,620	14 00 N	60 59 W	89
Catalonia (region), Spain		41 15 N	02 00 E	42
Caucasus (mts.), Europe		42 30 N	45 00 E	45
Cayenne,* Fr. Guiana	50,675	04 56 N	52 20 W	95
Cayman (isls.), U.K.	43,103	19 30 N	80 40 W	88
Cebu, Phil.	662,299	10 18 N	123 54 E	57
Cebu (isl.), Phil.		10 18 N	123 54 E	57
Cedar Rapids, Iowa, U.S.	120,758	41 59 N	91 40 W	83
Celebes (isl.), Indon.	14,111,444	02 00 S	121 00 E	57
Central African Republic	**3,742,482**	**06 00 N**	**20 00 E**	**69**
Ceuta, Spain	71,926	35 52 N	05 20 W	68
Ceylon (isl.), Sri Lanka		07 00 N	81 00 E	53
Chad	**9,538,544**	**15 00 N**	**18 00 E**	**69**
Chad (lake), Africa		13 15 N	14 30 E	68
Chaleur (bay), N.B.,Qué., Can.		48 00 N	65 00 W	85
Champaign, Ill., U.S.	67,518	40 07 N	88 14 W	84
Champlain (lake), Can.,U.S.		44 30 N	73 20 W	84
Changchun, China	1,697,620	43 53 N	125 18 E	55
Chang (Yangtze) (river), China		31 48 N	121 10 E	55
Changsha, China	1,077,180	28 12 N	112 59 E	55
Channel (isls.), U.K.	150,000	49 30 N	02 30 W	42
Chaozhou, China	289,116	23 40 N	116 38 E	55
Chapel Hill, N.C., U.S.	48,715	35 54 N	79 03 W	87
Charleston, S.C., U.S.	96,650	32 47 N	79 56 W	87
Charleston,* W. Va., U.S.	53,421	38 21 N	81 38 W	87
Charlotte, N.C., U.S.	540,828	35 13 N	80 50 W	87
Charlottesville, Va., U.S.	45,049	38 02 N	78 29 W	87
Charlottetown,* P.E.I., Can.	32,245	46 14 N	63 08 W	85
Chattanooga, Tenn., U.S.	155,554	35 02 N	85 18 W	87
Chelyabinsk, Russia	1,129,661	55 10 N	61 24 E	45
Chelyuskin (cape), Russia		77 45 N	104 30 E	47
Chemnitz, Germany	263,222	50 40 N	12 55 E	42
Chengdu, China	1,719,452	30 40 N	104 04 E	54
Chesapeake (bay), Md.,Va., U.S.		38 35 N	76 25 W	84
Chennai (Madras), India	4,216,268	13 05 N	80 15 E	53
Cheshskaya (bay), Russia		67 30 N	47 00 E	43
Chesterfield (inlet), Nun., Can.		63 40 N	91 45 W	76
Cheyenne,* Wyo., U.S.	53,011	41 08 N	104 49 W	81
Chiba, Japan	887,164	35 36 N	140 07 E	55
Chicago, Ill., U.S.	2,896,016	41 52 N	87 37 W	84
Chico, Calif., U.S.	59,954	39 43 N	121 50 W	82
Chicoutimi, Qué., Can.	60,008	48 25 N	71 06 W	85
Chidley (cape), Newf., Can.		60 23 N	64 26 W	77
Chihuahua, Mex.	657,876	28 38 N	106 05 W	89
Chile	**15,827,180**	**32 00 S**	**71 00 W**	**91**
Chilliwack, Br. Col., Can.	62,927	49 10 N	121 55 W	80
Chiloé (isl.), Chile		42 00 S	74 00 W	96
Chimborazo (mt.), Ecuador		01 28 S	78 48 W	94
China	**1,294,629,555**	**35 00 N**	**105 00 E**	**54**
Chişinău,* Moldova	665,000	47 00 N	28 50 E	44
Chittagong, Bangladesh	1,560,000	22 15 N	91 55 E	53
Chongqing, China	2,265,137	29 34 N	106 35 E	54
Chonos (arch.), Chile		45 00 S	74 00 W	96
Christchurch, N.Z.	316,224	43 32 S	172 39 E	59
Christmas (isl.), Kiribati		10 30 S	105 40 E	13
Chuckchi (pen.), Russia		66 00 N	175 00 W	47
Churchill (river), Man., Can.		58 47 N	94 11 W	76
Churchill, Man., Can.	963	58 46 N	94 10 W	76
Cimarron (river), U.S.		36 07 N	96 30 W	81
Cincinnati, Ohio, U.S.	331,285	39 06 N	84 31 W	84
Ciudad Guayana, Ven.	453,047	08 22 N	62 40 W	94
Ciudad Juárez, Mex.	1,187,275	31 44 N	106 29 W	89
Clarksville, Tenn., U.S.	103,455	36 31 N	87 21 W	84
Clearwater, Fla., U.S.	108,787	27 58 N	82 48 W	87
Cleveland, Ohio, U.S.	478,403	41 30 N	81 41 W	84
Clipperton (isl.), Fr.		10 13 N	109 10 W	12
Cluj-Napoca, Romania	332,297	46 45 N	23 36 E	44
Coast Ranges (mts.), Br. Col.,Yukon Terr., Can.		42 00 N	123 15 W	76
Cocos (isls.), Austl.	630	12 30 S	96 50 E	48
Cod (cape), Mass., U.S.		41 42 N	70 04 W	85
Cologne, Germany	962,507	51 00 N	07 00 E	42
Colombia	**42,310,775**	**05 00 N**	**74 00 W**	**94**
Colombo,* Sri Lanka	642,163	06 55 N	79 50 E	53
Colorado (river), Arg.		39 51 S	62 08 W	96
Colorado (river), Mexico,U.S.		31 49 N	114 45 W	82
Colorado (river), Texas, U.S.		28 52 N	96 02 W	83
Colorado (state), U.S.	4,301,261	39 00 N	105 30 W	82
Colorado Springs, Colo., U.S.	360,890	38 50 N	104 48 W	83
Columbia, Mo., U.S.	84,531	38 57 N	92 20 W	86
Columbia (plat.), U.S.		46 00 N	118 00 W	80
Columbia (river), Ore.,Wash., U.S.		46 15 N	123 40 W	80
Columbia,* S.C., U.S.	116,278	34 00 N	81 02 W	87
Columbus, Ga., U.S.	186,291	32 27 N	84 59 W	87
Columbus,* Ohio, U.S.	711,470	39 57 N	83 00 W	84
Comorin (cape), India		07 37 N	77 28 E	53
Comoros	**651,901**	**12 00 S**	**44 00 E**	**65**
Conakry,* Guinea	1,091,483	09 31 N	13 42 W	68
Concepción, Chile	326,784	36 50 S	73 01 W	96
Concord, Calif., U.S.	121,780	37 58 N	122 01 W	82
Concord,* N.H., U.S.	40,687	43 12 N	71 32 W	85
Concord,* N.C., U.S.	55,977	35 24 N	80 34 W	87
Congo (basin), D.R. Congo		00 00	22 00 E	69
Congo (river), Congo,D.R. Congo		06 05 S	12 20 E	70
Congo, Dem. Rep. of the	**58,317,930**	**02 00 S**	**24 00 E**	**65**
Congo, Rep. of the	**2,998,040**	**00 00**	**15 00 E**	**65**
Connecticut (state), U.S.	3,405,565	41 38 N	72 45 W	85
Constantine, Alg.	449,602	36 23 N	06 38 E	68
Cook (isls.), N.Z.	21,008	20 00 S	158 00 W	63
Cook (mt.), N.Z.		43 36 S	170 08 E	59
Cook (strait), N.Z.		41 15 S	174 30 E	59
Coppermine (river), N.W. Terrs., Nun., Can.		66 30 N	115 00 W	76
Copenhagen,* Denmark	495,699	55 40 N	12 35 E	43
Coral (sea)		14 00 S	156 00 E	59
Córdoba, Arg.	1,284,582	31 25 S	64 10 W	96
Córdoba, Spain	315,948	37 54 N	04 46 W	42
Corfu (isl.), Greece		39 38 N	19 56 E	44
Corinth (gulf), Greece		38 19 N	22 04 E	44
Cork, Ireland	123,338	51 55 N	08 30 W	42
Corner Brook, Newf., Can.	20,103	48 57 N	57 57 W	85
Cornwall, Ont., Can.	48,287	45 02 N	74 44 W	84
Coromandel Coast, India		13 00 N	80 15 E	53
Corpus Christi, Texas, U.S.	277,454	27 47 N	97 25 W	86
Corsica (isl.), Fr.	260,196	42 00 N	09 00 E	42
Corvallis, Ore., U.S.	49,322	44 34 N	123 16 W	80
Costa Rica	**3,956,507**	**10 00 N**	**84 00 W**	**88**
Côte d'Ivoire	**17,327,724**	**07 00 N**	**05 00 W**	**68**
Cotonou, Benin	536,827	06 21 N	02 26 E	68
Council Bluffs, Iowa, U.S.	58,268	41 15 N	95 51 W	81
Coventry, Eng., U.K.	299,316	52 25 N	01 33 W	42
Cranbrook, Br. Col., Can.	18,476	49 30 N	115 46 W	80
Crater Lake Nat'l Pk., Ore., U.S.		42 30 N	122 30 W	80
Crete (isl.), Greece	578,251	35 15 N	25 00 E	44
Crimea (pen.), Ukraine		45 00 N	34 00 E	44
Croatia	**4,435,960**	**45 30 N**	**16 00 E**	**44**
Cuba	**11,308,764**	**22 00 N**	**80 00 W**	**89**
Cumberland (pen.), Nun., Can.		66 00 N	65 00 W	77
Cumberland (sound), Nun., Can.		64 00 N	67 00 W	77
Curaçao (isl.), Neth. Ant.	151,448	12 11 N	69 00 W	89
Curitiba, Brazil	841,882	25 25 S	49 15 W	96
Cyclades (isls.), Greece		37 00 N	25 00 E	44
Cyprus	**775,927**	**35 00 N**	**33 00 E**	**52**
Czech Republic	**10,246,178**	**49 00 N**	**17 00 E**	**44**
Czectochowa, Poland	256,578	50 49 N	19 06 E	44

NAME	POPULATION	LATITUDE	LONGITUDE	PAGE
D				
Da Hinggan (mts.), China		48° 30′ N	120° 00′ E	55
Dakar,* Senegal	1,641,358	14 40 N	17 28 W	68
Dalian, China	1,632,152	38 55 N	121 39 E	55
Dallas, Texas, U.S.	1,188,580	32 47 N	96 47 W	86
Damascus,* Syria	1,549,000	33 35 N	36 28 E	52
Damavand (mt.), Iran		35 57 N	52 08 E	52
Da Nang, Vietnam	369,734	16 04 N	108 13 E	56
Danube (river), Europe		45 20 N	29 40 E	44
Dardanelles (strait), Turkey		40 07 N	26 23 E	44
Dar es Salaam,* Tanzania	1,360,850	06 48 S	39 17 E	70
Darling (river), Austl.		32 00 S	142 57 E	59
Dartmouth, N.S., Can.	65,629	44 40 N	63 34 W	85
Darwin, Austl.	68,694	12 27 S	130 50 E	59
Davao, Phil.	1,006,840	07 18 N	125 25 E	57
Davenport, Iowa, U.S.	98,359	41 31 N	90 35 W	81
Davis (strait), Can.,Greenland		66 30 N	58 00 W	77
Davis, Calif., U.S.	60,308	38 32 N	121 44 W	82
Dawson, Yukon Terr., Can.	1,251	64 04 N	139 27 W	76
Dayton, Ohio, U.S.	166,179	39 45 N	84 11 W	84
Daytona Beach, Fla., U.S.	64,112	29 12 N	81 01 W	87
Dead (sea), Asia		31 30 N	35 30 E	52
Dease (strait), Nun., Can.		68 00 N	108 00 E	76
Death Valley Nat'l Park, Calif., U.S.		37 00 N	117 07 W	82
Debrecen, Hungary	212,335	47 32 N	21 38 E	44
Decatur, Ala., U.S.	53,929	34 36 N	86 59 W	87
Decatur, Ill., U.S.	81,860	39 50 N	88 57 W	81
Deccan (plat.), India		17 00 N	78 00 E	53
Delaware (state), U.S.	783,600	39 00 N	75 30 W	84
Delgado (cape), Moz.		10 41 S	40 38 E	70
Delhi, India	9,817,439	28 29 N	77 15 E	53
Denmark	**5,413,392**	**56 00 N**	**10 30 E**	**43**
Denver,* Colo., U.S.	554,636	39 44 N	104 59 W	83
Des Moines,* Iowa, U.S.	198,682	41 35 N	93 37 W	81
Detroit, Mich., U.S.	951,270	42 20 N	83 02 W	84
Devon (isl.), Nun., Can.		75 00 N	86 00 W	77
Dezhneva (cape), Russia		66 05 N	169 40 W	47
Dhaka,* Bangladesh	3,637,892	23 45 N	90 25 E	53
Diefenbaker (lake), Sask., Can.		50 30 N	107 00 W	80
Diego Garcia (isl.), U.K.		07 36 S	72 28 E	13
Dili,* East Timor	13,000	08 35 S	125 35 E	57
Dinaric Alps (mts.), Bosnia and Herzegovina,Croatia		43 30 N	17 00 E	44
District of Columbia, U.S.	572,059	38 54 N	77 01 W	84
Diyarbakir, Turkey	381,144	37 55 N	40 14 E	44
Dixon (strait), Can.,U.S.		54 00 N	132 00 W	76
Djibouti	**466,900**	**12 00 N**	**43 00 E**	**69**
Djibouti,* Djibouti	200,000	11 35 N	43 09 E	69
Dnipropetrovs'k, Ukraine	1,189,900	48 27 N	35 01 E	44
Dnipro (river), Ukraine		46 30 N	32 36 E	44
Dnister (river), Moldova,Ukraine		46 20 N	30 18 E	44
Doğukaradeniz (mts.) Turkey		40 30 N	39 00 E	44
Doha,* Qatar	217,294	25 17 N	51 32 E	52
Dolphin and Union (strait), Nun., Can.		69 00 N	116 00 W	76
Dominica	**69,278**	**15 25 N**	**61 20 W**	**89**
Dominican Republic	**8,833,634**	**19 00 N**	**70 00 W**	**89**
Don (river), Russia		47 04 N	39 18 E	44
Donets (river), Ukraine		47 36 N	40 54 E	44
Donets'k, Ukraine	1,121,400	48 00 N	37 48 E	44
Dortmund, Germany	590,213	51 30 N	07 30 E	42
Dothan, Ala., U.S.	57,737	31 13 N	85 23 W	87
Douala, Cameroon	1,029,731	04 03 N	09 37 E	68
Douro (river), Port.,Spain		41 09 N	08 39 W	42
Dover (strait), Europe		51 00 N	01 30 E	42
Dover,* Del., U.S.	32,135	39 10 N	75 31 W	84
Drake (passage), Antarctica,S. America		60 00 S	67 00 W	96
Dresden, Germany	476,668	51 10 N	13 45 E	42
Drummondville, Qué., Can.	46,599	46 53 N	72 29 W	85
Dubayy, United Arab Emirates	669,181	25 15 N	55 17 E	44
Dublin,* Ire.	495,101	53 20 N	06 10 W	42
Dubrovnik, Croatia	30,436	42 38 N	18 07 E	44
Dubuque, Iowa, U.S.	57,686	42 30 N	90 40 W	81
Duluth, Minn., U.S.	86,918	46 47 N	92 06 W	81
Dundee, Scot.	151,010	56 30 N	02 58 W	42
Durango, Mex.	427,135	24 02 N	104 40 W	89
Durango, Colo., U.S.	13,922	37 16 N	107 51 W	82
Durban, S. Afr.	669,242	29 51 S	31 00 E	70
Durham, N.C., U.S.	187,035	35 59 N	78 54 W	87
Dushanbe,* Tajik.	602,000	38 33 N	68 48 E	46
Düsseldorf, Germany	568,855	51 20 N	06 40 E	42
Dvina, Northern (river), Russia		64 32 N	40 37 E	46
E				
East China (sea), China, Japan		30° 00′ N	125° 00′ E	55
Easter (isl.), Chile	2,764	27 08 S	109 25 W	63
Eastern Ghats (mts.), India		17 30 N	83 00 E	53
East London, S. Afr.	135,560	33 01 S	27 55 E	70
Eastmain (river), Qué., Can.		53 00 N	75 00 W	77
East Timor	**1,019,252**	**08 40 S**	**126 00 E**	**57**
Eau Claire (lake), Qué., Can.		56 00 N	75 00 W	77
Eau Claire, Wis., U.S.	61,704	44 48 N	91 30 W	81
Ebro (river), Spain		40 43 N	00 54 E	42
Ecatepec, Mex.	1,621,827	19 35 N	99 04 W	88
Eclipse (sound), Nun., Can.		72 00 N	80 00 W	77
Ecuador	**13,971,798**	**01 00 S**	**79 00 W**	**94**
Edinburgh,* Scot.	447,550	55 55 N	03 10 W	42
Edmonton,* Alta., Can.	666,104	53 33 N	113 28 W	80
Edmundston, N.B., Can.	17,373	47 22 N	68 20 W	85
Edward (lake), D.R. Congo,Uganda		00 20 S	29 35 E	69
Edwards (plat.), Texas, U.S.		30 30 N	101 00 W	83
Efate (isl.), Vanuatu		17 40 S	168 23 E	62
Egypt	**76,117,421**	**27 00 N**	**30 00 E**	**69**
Elbe (river), Ger.		53 30 N	09 45 E	42
Elbert (mt.), Colo., U.S.		39 06 N	106 27 W	82
El'brus (mt.), Georgia,Russia		43 21 N	42 26 E	45
Elburz (mts.), Iran		36 00 N	52 00 E	52
El Cajon, Calif., U.S.	94,869	32 47 N	116 57 W	82
Elgin, Ill., U.S.	94,487	42 02 N	88 17 W	84
Elkhart, Ind., U.S.	51,874	41 41 N	85 58 W	84
Ellesmere (isl.), Nun., Can.		79 00 N	82 00 W	77
El Paso, Texas, U.S.	563,662	31 45 N	106 29 W	82
El Salvador	**6,587,541**	**13 30 N**	**89 00 W**	**88**
Enewetak (isl.), Marshall Isls.		11 11 N	162 21 E	62
England, U.K.	49,138,831	53 00 N	01 00 W	42
English (chan.), Fr.,U.K.		50 00 N	02 30 W	42
Equatorial Guinea	**523,051**	**01 30 N**	**10 00 E**	**68**
Erie (lake), Can.U.S.		42 20 N	81 00 W	84
Erie, Pa., U.S.	103,717	42 07 N	80 05 W	84
Eritrea	**4,447,307**	**15 00 N**	**40 00 E**	**69**
Erzgebirge (mts.), Czech. Rep.,Ger.		50 30 N	13 00 E	42
Esfahān, Iran	1,266,072	32 40 N	51 38 E	52
Espíritu Santo (isl.), Vanuatu		15 15 S	166 55 E	62
Essen, Germany	599,515	51 30 N	07 00 E	42
Estonia	**1,401,945**	**59 00 N**	**26 00 E**	**43**
Ethiopia	**67,851,281**	**10 00 N**	**40 00 E**	**69**
Eugene, Ore., U.S.	137,893	44 03 N	123 05 W	80
Euphrates (river), Asia		38 00 N	39 05 E	52
Europe (cont.)	729,075,181			39
Evans (strait), Nun., Can.		63 00 N	81 00 W	77
Evans (mt.), Colo., U.S.		39 34 N	105 38 W	83
Evansville, Ind., U.S.	121,582	37 58 N	87 33 W	84
Everest (mt.), China,Nepal		27 58 N	87 05 E	53
Everett , Wash., U.S.	91,488	47 58 N	122 12 W	80
Everglades Nat'l Park, Fla., U.S.		25 15 N	81 00 W	87
Eyre (lake), Austl.		28 30 S	137 15 E	59
F				
Fairbanks, Alaska, U.S.	30,224	64° 51′ N	147° 43′ W	78
Fairfield, Calif., U.S.	96,178	38 15 N	122 02 W	82
Fairweather (mt.), Br. Col., Can.		58 15 N	137 29 W	82
Faisalabad, Pak.	1,104,209	31 25 N	73 05 E	53
Falkland (isls.), U.K.	2,967	52 00 S	59 00 W	96
Fall River, Mass., U.S.	91,938	41 42 N	71 09 W	85
Farīdābād, India	1,054,981	28 26 N	77 19 E	53
Fargo, N.D., U.S.	90,599	46 52 N	96 47 W	81
Faroe (isls.), Den.	46,345	62 00 N	07 00 W	39
Fayetteville, Ark., U.S.	58,047	36 03 N	94 09 W	83
Fayetteville, N.C., U.S.	121,015	35 03 N	78 52 W	87
Fear (cape), N.C., U.S.		33 50 N	77 58 W	87
Ferrara, Italy	131,713	44 50 N	11 40 E	42
Fès, Morocco	508,520	34 02 N	04 59 E	68
Fezzan (region), Libya		27 00 N	14 00 E	68
Fiji	**880,874**	**17 00 S**	**179 00 E**	**62**
Finisterre (cape), Spain		42 53 N	09 16 W	42
Finland	**5,214,512**	**64 00 N**	**26 00 E**	**43**
Finland (gulf), Europe		60 00 N	27 00 E	43
Fisher (strait), Nun., Can.		63 00 N	83 00 W	77
Flagstaff, Ariz., U.S.	52,894	35 12 N	111 39 W	82
Flin Flon, Man.-Sask., Can.	6,267	54 46 N	101 53 W	76
Flint, Mich., U.S.	124,943	43 00 N	83 41 W	84
Florence, Italy	374,501	43 46 N	11 13 E	42
Flores (isl.), Indon.		08 30 S	121 00 E	57
Flores (sea), Indon.		05 39 S	119 54 E	56
Florida (keys), Fla., U.S.		24 44 N	81 00 W	87
Florida (state), U.S.	15,982,378	28 00 N	82 00 W	87
Florida (straits), Cuba,U.S.		24 00 N	82 00 W	88
Forillon Nat'l Pk., Qué., Can.		49 00 N	64 30 W	85
Fortaleza, Brazil	1,026,787	03 41 S	38 33 W	95
Fort Collins, Colo., U.S.	118,652	40 35 N	105 04 W	83
Fort-de-France,* Mart.	94,778	14 36 N	61 05 W	89
Fort Frances, Ont., Can.	8,275	48 37 N	93 25 W	81
Fort Lauderdale, Fla., U.S.	152,397	26 07 N	80 08 W	87
Fort McMurray, Alta., Can.	41,466	56 44 N	111 23 W	76
Fort Myers, Fla., U.S.	48,208	26 38 N	81 52 W	87
Fort Nelson, Br. Col., Can.	4,188	58 49 N	122 36 W	76
Fort Peck (lake), Mont., U.S.		47 31 N	106 30 W	80
Fort Saint John, Br. Col., Can.	16,034	56 15 N	120 51 W	76
Fort Smith, Ark., U.S.	80,268	35 23 N	94 24 W	86
Fort Smith, N.W. Terrs., Can.	2,185	60 00 N	112 00 W	76
Fort Wayne, Ind., U.S.	205,727	41 04 N	85 08 W	84
Fort Worth, Texas, U.S.	534,694	32 45 N	97 19 W	86
Foxe (chan.), Nun., Can.		65 00 N	81 00 W	77
Foxe (pen.), Nun., Can.		65 00 N	76 00 W	77
Foxe Basin (bay), Nun., Can.		68 00 N	78 00 W	77
France	**60,424,213**	**47 00 N**	**02 00 E**	**42**
Frankfort,* Ky., U.S.	27,741	38 12 N	84 52 W	84
Frankfurt, Germany	643,821	50 10 N	08 30 E	42
Franklin D. Roosevelt (lake), Wash., U.S.		49 00 N	118 00 W	80
Franz Josef Land (isls.), Russia		81 00 N	51 00 E	46
Fraser (river), Br. Col., Can.		49 08 N	123 10 W	80
Frederick, Md., U.S.	52,767	39 25 N	77 24 W	84
Fredericton,* N.B., Can.	47,560	45 57 N	66 41 W	85
Freetown,* Sierra Leone	469,776	08 29 N	13 13 W	68
French Guiana, Fr.	191,309	04 00 N	53 00 W	95
French Polynesia, Fr.	266,339	15 00 S	140 00 W	63
Fresno, Calif., U.S.	427,652	36 45 N	119 46 W	82
Frobisher (bay), Nun., Can.		63 00 N	66 00 W	77
Frozen (strait), Nun., Can.		65 00 N	81 30 W	77
Fukuoka, Japan	1,341,470	33 35 N	130 24 E	55
Funafuti,* Tuvalu	2,120	08 31 S	179 08 E	62
Fundy (bay), Can.,U.S.		45 00 N	66 00 W	85
Fundy Nat'l Pk., N.B., Can.		46 00 N	65 00 W	85
Fury and Hecla (strait), Nun., Can.		70 00 N	84 00 W	77
Fushun, China	1,210,477	41 52 N	123 53 E	55
Fuzhou, China	889,920	26 05 N	119 19 E	55
G				
Gabon	**1,355,246**	**00° 00′**	**12° 00′ E**	**68**
Gaborone,* Bots.	174,583	24 40 S	25 54 E	70
Gainesville, Fla., U.S.	95,447	29 39 N	82 19 W	87
Galápagos (isls.), Ecuador	10,207	00 15 S	90 00 W	12
Galaţi, Romania	327,975	45 26 N	28 03 E	44
Galesburg, Ill., U.S.	33,706	40 57 N	90 22 W	84
Galveston, Texas, U.S.	57,247	29 18 N	94 48 W	86
Gambia, The	**1,546,848**	**13 30 N**	**15 30 W**	**68**
Gäncä, Azer.	294,100	40 40 N	46 22 E	45
Ganges (river), Bangladesh,India		26 00 N	80 15 E	53
Garonne (river), Fr.		45 01 N	00 36 W	42
Gary, Ind., U.S.	102,746	41 35 N	87 20 W	84
Gaspé, Qué., Can.	14,932	48 50 N	64 29 W	85
Gaspé (cape), Qué., Can.		48 50 N	64 00 W	85
Gaspé (pen.), Qué., Can.		48 30 N	65 00 W	85
Gastonia, N.C., U.S.	66,277	35 15 N	81 11 W	87
Gatineau, Qué., Can.	217,609	45 29 N	75 40 W	84
Gaza Strip	1,324,991	31 30 N	34 30 E	52
Gaziantep, Turkey	603,434	37 05 N	37 22 E	44
Gdańsk, Poland	462,076	54 20 N	18 30 E	43
Gdynia, Poland	251,303	54 32 N	18 33 E	43
Geneva (lake), Fr.,Switz.		46 25 N	06 25 E	42
Geneva, Switz.	173,549	46 12 N	06 10 E	42
Genoa, Italy	632,366	44 25 N	08 55 E	42
Georgetown,* Guyana	72,049	06 49 N	58 10 W	94
George Town, Malaysia	219,376	05 25 N	100 19 E	56
Georgia	**4,909,633**	**42 00 N**	**43 00 E**	**45**
Georgia (state), U.S.	8,186,453	32 30 N	83 15 W	87
Georgian (bay), Ont., Can.		45 15 N	80 45 W	84
Germany	**82,424,609**	**51 00 N**	**10 00 E**	**42**
Ghana	**20,757,032**	**07 00 N**	**01 00 W**	**68**
Ghent (Gent), Belgium	230,246	51 10 N	03 40 E	42
Gibraltar (strait), Mor.,Spain		35 55 N	05 35 W	42
Gibraltar, U.K.	27,833	36 08 N	05 22 W	42
Gijón, Spain	269,644	43 32 N	05 40 W	42
Glace Bay, N.S., Can.	21,187	46 12 N	59 57 W	85
Glacier Nat'l Park, Br. Col., Can.		51 00 N	118 00 W	80
Glacier Nat'l Park, Mont., U.S.		48 35 N	114 00 W	80
Glasgow, Scot.	618,430	55 50 N	04 10 W	42
Gobi (desert), China,Mongolia		43 00 N	110 00 E	54
Godavari (river), India		19 00 N	79 00 E	53
Godwin Austen (K2) (mt.), China,Pak.		35 53 N	76 30 E	53
Goiânia, Brazil	912,436	16 40 S	49 16 W	95
Good Hope (cape), S. Afr.		34 21 S	18 29 E	70
Göteborg, Sweden	433,020	57 43 N	11 58 E	43
Gotland (isl.), Sweden	57,313	57 45 N	18 45 E	43
Gouin (res.), Qué., Can.		48 30 N	75 30 W	84
Grampians (mts.), Scot.,U.K.		56 45 N	04 30 W	42
Granada, Spain	271,180	37 11 N	03 36 W	42
Gran Chaco (region), Arg.,Para.		24 00 S	62 00 W	96
Grand (lake), Newf., Can.		49 00 N	58 00 W	85
Grand Canyon Nat'l Park, Ariz., U.S.		36 03 N	112 08 W	82
Grande Prairie, Alta., Can.	36,483	55 10 N	118 48 W	76
Grand Falls, Newf., Can.	5,858	48 56 N	55 40 W	85
Grand Forks, N.D., U.S.	49,321	47 55 N	97 02 W	81
Grand Rapids, Mich., U.S.	197,800	42 57 N	85 40 W	84
Grand Teton (mt.), Wyo., U.S.		43 44 N	110 48 W	80
Grand Teton Nat'l Park, Wyo., U.S.		43 45 N	110 45 W	80
Graz, Austria	237,810	47 00 N	15 30 E	42
Great Australian Bight (bay), Austl.		33 00 S	130 00 E	59
Great Barrier (reef), Austl.		16 00 S	145 50 E	59
Great Bear (lake), N.W. Terrs., Can.		66 00 N	121 00 W	76
Great Britain (isl.), U.K.	57,103,927	54 00 N	02 00 W	42
Great Dividing Range (mts.), Austl.		35 00 S	149 35 E	59
Great Falls, Mont. U.S.	56,690	47 30 N	111 18 W	80
Great Indian (desert), India		28 00 N	73 00 E	53
Great Plains (plain), Can.,U.S.		46 00 N	102 00 W	81
Great Rift (valley), Tanz.,Zambia		09 00 N	31 00 E	69
Great Salt (lake), Ut. U.S.		41 05 N	112 30 W	82
Great Sandy (desert), Austl.		20 00 S	124 00 E	59
Great Slave (lake), N.W. Terrs., Can.		61 00 N	114 00 W	76
Great Victoria (desert), Austl.		27 00 S	130 00 E	59
Greater Antilles (isls.), N. America		18 00 N	74 00 W	89
Greece	**10,647,529**	**39 00 N**	**23 00 E**	**44**
Greeley, Colo., U.S.	76,930	40 25 N	104 42 W	83
Green Bay, Wis., U.S.	102,313	44 30 N	88 00 W	84
Greenland (isl.), Den.	56,384	70 00 N	40 00 W	73
Greenland (sea)		75 00 N	15 00 W	71
Greensboro, N.C., U.S.	223,891	36 04 N	79 47 W	87
Greenville, N.C., U.S.	60,476	35 36 N	77 23 W	87
Greenville, S.C., U.S.	56,002	34 51 N	82 23 W	87
Grenada	**89,357**	**12 05 N**	**61 40 W**	**89**
Grenoble, Fr.	156,203	45 10 N	05 43 E	42
Gros Morne Nat'l Pk., Newf., Can.		49 30 N	58 00 W	85
Guadalajara, Mex.	1,646,183	20 40 N	103 20 W	88
Guadalcanal (isl.), Sol. Is.	61,243	09 40 S	160 15 E	62
Guadalupe (isl.), Mex.		29 11 N	118 17 W	73
Guadalupe (mt.), Texas, U.S.		31 53 N	104 51 W	83
Guadarrama (mts.), Spain		41 00 N	03 30 W	42
Guadeloupe (isl.), Fr.	444,515	16 15 N	61 35 W	89
Guajira (pen.), Col.		11 30 N	72 45 W	94
Guam (isl.), U.S.	160,796	13 30 N	144 47 E	62
Guangzhou, China	2,891,643	23 07 N	113 15 E	55
Guatemala	**14,280,596**	**15 30 N**	**90 15 W**	**88**
Guatemala,* Guat.	823,301	14 37 N	90 31 W	88
Guayaquil, Ecuador	1,513,437	02 12 S	79 53 W	94
Guelph, Ont., Can.	106,920	43 33 N	80 15 W	84
Guiana Highlands (plat.), S. America		05 00 N	60 00 W	94
Guinea	**9,246,462**	**10 00 N**	**11 00 W**	**68**
Guinea (gulf), Africa		03 00 N	04 00 E	68
Guinea-Bissau	**1,388,363**	**11 50 N**	**15 00 W**	**68**
Guiyang, China	1,009,399	26 35 N	106 43 E	54
Gulfport, Miss., U.S.	71,127	30 22 N	89 05 W	87
Guwāhati, India	808,021	26 10 N	91 45 E	53
Guyana	**705,803**	**05 00 N**	**59 00 W**	**94**

Index of the World

Index of the World

NAME	POPULATION	LATITUDE	LONGITUDE	PAGE
New Caledonia (isl.), Fr.	213,679	21 30 S	165 30 E	62
Newcastle, Austl.	270,324	32 55 S	151 45 E	59
Newcastle upon Tyne, Eng., U.K.	189,150	55 00 N	01 35 W	42
New Delhi,* India	294,783	28 19 N	77 15 E	53
Newfoundland (isl.), Newf., Can.		49 30 N	57 30 W	85
Newfoundland and Labrador (prov.), Can.	512,930	51 30 N	55 45 W	77
New Guinea (isl.), Indon.,P.N.G.		05 00 S	141 00 E	57
New Hampshire (state), U.S.	1,235,786	43 30 N	71 45 W	85
New Haven, Conn., U.S.	123,626	41 19 N	72 55 W	85
New Ireland (isl.), P.N.G.		04 00 S	152 00 E	62
New Jersey (state), U.S.	8,414,350	40 00 N	74 30 W	84
Newmarket, Ont., Can.	65,788	44 03 N	79 28 W	84
New Mexico (state), U.S.	1,819,046	34 30 N	106 00 W	82
New Orleans, La., U.S.	484,674	29 57 N	90 04 W	87
Newport News, Va., U.S.	180,150	36 58 N	76 25 W	84
New Siberian (isls.), Russia		75 00 N	142 00 E	47
New South Wales (state), Austl.	6,371,745	32 00 S	147 00 E	59
New York, N.Y., U.S.	8,008,278	40 45 N	74 00 W	84
New York (state), U.S.	18,976,457	43 00 N	76 00 W	84
New Zealand	**3,993,817**	**41 00 S**	**173 00 E**	**59**
Niagara Falls, Ont., Can.	78,815	43 06 N	79 04 W	84
Niagara Falls, N.Y., U.S.	55,593	43 05 N	79 03 W	84
Niamey,* Niger	392,169	13 31 N	02 07 E	68
Nicaragua	**5,232,216**	**13 00 N**	**85 00 W**	**88**
Nicaragua (lake), Nic.		11 30 N	85 30 W	88
Nice, Fr.	345,892	43 42 N	07 16 E	42
Nicobar (isls.), India	51,000	07 45 N	93 30 E	53
Nicosia,* Cyprus	47,036	35 12 N	33 22 E	52
Niger	**11,360,538**	**17 00 N**	**08 00 E**	**68**
Niger (river), Africa		04 17 N	06 04 E	68
Nigeria	**137,253,133**	**09 00 N**	**08 00 E**	**68**
Niihau (isl.), Hawaii, U.S.		21 53 N	160 10 W	78
Nile (river), Africa		31 50 N	32 00 E	69
Ningbo, China	548,277	29 54 N	121 32 E	55
Nipigon (lake), Ont., Can.		49 30 N	89 00 W	84
Nipissing (lake), Ont., Can.		46 30 N	79 30 W	84
Niue (isl.), N.Z.	2,145	19 02 S	169 52 W	63
Nizhniy Novgorod, Russia	1,425,316	56 20 N	44 00 E	45
Norfolk (isl.), Austl.	1,853	29 02 S	167 57 W	62
Norfolk, Va., U.S.	234,403	36 50 N	76 17 W	84
Norman, Okla., U.S.	95,694	35 13 N	97 26 W	86
Normandy (region), Fr.		49 00 N	00 00	42
Norrköping, Sweden	120,478	58 30 N	16 10 E	43
Norrland (region), Sweden		66 00 N	20 00 E	43
North (cape), Norway		71 11 N	25 40 E	39
North (isl.), N.Z.	2,829,798	39 00 S	176 00 E	59
North (sea), Europe		55 20 N	03 00 E	42
North America (cont.)	508,788,254			73
North Battleford, Sask., Can.	13,692	52 46 N	108 17 W	80
North Bay, Ont., Can.	51,895	46 19 N	79 28 W	84
North Carolina (state), U.S.	8,049,313	35 30 N	79 00 W	87
North Cascades Nat'l Pk., Wash., U.S.		49 00 N	122 00 W	80
North Dakota (state), U.S.	642,200	47 30 N	100 30 W	81
North Korea	**22,697,553**	**40 00 N**	**127 00 E**	**55**
Northern Ireland, U.K	1,685,267	54 30 N	06 30 W	42
Northern Marianas (isls.), U.S.	78,252	18 00 N	145 45 E	62
Northern Territory, Austl.	210,664	20 00 S	134 00 E	59
North Magnetic Pole		75 00 N	100 00 W	71
North Saskatchewan (river), Alta.,Sask., Can.		53 00 N	110 00 W	80
Northwest Territories, Can.	37,360	64 00 N	120 00 W	76
Norton (sound), Alaska, U.S.		64 00 N	164 00 W	78
Norwalk, Conn., U.S.	82,951	41 07 N	73 25 W	84
Norway	**4,574,560**	**65 00 N**	**11 00 E**	**43**
Norwegian (sea), Europe		70 00 N	00 00	39
Notre Dame (bay), Newf., Can.		49 30 N	55 00 W	85
Notre Dame (mts.), Can.,U.S.		48 00 N	68 00 W	85
Nottingham, Eng., U.K.	270,222	52 58 N	01 10 W	42
Nouakchott,* Mauritania	390,000	18 06 N	15 57 W	68
Nouméa,* New Cal.	65,110	22 17 S	166 26 E	62
Nova Scotia (prov.), Can.	908,007	45 00 N	63 00 W	85
Novaya Zemlya (isls.), Russia		74 00 N	57 00 E	46
Novosibirsk, Russia	1,423,860	55 02 N	82 53 E	46
Nubian (desert), Sudan		21 00 N	33 00 E	69
Nuku'alofa,* Tonga	21,383	21 08 S	175 12 E	63
Nürnberg, Germany	486,628	49 20 N	11 05 E	42
Nunavut (terr.), Can.	26,795	64 00 N	90 00 W	76
Nuuk (Godthab),* Greenland	12,233	64 11 N	51 45 W	73
Nyasa (lake), Africa		12 00 S	34 30 E	70

O

NAME	POPULATION	LATITUDE	LONGITUDE	PAGE
Oahe (lake), N.D.,S.D., U.S.		46° 00′ N	101° 00′ W	81
Oahu (isl.), Hawaii, U.S.		21 30 N	158 00 W	78
Oakland, Calif., U.S.	399,484	37 48 N	122 16 W	82
Ob' (river), Russia		66 45 N	69 07 E	46
Oceanside, Calif., U.S.	161,029	33 11 N	117 22 W	82
Odense, Denmark	143,029	55 24 N	10 23 E	43
Oder (river), Ger.,Poland		53 30 N	14 30 E	42
Odesa, Ukraine	1,095,800	46 29 N	30 44 E	44
Odessa, Texas, U.S.	90,943	31 50 N	102 22 W	83
Ogbomosho, Nigeria	660,000	08 08 N	04 16 E	68
Ogden, Utah, U.S.	77,226	41 13 N	111 58 W	82
Ohio (river), U.S.		36 59 N	89 08 W	84
Ohio (state), U.S.	11,353,140	40 00 N	82 45 W	84
Oka (river), Russia		56 00 N	43 57 E	43
Okeechobee (lake), Fla., U.S.		27 00 N	80 50 W	87
Okhotsk (sea), Russia		55 00 N	150 00 E	47
Okinawa (isls.), Japan	1,240,000	26 30 N	128 00 E	55
Oklahoma (state), U.S.	3,450,654	35 30 N	97 30 W	86
Oklahoma City,* Okla., U.S.	506,132	35 28 N	97 31 W	86
Olenek (river), Russia		73 00 N	119 55 E	47
Olympia,* Wash., U.S.	42,514	47 02 N	122 54 W	80
Olympic Nat'l Park, Wash., U.S.		47 45 N	123 40 W	80
Olympus (mt.), Wash., U.S.		47 48 N	123 42 W	80
Omaha, Neb., U.S.	390,007	41 15 N	95 56 W	83
Oman	**2,903,165**	**21 00 N**	**57 00 E**	**52**
Oman (gulf), Asia		24 30 N	58 45 E	52
Omdurman, Sudan	228,773	15 37 N	32 30 E	69
Omsk, Russia	1,163,885	55 00 N	73 24 E	46
Onega (bay), Russia		64 15 N	37 00 E	43
Onega (lake), Russia		61 30 N	35 00 E	43
Ontario (lake), Can.,U.S.		43 40 N	78 00 W	84
Ontario (prov.), Can.	11,410,046	50 00 N	87 00 W	76
Oradea, Rom.	223,680	47 03 N	21 54 E	44
Oran, Algeria	528,525	35 43 N	00 38 W	68
Orange (river), Namibia,S. Afr.		28 39 S	16 29 E	70
Oregon (state), U.S.	3,421,399	44 00 N	120 30 W	80
Orenburg, Russia	554,144	51 45 N	55 06 E	45
Orillia, Ont., Can.	29,121	44 37 N	79 25 W	84
Orinoco (river), Ven.		09 00 N	60 45 W	94
Orkney (isls.), U.K.	19,245	59 00 N	03 00 W	42
Orlando, Fla., U.S.	185,951	28 32 N	81 22 W	87
Osaka, Japan	2,598,774	34 40 N	135 30 E	55
Oshawa, Ont., Can.	139,051	43 54 N	78 51 W	84
Oshkosh, Wis., U.S.	62,916	44 00 N	88 31 W	84
Oslo,* Norway	507,831	59 55 N	10 40 E	43
Ostrava, Czech Rep.	319,293	49 45 N	18 20 E	44
Otranto (strait), Europe		40 30 N	19 00 E	44
Ottawa (river), Ont.,Qué., Can.		45 26 N	74 00 W	84
Ottawa,* Ont., Can.	774,072	45 25 N	75 42 W	84
Ouagadougou,* Burkina Faso	441,514	12 22 N	01 30 W	68
Oulu, Finland	109,094	65 00 N	25 28 E	43
Owen Sound, Ont., Can.	22,161	44 34 N	80 51 W	84
Owensboro, Ky., U.S.	54,067	37 46 N	87 06 W	87
Oxford, Eng., U.K.	118,795	51 45 N	01 15 W	42
Oxnard, Calif., U.S.	170,358	34 12 N	119 10 W	82

P

NAME	POPULATION	LATITUDE	LONGITUDE	PAGE
Pacific Rim Nat'l Pk., Br. Col., Can.		49° 00′ N	125° 00′ W	80
Pago Pago,* Amer. Samoa	4,278	14 17 S	170 40 W	63
Pakistan	**153,705,278**	**30 00 N**	**69 00 E**	**49**
Palau	**20,016**	**07 30 N**	**134 30 E**	**62**
Palembang, Indonesia	1,084,251	02 55 S	104 55 E	56
Palawan (isl.), Phil.		10 30 N	118 30 E	56
Palermo, Italy	679,290	38 07 N	13 20 E	44
Palikir,* Micronesia, Fed. States of	6,200	06 57 N	158 15 E	63
Palma, Spain	322,008	39 34 N	02 39 E	42
Palo Alto, Calif., U.S.	58,598	37 26 N	122 08 W	82
Pamir (plat.), China,Tajik.		38 00 N	73 50 E	54
Pampas (plains), Arg.		35 00 S	63 00 W	96
Panama	**3,000,463**	**08 30 N**	**80 00 W**	**88**
Panamá,* Panama	455,902	08 57 N	79 32 W	89
Panama (canal), Panama		08 58 N	79 31 W	89
Panay (isl.), Phil.		10 42 N	122 33 E	57
Pangnirtung, Nun., Can.	1,276	66 08 N	65 44 W	77
Papeete,* Fr. Polynesia	23,555	17 32 S	149 34 W	63
Papua (gulf), P.N.G.		08 30 S	145 00 E	57
Papua New Guinea	**5,420,280**	**06 00 S**	**148 00 E**	**62**
Paraguay	**6,191,368**	**24 00 S**	**58 00 W**	**91**
Paraguay (river), S. America		27 18 S	58 36 W	94
Paramaribo,* Suriname	180,000	05 50 N	55 09 W	95
Paraná (river), Arg.		31 44 S	60 32 W	96
Paris,* Fr.	2,147,857	48 45 N	02 20 E	42
Parry (chan.), Nun., Can.		74 30 N	100 00 W	76
Parry Sound, Ont., Can.	6,124	45 20 N	80 02 W	84
Pasadena, Calif., U.S.	133,936	34 08 N	118 09 W	82
Patagonia (region), Arg.		44 00 S	68 00 W	96
Patna, India	917,243	25 36 N	85 07 E	53
Patos (lagoon), Brazil		31 00 S	51 20 W	96
Pawtucket, R.I., U.S.	72,958	41 52 N	71 23 W	85
Peace (river), Alta.,Br. Col., Can.		58 59 N	111 25 W	76
Peace River, Alta., Can.	6,240	56 14 N	117 17 W	76
Pechora (river), Russia		67 40 N	52 30 E	43
Pecos (river), Texas, U.S.		29 40 N	101 40 W	83
Peel (river), N.W. Terrs.,Yukon Terr., Can.		67 41 N	134 32 W	76
Peel (sound), Nun., Can.		73 00 N	97 00 W	76
Peipus (lake), Estonia,Russia		58 45 N	27 30 E	43
Pemba (isl.), Tanz.	314,000	05 15 S	39 45 E	70
Pennsylvania (state), U.S.	12,281,054	41 00 N	77 30 W	84
Pensacola, Fla., U.S.	56,255	30 25 N	87 13 W	87
Penticton, Br. Col., Can.	30,985	49 30 N	119 35 W	80
Penza, Russia	547,623	53 12 N	45 03 E	45
Peoria, Ill., U.S.	112,936	40 41 N	89 35 W	84
Péribonca (river), Qué., Can.		50 30 N	71 00 W	77
Perm', Russia	1,091,056	58 00 N	56 15 E	45
Persian (gulf), Asia		26 30 N	52 45 E	52
Perth, Austl.	1,162,716	31 55 S	115 50 E	59
Peru	**28,863,494**	**10 00 S**	**75 00 W**	**94**
Peshāwar, Pakistan	566,248	34 01 N	71 33 E	53
Petare, Ven.	338,417	10 29 N	66 49 W	94
Peterborough, Ont., Can.	73,303	44 18 N	78 19 W	84
Petersburg, Va., U.S.	33,740	37 13 N	77 24 W	84
Petropavlovsk-Kamchatskiy, Russia	265,254	53 01 N	158 39 E	47
Philadelphia, Pa., U.S.	1,517,550	39 57 N	75 10 W	84
Philippine (sea)		19 00 N	135 00 E	57
Philippines	**86,241,697**	**12 00 N**	**122 00 E**	**57**
Phnom Penh,* Cambodia	620,000	11 33 N	104 55 E	56
Phoenix (isls.), Kiribati		03 43 S	171 00 W	63
Phoenix,* Ariz., U.S.	1,321,045	33 27 N	112 05 W	82
Pierre,* S.D., U.S.	13,876	44 22 N	100 21 W	81
Pietermaritzburg, S. Afr.	223,518	29 37 S	30 16 E	70
Pikes Peak (mt.), Colo., U.S.		38 50 N	105 02 W	83
Pilcomayo (river), S. America		25 16 S	57 43 W	96
Pine Bluff, Ark., U.S.	55,085	34 13 N	92 00 W	83
Pipmuacan (res.), Qué., Can.		49 30 N	70 30 W	85
Pisa, Italy	91,977	43 45 N	10 21 E	42
Pitcairn (isls.), U.K.	47	25 05 S	130 05 W	63
Pittsburgh, Pa., U.S.	334,563	40 26 N	80 00 W	84
Platte (river), U.S.		41 05 N	95 55 W	83
Ploieşti, Rom.	253,623	44 57 N	26 02 E	44
Plovdiv, Bulgaria	341,374	42 09 N	24 45 E	44
Plymouth, Eng., U.K.	245,295	50 24 N	04 07 W	42
Plzeň, Czech Rep.	166,274	49 45 N	13 22 E	44
Po (river), Italy		45 00 N	12 25 E	42
Pocatello, Idaho, U.S.	51,466	42 52 N	112 26 W	80
Pohnpei (isl.), Micronesia	33,372	06 54 N	158 14 E	62
Pointe-Noire, Congo	576,000	04 46 S	11 51 E	70
Poland	**38,626,349**	**52 00 N**	**19 00 E**	**39**
Polynesia (region)		10 00 S	160 00 W	63
Pomerania (region), Poland		53 00 N	16 30 E	43
Pontiac, Mich., U.S.	66,337	42 38 N	83 17 W	84
Poopó (lake), Bolivia		19 10 S	67 00 W	94
Portage la Prairie, Man., Can.	12,976	49 58 N	98 18 W	80
Port Arthur, Texas, U.S.	57,755	29 54 N	93 55 W	86
Port-au-Prince,* Haiti	690,168	18 83 N	72 21 W	89
Port Elizabeth, S. Afr.	775,255	33 58 S	25 37 E	70
Portland, Maine, U.S.	64,249	43 39 N	70 16 W	85
Portland, Ore., U.S.	529,121	45 31 N	122 40 W	80
Port Louis,* Mauritius	143,509	20 10 S	57 30 E	13
Port Moresby,* P.N.G.	193,242	09 29 S	147 09 E	57
Porto, Portugal	310,637	41 10 N	08 36 W	42
Porto Alegre, Brazil	1,237,223	30 02 S	51 14 W	96
Port of Spain,* Trinidad and Tobago	50,878	10 39 N	61 31 W	89
Porto-Novo,* Benin	179,138	06 28 N	02 38 E	68
Port Said, Egypt	460,000	31 16 N	32 18 E	69
Portsmouth, Eng., U.K.	174,690	50 47 N	01 05 W	42
Portsmouth, Va., U.S.	100,565	36 49 N	76 20 W	87
Portugal	**10,119,250**	**39 00 N**	**08 00 W**	**42**
Port-Vila,* Vanuatu	29,356	17 44 S	168 19 E	62
Poznań, Poland	586,908	52 25 N	16 58 E	44
Prague,* Czech Rep.	1,178,576	50 05 N	14 20 E	44
Pretoria,* S. Afr.	692,348	25 45 S	28 11 E	70
Prince Albert, Sask., Can.	34,291	53 12 N	105 46 W	81
Prince Albert (pen.), N.W. Terrs., Can.		73 00 N	115 00 W	76
Prince Albert (sound), N.W. Terrs., Can.		71 00 N	115 00 W	76
Prince Albert Nat'l Pk., Sask., Can.		54 00 N	106 00 W	80
Prince Edward Island (prov.), Can.	135,294	46 20 N	63 30 W	85
Prince George, Br. Col., Can.	72,406	53 55 N	122 45 W	80
Prince of Wales (isl.), Nun., Can.		72 30 N	98 30 W	76
Prince of Wales (str.), N.W. Terrs., Can.		75 00 N	118 00 W	76
Prince Rupert, Br. Col., Can.	14,643	54 19 N	130 19 W	76
Prince William (sound), Alaska, U.S.		61 00 N	144 00 W	76
Provence (region), Fr.		43 30 N	06 00 E	42
Providence,* R.I., U.S.	173,618	41 49 N	71 24 W	85
Provo, Utah, U.S.	105,166	40 14 N	111 39 W	82
Prut (river), Moldova,Rom.		45 29 N	28 13 E	44
Puebla, Mex.	1,271,673	19 03 N	98 10 W	88
Pueblo, Colo, U.S.	102,121	38 16 N	104 35 W	83
Puerto Rico, U.S.	3,957,988	18 15 N	66 30 W	89
Puget (sound), Wash., U.S.		47 30 N	122 29 W	80
Pune, India	2,540,069	18 30 N	73 45 E	53
Purus (river), Brazil		03 43 S	61 28 W	94
Pusan, S. Korea	3,655,437	35 06 N	129 03 E	55
P'yongyang,* N. Korea	2,639,448	39 01 N	125 45 E	55
Pyrenees (mts.), Europe		42 45 N	00 05 E	42

Q

NAME	POPULATION	LATITUDE	LONGITUDE	PAGE
Qu'Appelle (river), Sask., Can.		50° 30′ N	104° 00′ W	81
Qaraghandy, Kazakhstan	596,000	49 50 N	73 10 E	46
Qatar	**840,290**	**25 30 N**	**51 15 E**	**52**
Qingdao, China	1,317,465	36 04 N	120 19 E	55
Qiqihar, China	1,065,676	47 19 N	123 55 E	55
Qom, Iran	777,677	34 39 N	50 54 E	52
Québec (prov.), Can.	7,237,479	52 00 N	72 00 W	77
Québec,* Qué., Can.	465,029	46 49 N	71 14 W	85
Queen Charlotte (isls.), Br. Col., Can.		53 00 N	132 00 W	76
Queen Charlotte (sound), Br. Col., Can.		51 30 N	130 00 W	76
Queen Elizabeth (isls.), N.W. Terrs.,Nun., Can.		77 00 N	100 00 W	77
Queen Maud Land (region), Antarctica		72 30 S	12 00 E	71
Queensland (state), Austl.	3,655,139	23 00 S	145 00 E	59
Quesnel, Br. Col., Can.	10,044	52 59 N	122 29 W	80
Quezon City, Phil.	1,989,419	14 38 N	121 03 E	57
Quincy, Mass., U.S.	88,025	42 15 N	71 00 W	85
Quito,* Ecuador	1,112,575	00 13 S	78 30 W	94

R

NAME	POPULATION	LATITUDE	LONGITUDE	PAGE
Rabat,* Mor.	916,544	34° 00′ N	06° 51′ W	68
Rabaul, P.N.G.	16,883	04 12 S	152 12 E	62
Race (cape), Newf., Can.		46 38 N	53 06 W	85
Racine, Wis., U.S.	81,855	42 43 N	87 47 W	84
Rainier (mt.), Wash., U.S.		46 51 N	121 46 W	80
Raleigh,* N.C., U.S.	276,093	35 47 N	78 38 W	87
Rankin Inlet, Nun., Can.	2,177	62 49 N	92 05 W	77
Rann of Kutch (salt lake), India		24 00 N	70 00 E	53
Rapid City, S.D., U.S.	59,607	44 05 N	103 14 W	81
Rarotonga (isl.), Cook Isls., N.Z.	11,225	21 14 S	159 46 W	63
Rāwalpindi, Pakistan	794,843	33 36 N	73 04 E	53
Reading, Pa., U.S.	81,207	40 20 N	75 55 W	84
Recife, Brazil	1,296,995	08 04 S	34 53 W	95
Red (river), U.S.		30 58 N	91 40 W	86
Red (sea), Africa,Asia		20 00 N	39 00 E	52
Red Deer, Alta., Can.	67,707	52 16 N	113 48 W	80
Red Deer (river), Alta., Can.		50 30 N	112 00 W	80
Redding, Calif., U.S.	80,865	40 35 N	122 23 W	80
Red River of the North (river), Can.,U.S.		49 00 N	97 14 W	81
Redwood Nat'l Pk., Calif., U.S.		41 30 N	124 00 W	82
Reggio di Calabria, Italy	179,509	38 06 N	15 39 E	44
Regina,* Sask., Can.	178,225	50 27 N	104 37 W	81
Reims, Fr.	191,325	49 15 N	04 00 E	42
Reindeer (lake), Man.,Sask., Can.		57 15 N	102 15 W	76
Rennes, Fr.	212,494	48 05 N	01 40 W	42
Reno, Nev., U.S.	180,480	39 31 N	119 48 W	82

Index of the World

NAME	POPULATION	LATITUDE	LONGITUDE	PAGE
Réunion (isl.), Fr.	766,153	21 00 S	55 30 E	13
Revelstoke, Br. Col., Can.	7,500	51 00 N	118 11 W	80
Revillagigedo (isls.), Mex.		19 00 N	111 30 W	73
Reyes (point), Calif., U.S.		38 00 N	123 00 W	82
Reykjavík,* Iceland	111,345	64 10 N	21 58 W	39
Rhine (river), Europe		52 00 N	04 00 E	42
Rhode Island (state), U.S.	1,048,319	41 49 N	71 30 W	85
Rhodes (isl.), Greece		36 15 N	28 00 E	44
Rhodope (mts.), Bulgaria,Greece.		41 50 N	24 00 E	44
Rhône (river), Europe		45 00 N	05 00 E	42
Richmond,* Va., U.S.	197,790	37 33 N	77 27 W	84
Riding Mountain Nat'l Pk., Man., Can.		50 30 N	100 00 W	81
Riga,* Latvia	764,328	56 55 N	24 15 E	43
Rijeka, Croatia	143,800	45 21 N	14 24 E	44
Rimouski, Qué., Can.	31,305	48 26 N	68 30 W	85
Rio de Janeiro, Brazil	5,473,909	22 54 S	43 15 W	95
Rio Grande (river), Mex.,U.S.		25 58 N	97 09 W	86
Riverside, Calif., U.S.	255,186	33 57 N	117 24 W	82
Rivière-du-Loup, Qué., Can.	17,772	47 50 N	69 32 W	85
Riyadh,* S. Ar.	1,800,000	24 45 N	46 45 E	52
Roanoke, Va., U.S.	94,911	37 16 N	79 56 W	84
Roberval, Qué., Can.	10,906	48 31 N	72 13 W	85
Robson (mt.), Br. Col., Can.		53 06 N	119 08 W	80
Rochester, Minn., U.S.	85,806	44 01 N	92 28 W	81
Rochester, N.Y., U.S.	219,773	43 09 N	77 37 W	84
Rockford, Ill., U.S.	150,115	42 16 N	89 05 W	84
Rocky (mts.), Can.,U.S.		50 00 N	117 00 W	73
Rocky Mount, N.C., U.S.	55,893	35 57 N	77 47 W	87
Rodrigues (isl.), Mauritius	35,779	19 45 S	63 25 E	13
Roes Welcome (sound), Nun., Can.		64 00 N	88 00 W	77
Romania	**22,355,551**	**46 00 N**	**25 00 E**	**44**
Rome,* Italy	2,655,970	41 54 N	12 30 E	42
Rosario, Arg.	894,645	32 57 S	60 40 W	96
Roseau,* Dominica	6,131	15 17 N	61 23 W	89
Ross Ice Shelf, Antarctica		81 30 S	175 00 W	71
Ross (sea), Antarctica		75 00 S	180 00	71
Rostov, Russia	1,012,649	47 15 N	39 53 E	45
Roswell, N.M., U.S.	45,293	33 23 N	104 31 W	83
Rotterdam, Neth.	589,707	51 55 N	04 25 E	42
Rotuma (isl.), Fiji	2,600	12 30 S	177 05 E	62
Rouyn-Noranda, Qué., Can.	28,270	48 15 N	79 01 W	84
Rub' al Khali (desert), Asia		20 00 N	52 00 E	52
Russia	**144,112,353**	**60 00 N**	**90 00 E**	**46**
Rwanda	**7,954,013**	**02 00 S**	**30 00 E**	**70**
Ryazan', Russia	524,097	54 38 N	39 44 E	43
Ryukyu (isls.), Japan	1,318,220	27 00 N	127 00 E	55

S

NAME	POPULATION	LATITUDE	LONGITUDE	PAGE
's Gravenhage (The Hague),* Neth.	455,287	52° 05′ N	04° 20′ E	42
Sabah (state), Malaysia	2,894,900	05 00 N	117 00 E	56
Sable (cape), N.S., Can.		43 24 N	65 37 W	85
Sable (isl.), N.S., Can.		43 55 N	60 00 W	85
Sacramento (mts.), N.M., U.S.		33 15 N	105 40 W	83
Sacramento,* Calif., U.S.	407,018	38 35 N	121 29 W	82
Saginaw, Mich., U.S.	61,799	43 25 N	83 58 W	84
Sahara (desert), Africa		23 00 N	10 00 E	68
Saigon (Ho Chi Minh City), Vietnam	2,899,753	10 47 N	106 41 E	56
Saint Albert, Alta., Can.	53,081	53 38 N	113 38 W	80
Saint Catharines, Ont., Can.	129,170	43 10 N	79 15 W	84
Saint Charles, Mo., U.S.	60,321	38 47 N	90 29 W	83
Saint Cloud, Minn., U.S.	59,107	45 33 N	94 09 W	81
Saint Elias (mts.), Can.,U.S.		61 00 N	140 00 W	76
Saint-Étienne, Fr.	183,522	45 25 N	04 25 E	42
Saint George (pt.), Calif., U.S.		41 46 N	124 14 W	80
Saint George, Utah, U.S.	49,663	37 06 N	113 35 W	82
Saint George's,* Grenada	4,788	12 03 N	61 45 W	89
Saint Helena (isl.), U.K.	7,415	15 58 S	05 21 W	65
Saint Helens (mt.), Wash., U.S.		46 11 N	122 12 W	80
Saint John, N.B., Can.	69,661	45 16 N	66 01 W	85
Saint John's,* Antigua and Barbuda	22,342	17 07 N	61 50 W	89
Saint John's,* Newf., Can.	99,182	47 34 N	52 43 W	85
Saint Joseph, Mo., U.S.	73,990	39 46 N	94 50 W	83
Saint Kitts and Nevis	**38,836**	**17 17 N**	**62 40 W**	**89**
Saint Lawrence (gulf), Can.		49 00 N	62 00 W	85
Saint Lawrence (isl.), Alaska, U.S.		63 00 N	170 00 W	78
Saint Lawrence (river), Can.,U.S.		49 30 N	66 00 W	85
Saint Louis, Mo., U.S.	348,189	38 37 N	90 12 W	83
Saint Lucia	**164,213**	**14 00 N**	**61 00 W**	**89**
Saint Paul,* Minn., U.S.	287,151	44 57 N	93 05 W	81
Saint Petersburg, Fla., U.S.	248,232	27 46 N	82 38 W	87
St. Petersburg (Leningrad), Russia	4,328,851	59 55 N	30 15 E	43
Saint Pierre & Miquelon (isls.), Fr.	6,995	46 47 N	56 21 W	85
Saint Vincent and the Grenadines	**117,193**	**13 15 N**	**61 15 W**	**89**
Saipan (isl.), N. Marianas, U.S.	62,392	15 12 N	145 45 E	62
Sakhalin (isl.), Russia	519,500	50 00 N	143 00 E	47
Sala y Gómez (isl.), Chile		26 27 S	105 28 W	12
Salado (river), Arg.		32 30 S	60 47 W	96
Salem,* Ore., U.S.	136,924	44 56 N	123 02 W	80
Salinas, Calif., U.S.	151,060	36 40 N	121 39 W	82
Salt Lake City,* Utah, U.S.	181,743	40 46 N	111 53 W	82
Salton Sea (lake), Calif., U.S.		33 15 N	115 48 W	82
Salvador, Brazil	2,070,296	13 00 S	38 30 W	95
Salween (river), China		25 00 N	98 45 E	54
Samar (isl.), Phil.		12 00 N	125 00 E	57
Samara, Russia	1,231,653	53 12 N	50 09 E	45
Samoa	**177,714**	**14 00 S**	**172 00 W**	**63**
Samsun, Turkey	303,979	41 17 N	36 20 E	44
Sanaa,* Yemen	972,000	15 21 N	44 12 E	52
San Angelo, Texas, U.S.	88,439	31 28 N	100 26 W	83
San Antonio, Texas, U.S.	1,144,646	29 25 N	98 30 W	83
San Bernardino, Calif., U.S.	185,401	34 06 N	117 17 W	82
San Diego, Calif., U.S.	1,223,400	32 43 N	117 09 W	82
San Francisco, Calif., U.S.	776,733	37 46 N	122 25 W	82
San Jose, Calif., U.S.	894,943	37 20 N	121 53 W	82
San José,* C.R.	279,000	09 56 N	84 05 W	88
San Juan,* P.R., U.S.	421,958	18 28 N	66 07 W	89
San Luis Obispo, Calif., U.S.	44,174	35 17 N	120 39 W	82
San Luis Potosí, Mex.	629,208	22 09 N	100 59 W	88
San Marino	**28,503**	**43 56 N**	**12 28 E**	**42**
San Marino,* San Marino	2,768	43 56 N	12 28 E	42
San Mateo, Calif., U.S.	92,482	37 33 N	122 19 W	82
San Miguel de Tucumán, Arg.	527,607	26 50 S	65 12 W	96
San Pedro Sula, Honduras	287,350	15 27 N	88 02 W	88
San Salvador (Watling) (isl.), Bahamas	465	24 02 N	74 28 W	89
San Salvador,* El Sal.	415,346	13 41 N	89 12 W	88
Santa Ana, Calif., U.S.	337,977	33 44 N	117 52 W	82
Santa Barbara, Calif., U.S.	92,325	34 25 N	119 42 W	82
Santa Cruz de la Sierra, Bolivia	694,616	17 48 S	63 10 W	94
Santa Fe, Arg.	489,506	31 38 S	60 43 W	96
Santa Fe,* N.M., U.S.	62,203	35 41 N	105 56 W	83
Santa Rosa, Calif., U.S.	147,595	38 26 N	122 42 W	82
Santiago,* Chile	4,298,240	33 26 S	70 42 W	96
Santiago, Dom. Rep.	365,463	19 27 N	70 42 W	89
Santiago de Cuba, Cuba	430,494	20 01 N	75 49 W	89
Santo André, Brazil	518,272	23 40 S	46 31 W	95
Santo Domingo,* Dom. Rep.	1,609,966	18 28 N	69 53 W	89
Santos, Brazil	415,554	23 57 S	46 19 W	95
São Francisco (river), Brazil		10 30 S	36 23 W	95
São Paulo, Brazil	10,434,252	23 33 S	46 37 W	95
São Roque (cape), Brazil		05 26 S	35 15 W	95
São Tomé,* São Tomé and Príncipe	43,420	00 20 N	06 44 E	68
São Tomé and Príncipe	**181,565**	**01 00 N**	**07 00 E**	**68**
Sapporo, Japan	1,822,368	43 04 N	141 22 E	55
Saragossa (Zaragoza), Spain	606,620	41 39 N	00 51 W	42
Sarajevo,* Bosnia and Herzegovina	529,021	43 52 N	18 25 E	44
Sarasota, Fla., U.S.	52,715	27 20 N	82 32 W	87
Saratov, Russia	899,173	51 34 N	46 02 E	45
Sarawak (state), Malaysia	2,027,900	02 30 N	113 00 E	56
Sardinia (isl.), Italy	1,648,044	40 00 N	09 00 E	42
Sarnia, Ont., Can.	74,566	42 58 N	82 23 W	84
Saskatchewan (prov.), Can.	978,933	54 00 N	106 00 W	76
Saskatchewan (river), Man.,Sask., Can.		53 11 N	99 17 W	81
Saskatoon, Sask., Can.	196,811	52 07 N	106 38 W	80
Satpura Range (mts.), India		21 25 N	76 10 E	53
Saudi Arabia	**25,100,425**	**24 00 N**	**45 00 E**	**52**
Sault Sainte Marie, Ont., Can.	74,566	46 31 N	84 20 W	84
Sava (river), Europe		44 51 N	20 27 E	44
Savai'i (isl.), Samoa	45,040	13 35 S	172 25 W	63
Savannah (river), Ga.,S.C., U.S.		32 03 N	80 55 W	87
Savannah, Ga., U.S.	131,510	32 05 N	81 06 W	87
Sayan (mts.), Russia		53 00 N	95 00 E	46
Schefferville, Qué., Can.	240	54 48 N	66 50 W	77
Schenectady, N.Y., U.S.	61,821	42 49 N	73 56 W	84
Scotia (sea), Antarctica		57 00 S	40 00 W	71
Scotland, U.K.	5,062,011	57 00 N	04 00 W	42
Scottsdale, Ariz., U.S.	202,705	33 29 N	111 56 W	82
Scranton, Pa., U.S.	76,415	41 24 N	75 39 W	84
Seattle, Wash., U.S.	563,374	47 36 N	122 20 W	80
Seine (river), Fr.		49 20 N	00 20 E	42
Selvas (region), Brazil		06 00 S	64 00 W	94
Semarang, Indon.	1,003,575	06 58 S	110 25 E	56
Sendai, Japan	1,008,130	38 15 N	140 53 E	55
Senegal	**10,852,147**	**15 00 N**	**15 00 W**	**68**
Senegal (river), Africa		15 51 N	17 29 W	68
Seoul,* S. Korea	9,853,972	37 34 N	127 00 E	55
Sept-Îles, Qué., Can.	23,791	50 12 N	66 22 W	85
Serbia and Montenegro	**10,663,022**	**44 00 N**	**21 00 E**	**44**
Severnaya Zemlya (isls.), Russia		79 30 N	98 00 E	46
Seville, Spain	724,148	37 24 N	06 00 W	42
Seychelles	**80,832**	**04 30 S**	**55 30 E**	**13**
Shanghai, China	7,551,236	31 14 N	121 30 E	55
Shannon (river), Ireland		52 39 N	09 00 W	42
Shaoxing, China	180,086	30 00 N	120 35 E	55
Shasta (mt.), Calif., U.S.		41 24 N	122 11 W	82
Shatt-al-'Arab (river), Iran,Iraq		30 00 N	48 30 E	52
Shawinigan, Qué., Can.	17,535	46 33 N	72 45 W	85
Sheboygan, Wis., U.S.	50,792	43 45 N	87 43 W	84
Sheffield, Eng., U.K.	431,607	53 22 N	01 30 W	42
Shelekhov (gulf), Russia		60 00 N	158 00 E	47
Shenyang, China	3,588,084	41 48 N	123 26 E	55
Sherbrooke, Qué., Can.	75,916	45 25 N	71 54 W	85
Shetland (isls.), U.K.	21,988	60 30 N	01 00 W	42
Shikoku (isl.), Japan	4,154,039	34 00 N	140 00 E	55
Shīrāz, Iran	1,053,025	29 37 N	52 33 E	52
Shijazhuang, China	1,065,392	36 03 N	114 29 E	55
Shreveport, La., U.S.	200,145	32 31 N	93 45 W	86
Sicily (isl.), Italy	5,076,700	37 00 N	14 00 E	44
Sicily (str.), Italy		37 30 N	12 00 E	42
Sidra (gulf), Libya		32 00 N	18 00 E	68
Sierra Leone	**5,883,889**	**08 00 N**	**12 00 W**	**68**
Sierra Madre Occidental (mts.), Mex.		26 00 N	106 20 W	89
Sierra Madre Oriental (mts.), Mex.		23 30 N	100 00 W	88
Sierra Nevada (mts.), Calif.,Nev., U.S.		38 00 N	119 30 W	82
Sikhote-Alin' (mts.), Russia		48 00 N	138 00 E	55
Silesia (region), Europe		51 30 N	17 00 E	44
Simcoe (lake), Ont., Can.		45 00 N	79 00 W	84
Simpson (pen.), Nun., Can.		68 00 N	89 00 W	76
Sinai (pen.), Egypt		29 00 N	34 00 E	52
Singapore	**4,767,974**	**01 17 N**	**103 51 E**	**56**
Singapore,* Singapore	2,987,000	01 17 N	103 51 E	56
Sioux City, Iowa, U.S.	85,013	42 29 N	96 23 W	81
Sioux Falls, S.D., U.S.	123,975	43 32 N	96 44 W	81
Sir Alexander (mt.), Br. Col., Can.		53 56 N	120 22 W	80
Sir James MacBrien (mt.), N.W. Terrs., Can.		62 00 N	127 40 W	76
Skagerrak (strait), Europe		58 00 N	09 30 E	43
Skeena (mts.), Br. Col., Can.		56 30 N	129 00 W	76
Skopje,* Macedonia	440,577	42 00 N	21 26 E	44
Slave (river), Alta.,N.W. Terrs., Can.		61 00 N	112 00 W	76
Slovakia	**5,423,567**	**48 30 N**	**19 00 E**	**44**
Slovenia	**1,938,282**	**46 00 N**	**15 00 E**	**44**
Smallwood (res.), Newf., Can.		54 00 N	64 00 W	77
Snake (river), U.S.		46 12 N	119 02 W	80
Society (isls.), Fr. Polynesia	184,224	17 00 S	152 00 W	63
Socotra (isl.), Yemen		12 30 N	54 00 E	52
Sofia,* Bulgaria	1,114,476	42 42 N	23 20 E	44
Solomon (sea), P.N.G.		08 00 S	152 00 E	62
Solomon Islands	**523,617**	**09 00 S**	**160 00 E**	**62**
Somalia	**8,304,601**	**05 00 N**	**47 00 E**	**69**
Somerset (isl.), Nun., Can.		73 30 N	93 30 W	76
South (isl.), N.Z.	906,753	44 00 S	171 00 E	59
South Africa	**42,718,530**	**30 00 S**	**25 00 E**	**70**
South America (cont.)	368,926,272			91
Southampton (isl.), Nun., Can.		64 45 N	84 30 W	77
Southampton, Eng., U.K.	210,138	50 55 N	01 28 W	42
South Australia (state), Austl.	1,467,261	31 00 S	136 00 E	59
South Bend, Ind., U.S.	107,789	41 40 N	86 15 W	84
South Carolina (state), U.S.	4,012,012	34 00 N	81 00 W	87
South China (sea), Asia		15 00 N	115 00 E	56
South Dakota (state), U.S.	754,844	44 30 N	100 30 W	81
South Georgia (isl.), U.K.		54 20 S	36 40 W	96
South Korea	**48,598,175**	**37 30 N**	**128 00 E**	**55**
South Orkney (isls.), U.K.		60 38 S	45 35 W	71
South Sandwich (isls.), U.K.		56 00 S	26 30 W	12
South Saskatchewan (river), Alta.,Sask., Can.		50 30 N	110 00 W	80
South Shetland (isls.), U.K.		62 00 S	58 00 W	71
Spain	**40,280,780**	**40 00 N**	**04 00 W**	**42**
Spokane, Wash., U.S.	195,629	47 39 N	117 25 W	80
Spratly (isls.), Asia		08 00 N	113 00 E	56
Springfield,* Ill., U.S.	111,454	39 48 N	89 38 W	84
Springfield, Mass., U.S.	152,082	42 06 N	72 35 W	85
Springfield, Mo., U.S.	151,580	37 13 N	93 18 W	83
Springfield, Ohio, U.S.	65,358	39 55 N	83 48 W	84
Springfield, Ore., U.S.	52,864	44 02 N	123 01 W	80
Sri Jayewardenepura Kotte,* Sri Lanka	109,000	06 54 N	79 54 E	53
Sri Lanka	**19,905,165**	**07 00 N**	**81 00 E**	**53**
Srinagar, India	894,940	34 07 N	74 45 E	53
Stamford, Conn., U.S.	117,083	41 03 N	73 32 W	84
Stanley,* Falk. Is.	1,557	51 42 S	57 51 W	96
Stanovoy (mts.), Russia		55 40 N	126 00 E	47
Stavanger, Norway	107,866	58 58 N	05 45 E	43
Stikine (river), Br. Col., Can.		56 37 N	132 21 W	76
Stockholm,* Sweden	674,680	59 16 N	18 00 E	43
Stockton, Calif., U.S.	243,771	37 57 N	121 17 W	82
Strasbourg, Fr.	267,051	48 35 N	07 45 E	42
Stuttgart, Germany	582,443	48 40 N	09 10 E	42
Subotica, Serb.	99,471	46 06 N	19 40 E	44
Sucre,* Bolivia	130,952	19 03 S	65 18 W	94
Sudan	**39,148,162**	**13 00 N**	**30 00 E**	**69**
Sudan (region), Africa		12 00 N	10 00 E	68
Sudbury, Ont., Can.	103,879	46 30 N	81 00 W	84
Sudd (swamp), Sudan		08 00 N	30 00 E	69
Sudeten (mts.), Europe		51 00 N	17 00 E	44
Suez (canal), Egypt		30 45 N	32 20 E	69
Sulu (arch.), Phil.		09 00 N	120 30 E	57
Sulu (sea), Phil.		09 08 N	120 00 E	57
Sumatra (isl.), Indon.	42,409,510	00 00	102 00 E	56
Sumba (isl.), Indon.		10 00 S	120 00 E	57
Sumba (strait), Indon.		08 30 S	122 00 E	56
Sumbawa (isl.), Indon.		08 30 S	117 26 E	56
Summerside, P.E.I., Can.	14,654	46 24 N	63 47 W	85
Sunda (isls.), Indon.		09 00 S	105 00 E	57
Sunda (strait), Indon.		06 28 S	105 24 E	56
Sundsvall, Sweden	93,733	62 23 N	17 19 E	43
Superior (lake), Can.,U.S.		87 00 N	48 00 W	84
Sur (pt.), Calif., U.S.		36 18 N	121 52 W	82
Surabaya, Indon.	2,410,417	07 16 S	112 44 E	56
Surat, India	2,433,787	21 10 N	72 50 E	53
Suriname	**436,935**	**04 00 N**	**56 00 W**	**95**
Surrey, Br. Col., Can.	347,825	49 08 N	122 51 W	80
Sutlej (river), Pak.		30 00 N	73 00 E	53
Suva,* Fiji	69,665	18 08 S	178 24 E	62
Svalbard (arch.), Norway	2,811	79 00 N	19 00 E	71
Swansea, Wales	171,038	51 58 N	03 55 W	42
Swaziland	**1,169,241**	**26 30 S**	**31 30 E**	**70**
Sweden	**8,986,400**	**62 00 N**	**16 00 E**	**43**
Swift Current, Sask., Can.	14,821	50 17 N	107 48 W	80
Switzerland	**7,450,867**	**46 48 N**	**08 00 E**	**42**
Sydney, Austl.	3,455,110	33 52 S	151 10 E	59
Sydney, N.S., Can.	33,913	46 09 N	60 11 W	85
Syracuse, N.Y., U.S.	147,306	43 03 N	76 09 W	84
Syrdariya (river), Kazak.		46 03 N	61 06 E	45
Syria	**18,016,874**	**35 00 N**	**38 00 E**	**52**
Szczecin, Poland	411,275	53 50 N	14 30 E	44

T

NAME	POPULATION	LATITUDE	LONGITUDE	PAGE
Tabrīz, Iran	1,191,043	38° 05′ N	46° 18′ E	52
Tacoma, Wash., U.S.	193,556	47 15 N	122 26 W	80
Taegu, Korea	2,473,990	35 52 N	128 36 E	55
Taejŏn, Korea	1,365,961	36 20 N	127 26 E	55
Tagus (river), Port.,Spain		38 45 N	09 00 W	42
Tahiti (isl.), Fr.	150,707	17 38 S	149 25 W	63
Tahoe (lake), Calif.,Nev., U.S.		38 30 N	120 00 W	82
Tai'an, China	705,940	36 12 N	117 07 E	55
T'aichung, Taiwan, China	849,549	24 09 N	120 41 E	55
T'aipei,* Taiwan, China	2,639,283	25 02 N	121 31 E	55
Taiwan	**22,749,838**	**24 00 N**	**121 00 E**	**55**
Taiyuan, China	1,514,347	37 52 N	112 35 E	55
Tajikistan	**7,011,556**	**39 00 N**	**71 00 E**	**46**
Takla Makan (desert), China		39 20 N	83 00 E	54
Tallahassee,* Fla., U.S.	150,624	30 26 N	84 17 W	87
Tallinn,* Estonia	404,000	59 25 N	24 45 E	43
Tampa, Fla., U.S.	303,447	27 57 N	82 27 W	87